Computers For Seniors

FOR

DUMMIES®

3RD EDITION

by Nancy Muir

WILEY

John Wiley & Sons, Inc.

Computers For Seniors For Dummies®, 3rd Edition

Published by
John Wiley & Sons, Inc.
111 River Street
Hoboken, NJ 07030-5774

www.wiley.com

For general information on our other products and services, please contact our Customer Care Department within the U.S. at 877-762-2974, outside the U.S. at 317-572-3993, or fax 317-572-4002.

For technical support, please visit www.wiley.com/techsupport.

Wiley publishes in a variety of print and electronic formats and by print-on-demand. Some material included with standard print versions of this book may not be included in e-books or in print-on-demand. If this book refers to media such as a CD or DVD that is not included in the version you purchased, you may download this material at http://booksupport.wiley.com. For more information about Wiley products, visit www.wiley.com.

Library of Congress Control Number: 2012949806

ISBN 978-1-118-11553-4 (pbk); ISBN 978-1-118-22425-0 (ebk); ISBN 978-1-118-23243-9 (ebk); ISBN 978-1-118-26249-8 (ebk)

Manufactured in the United States of America

10 9 8 7 6

WILEY

About the Author

Nancy Muir worked in regional theater and video production, as well as teaching English in Japan before starting her career in technology. She worked at Symantec and then in computer book publishing starting about 20 years ago. She runs two websites (iPadMadeClear.com and TechSmartSenior.com) and writes on a variety of technology topics. Nancy also writes a column on computers and the Internet for Retirenet. com. With almost 100 books to her credit, Nancy continues to enjoy learning about new technologies and gadgets and helping others enjoy them as well.

Dedication

To Allegra Clarkson with thanks for supporting me throughout the writing of this book.

Author's Acknowledgments

As with all books this book was a team effort. Katie Mohr is the person who led the vision for the book and is kind enough to continue to work with me on this and other projects. Leading the team in the trenches was Blair Pottenger, the best editor I've ever worked with. Thanks for your usual stellar job, Blair. The copy editor Heidi Unger and tech editor Sharon Mealka helped to make sure the book is accurate and literate. Finally, thanks to readers who have offered suggestions in the past so we can try to make this book better in each edition.

Publisher's Acknowledgments

We're proud of this book; please send us your comments at http://dummies.custhelp.com. For other comments, please contact our Customer Care Department within the U.S. at 877-762-2974, outside the U.S. at 317-572-3993, or fax 317-572-4002.

Some of the people who helped bring this book to market include the following:

Acquisitions and Editorial

Project Editor: Blair J. Pottenger

Acquisitions Editor: Katie Mohr

Copy Editor: Heidi Unger

Technical Editor: Sharon Mealka

Editorial Manager: Kevin Kirschner

Editorial Assistant: Leslie Saxman

Sr. Editorial Assistant: Cherie Case

Cover Photo: © Joshua Hodge Photography/ iStockphoto.com

Cartoons: Rich Tennant (www.the5thwave.com)

Composition Services

Project Coordinator: Patrick Redmond

Layout and Graphics: Joyce Haughey, Corrie Niehaus

Proofreaders: Melissa D. Buddendeck, John Greenough

Indexer: Potomac Indexing, LLC

Publishing and Editorial for Technology Dummies

Richard Swadley, Vice President and Executive Group Publisher

Andy Cummings, Vice President and Publisher

Mary Bednarek, Executive Acquisitions Director

Mary C. Corder, Editorial Director

Publishing for Consumer Dummies

Kathleen Nebenhaus, Vice President and Executive Publisher

Composition Services

Debbie Stailey, Director of Composition Services

Table of Contents

Introduction 1

    About This Book 1

    Foolish Assumptions 2

    Why You Need This Book 2

    How This Book Is Organized 2

    Get Going! 4

    For Windows 8.1 Users 4

Part 1: Get Going! 5

  Chapter 1: Buying a Computer 7

    Understand All You Can Do with Computers 8

    Understand Hardware and Software 11

    Explore Types of Computers 13

    Choose a Version of Windows 16

    Choose a Price Range 17

    Select a Monitor 19

    Choose an Optical Drive 21

    Understand Processor Speed and Memory 22

    Determine How You'll Connect to the Internet 24

    Buy a Customized Computer 25

  Chapter 2: Setting Up Your Computer 27

    Connect the Monitor, Keyboard, and Mouse 28

    Use the Mouse 29

    Work with a Touchscreen 30

    Use Shortcuts 31

    Log on to Windows 8 31

    Set the Date and Time 33

    Create a New User Account 35

    Switch User Accounts 38

Change the User Account Type 38

Shut down Your Computer 40

Chapter 3: Getting around Windows 8 41

Understand Changes in Windows 8 42

Work with the Start Screen 43

Display the Charms Bar 46

Search for Files, Settings, and Apps 47

View Recent Apps 49

Work with Windows 8 Using a Touchscreen Device....................50

Explore the Desktop..50

Work with Frequently Used Programs..52

Arrange Icons on the Desktop..54

Empty the Recycle Bin 55

Find a File or Open an Application with File Explorer 56

Create a Shortcut to a File or Folder 57

Switch between Programs..58

Resize Windows 59

Chapter 4: Setting Up Your Display 61

Customize Windows's Appearance..62

Set Your Screen's Resolution 63

Change the Start Screen Background and Color...........................65

Change the Lock Screen Picture 66

Change Your Account Picture 67

Change the Desktop Background 70

Choose a Desktop Theme..72

Set Up a Screen Saver...73

**Chapter 5: Getting Help with Vision, Hearing,
and Dexterity Challenges.. 75**

Use Tools for the Visually Challenged...76

Replace Sounds with Visual Cues 78

Make Text Larger or Smaller..79

Set Up Speech Recognition...81

Modify How Your Keyboard Works 84

Use the Onscreen Keyboard Feature 86

Set Up Keyboard Repeat Rates 88

Customize Mouse Behavior..89

Change the Cursor 91

Chapter 6: Setting Up Printers and Scanners......................93

Install a Printer..94

Add a Printer Manually..95

Set a Default Printer..98

Set Printer Preferences 100

View Currently Installed Printers 103

Remove a Printer.. 104

Install a Plug-and-Play Scanner.. 105

Install a Scanner Manually 105

Modify Scanner Settings 106

Chapter 7: Getting Help...109

Search Windows Help and Support.................................... 110

Get Help Getting Started with Windows 8......................... 112

Find Information about Using the Start Screen 114

Get Answers from the Windows Community...................... 115

Switch between Online and Offline Help........................... 117

Connect to Remote Assistance 118

Part II: Getting Things Done with Software............................. 123

Chapter 8: Working with Software Programs 125

Launch a Program 126

Move Information between Programs................................. 128

Set Program Defaults 130

Remove a Program 131

Chapter 9: Working with Files and Folders 135

Understand How Windows Organizes Data....................... 136

Access Recently Used Items 138

Locate Files and Folders in Your Computer 139

Search for Online Content 141

Move a File or Folder 142

Rename a File or Folder 145

Create a Shortcut to a File or Folder 146

Delete a File or Folder 147

Create a Compressed File or Folder 148

Add a File to Your Favorites List 150

Back Up Files 152

**Chapter 10: Working with the Weather, People,
and Calendar Apps** **153**

Display Weather Views 154

Specify a Place in Weather 156

Explore Weather around the World 157

Add a Contact 159

Edit Contact Information 161

Send E-mail to Contacts 163

View Contacts' Latest Postings 164

Pin a Contact 166

Add an Event to Your Calendar 167

Invite People to an Event 169

Part III: Going Online **171**

Chapter 11: Understanding Internet Basics **173**

Understand What the Internet Is 174

Explore Different Types of Internet Connections 176

Set Up an Internet Connection 179

Practice Navigation Basics with the Start Screen IE App 181

Practice Navigation Basics with the Desktop IE App 183

Understand Tabs in Browsers 184

Understand Home Pages 185

Set Up a Home Page in Desktop IE 186

Chapter 12: Browsing the Web with Internet Explorer... 189

Understand Differences between the Two Versions of IE 190

Search the Web 192

Find Content on a Web Page Using Start Screen IE 195

Pin a Web Page to the Start Screen 196

Add a Website to Favorites 197

Organize Favorites 198

View Your Browsing History using Desktop IE 199

Customize the Internet Explorer Toolbar 201

View RSS Feeds 202

Print a Web Page 204

Use Start Screen IE 11 Settings 205

Chapter 13: Staying Safe While Online 207

Understand Technology Risks on the Internet 208

Use Suggested Sites 211

Download Files Safely 212

Turn on InPrivate Browsing 214

Use SmartScreen Filter 215

Change Privacy Settings 216

Understand Information Exposure 218

Keep Your Information Private 222

Spot Phishing Scams and Other E-mail Fraud 224

Create Strong Passwords 226

Chapter 14: Keeping In Touch with Mail 229

Set Up an Internet-Based E-mail Account 230

Set Up Accounts in Mail 232

Get to Know Mail 234

Open Mail and Receive Messages 236

Create and Send E-mail 238

Send an Attachment 240

Read a Message 241

Reply to a Message 242

Forward E-mail 243

Make Account Settings in Mail 244

Chapter 15: Working in the Cloud **249**

    Use Applications Online 250

    Add Files to SkyDrive.. 252

    Share Files Using SkyDrive 253

    Create a New SkyDrive Folder... 255

    Share a SkyDrive Folder with Others................................ 256

    Turn On the Sync Feature... 257

    Choose which Settings You Want to Sync......................... 258

Chapter 16: Connecting with People Online **261**

    Use Discussion Boards and Blogs..................................... 262

    Participate in Chat 264

    Send and Receive Instant Messages (IMs) 266

    Work with the Messaging App 267

    Use Webcams 270

    Get an Overview of Collaborative and Social Networking Sites 271

    Sign Up for a Social Networking Service.......................... 273

    Understand How Online Dating Works.............................. 275

    Select a Dating Service 277

    Share Content with Others.. 278

Part IV: Having Fun **281**

Chapter 17: Getting Visual: Using Windows Media Player, Video, and Camera **283**

    Work with Media Software... 284

    Buy Video Content at the Windows Store......................... 286

    Play Movies with Windows Media Player 289

    Upload Photos from Your Digital Camera 291

    Take Pictures and Videos with the Windows 8 Camera App 292

    View a Digital Image in the Photos App 293

    Share a Photo 295

    Run a Slide Show in Photos.. 297

Chapter 18: Playing Music in Windows 8 .... **299**

Set Up Speakers 300

Adjust System Volume 301

Make Settings for Ripping Music 303

Find Music with Windows 8's Integrated Search 305

Buy Music from the Windows Store 306

Create a Playlist 309

Burn Music to a CD/DVD 311

Sync with a Music Device 312

Play Music with Windows Media Player 314

Chapter 19: Going Shopping Online **317**

Search for Items 318

Compare Prices 319

Verify If a Store is Trustworthy 320

Read Customer Reviews 321

Buy through Auction Sites 322

Find Coupons 323

Manage a Shopping Cart 324

Use Various Payment Methods 326

Understand Shipping Options 327

Part V: Windows Toolkit **329**

Chapter 20: Working with Networks **331**

Join a Homegroup 332

Make a Connection to a Network 333

Specify What You Want to Share over a Network 334

Set Up a Wireless Network 336

Make Your Computer Discoverable to Bluetooth 338

Connect to Bluetooth Devices 339

Go Online Using Your Cellular Network 340

Chapter 21: Protecting Windows **343**

Understand Computer Security 344

Understand Windows Update Options 345

Run Windows Update 347

Set Up Trusted and Restricted Websites 348

Enable Windows Firewall 351

Change Your Password 353

Allow Firewall Exceptions 355

Chapter 22: Maintaining Windows **357**

Shut Down a Nonresponsive Application 358

Create a System Restore Point 359

Restore Your PC 361

Refresh Your PC 364

Reset Your PC 365

Defragment a Hard Drive 367

Free Disk Space 368

Delete Temporary Internet Files by Using Internet Explorer 370

Schedule Maintenance Tasks 372

Troubleshoot Software Problems 374

Index **377**

Introduction

Computers for consumers have come a long way in just 20 years or so. They're now at the heart of the way many people communicate, shop, and learn. They provide useful tools for tracking information, organizing finances, and being creative.

During the rapid growth of the personal computer, you might have been too busy to jump in and learn the ropes, but you now realize how useful and fun working with a computer can be.

This book can help you get going with computers quickly and painlessly.

About This Book

This book is specifically written for mature people like you — folks who are relatively new to using a computer and want to discover the basics of buying a computer, working with software, and getting on the Internet. In writing this book, I've tried to take into account the types of activities that might interest a 50-plus year old who's discovering computers for the first time.

Conventions Used in This Book

This book uses these conventions to help you find your way around:

➡ When you have to type something in a text box, I put it in **bold** type. Whenever I mention a website address, I put it in another font, `like this`. Figure references are also in bold, to help you find them.

➡ For menu commands, I use the ⇨ symbol to separate menu choices. For example, choose Tools⇨Internet Options. The ⇨ symbol is just my way of saying, "Open the Tools menu and then click Internet Options."

➡ Callouts for figures draw your attention to an action you need to perform. In some cases, points of interest in a figure might be circled. The text tells you what to look for; the circle makes it easy to find.

 Tip icons point out insights or helpful suggestions related to tasks in the steps list.

Foolish Assumptions

This book is organized by sets of tasks. These tasks start from the very beginning, assuming you know little about computers, and guide you through the most basic steps in easy-to-understand language. Because I assume you're new to computers, the book provides explanations or definitions of technical terms to help you out.

All computers are run by software called an *operating system*, such as Windows. The latest version is Windows 8. Because Microsoft Windows–based personal computers (PCs) are the most common type, the book focuses mostly on Windows 8 functionality.

Why You Need This Book

Working with computers can be a daunting prospect to people who are coming to them later in life. Your grandchildren may run rings around you when it comes to technology, and you might have fallen for that old adage, "You can't teach an old dog new tricks." However, with the simple step-by-step approach of this book, you can get up to speed with computers and overcome any technophobia you might have experienced.

You can work through this book from beginning to end or simply open up a chapter to solve a problem or help you learn a new skill whenever you need it. The steps in each task get you where you want to go quickly, without a lot of technical explanation. In no time, you'll start picking up the skills you need to become a confident computer user.

How This Book Is Organized

This book is conveniently divided into several handy parts to help you find what you need.

➠ **Part I: Get Going!:** If you need to buy a computer or get started with the basics of using a computer, this part is for you. These chapters help you explore the different specifications, styles, and price ranges for computers and discover how to set up your computer right out of the box, including hooking it up to a printer. These chapters provide information for exploring the Windows 8 interface when you first turn on your computer, to customize Windows to work the way you want it to. Finally, I provide information on using the Help system that's part of Windows.

➠ **Part II: Getting Things Done with Software:** Here's where you start working with that new computer. I explain the preinstalled apps that come with Windows 8 as well as how to buy new apps in the Windows Store. This is also the part where you explore how Windows organizes files and folders. Chapters in this part also introduce you to the built-in Windows apps People, Calendar, and Weather.

➠ **Part III: Going Online:** It's time to get online! The chapters in this part help you understand what the Internet is and what tools and functions it makes available to you. Find out how to explore the Internet with a web browser; how to stay in touch with people via e-mail, instant messaging, chat, and blogs; and how to use tools stored in the cloud to share files and connect with others.

➠ **Part IV: Having Fun:** Time for a break to play movies, take and view photos and videos, and play some toe-tapping music. That's all covered in this part of the book.

➠ **Part V: Windows Toolkit:** Now that you have a computer, you have certain responsibilities toward it (just like having a child or puppy!). In this case, you might start by connecting it with other computers in a home network. Next, you need to protect the data on your computer, which you can do using Windows and Internet Explorer tools. In addition, you need to perform some routine maintenance tasks to keep your hard drive uncluttered and virus free.

Get Going!

Whether you need to start from square one and buy yourself a computer or you're ready to just start enjoying the tools and toys your current computer makes available, it's time to get going, get online, and get computer savvy.

For Windows 8.1 Users

This book was written based on Windows 8 and updated with information for Windows 8.1 users. You can upgrade to 8.1 for free by downloading it from the Windows Store (click Store on the Start screen).

Part I
Get Going!

The 5th Wave   By Rich Tennant

Buying a Computer

*I*f you've never owned a computer and now face purchasing one for the first time, deciding what to get can be a somewhat daunting experience. There are lots of technical terms to figure out and various pieces of *hardware* (the physical pieces of your computer such as the monitor and keyboard) and *software* (the brains of the computer that help you create documents and play games, for example) that you need to understand.

In this chapter, I introduce you to the world of activities your new computer makes available to you, and I provide the information you need to choose just the right computer for you. Remember as you read through this chapter that figuring out what you want to do with your computer is an important step in determining which computer you should buy. You have to consider how much money you want to spend, how you'll connect your computer to the Internet, and how much power and performance you'll require from your computer.

Get ready to . . .

➡ Understand All You Can Do with Computers 8

➡ Understand Hardware and Software 11

➡ Explore Types of Computers 13

➡ Choose a Version of Windows 16

➡ Choose a Price Range 17

➡ Select a Monitor 19

➡ Choose an Optical Drive 21

➡ Understand Processor Speed and Memory 22

➡ Determine How You'll Connect to the Internet 24

➡ Buy a Customized Computer 25

Understand All You Can Do with Computers

Congratulations — in your life you've been witness to a remarkable revolution. In just a few decades, computers have moved from being expensive behemoths that lived in corporate basements to being personal productivity and entertainment tools. They've empowered people to connect around the world in unprecedented ways, and they've made common tasks much easier to handle.

The following list walks you through some of the things your computer will enable you to do. Depending on what activities are important to you, you can make a more-informed purchasing choice.

➡ **Keep in touch with friends and family.** The Internet makes it possible to communicate with other people via e-mail; share video images using built-in video recorders or webcams (tiny, inexpensive video cameras that capture and send your image to another computer); and make phone calls using a technology called VoIP (Voice over Internet Protocol), which uses your computer and Internet connection to place calls. You can also chat with others by typing messages and sending them through your computer using a technology called *instant messaging* (IM). These messages are exchanged in real time, so that you and your grandchild, for example, can see and reply to text or share images immediately. Part III of this book explains these topics in more detail.

➡ **Research any topic from the comfort of your home.** Online, you can find many reputable websites that help you get information on anything from expert medical advice to the best travel deals. You can read news from around the corner or around the world. You can visit government websites to find out information about your taxes, Social Security, and more, or even go to entertainment sites to look up your local television listings or movie reviews.

➡ **Create greeting cards, letters, or home inventories.**
Whether you're organizing your holiday card list,
tracking sales for your home business, or figuring out
a monthly budget, computer programs can help. For
example, **Figure 1-1** shows a graph that the Excel
program created from data in a spreadsheet.

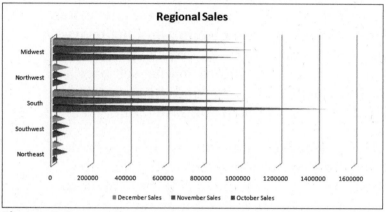

Figure 1-1

➡ **Pursue hobbies such as genealogy or sports.** You
can research your favorite teams online (see **Figure
1-2**) or connect with people who have the same
interests. The online world is full of special-interest
discussion groups where you can talk about your
interests with others.

➡ **Play interactive games with others over the
Internet.** You can play everything from shuffleboard
to poker or participate in action games in virtual
worlds.

➡ **Share and create photos, drawings, and videos.** If
you have a digital camera, you can transfer photos to
your computer (called *uploading*) or copy photos off
the Internet (if their copyright permits it) and share
them in e-mails or use them to create your own
greeting cards. If you're artistically inclined, you can
create digital drawings. Many popular websites make
sharing your homemade videos easy, too. If you

have a digital video camera and editing software, you can use editing tools to make a movie and share it with others via video-sharing sites such as YouTube or by e-mail. Steven Spielberg, look out!

➟ **Shop online and compare products easily, day or night.** You can shop for anything from a garden shed to travel deals or a new camera. Using handy shopping site features, you can easily compare prices from several stores or read customer product reviews. Websites such as www.nextag.com list product prices from a variety of vendors on one web page, so you can find the best deals. Beyond the convenience, all this information can help you save money.

➟ **Manage your financial life.** You can do your banking or investing online and get up-to-the-minute data about your bank account, credit card balances, and investments. And if you're online savvy, you can do this all without fear of having your financial data stolen (see Chapter 13 for more about this).

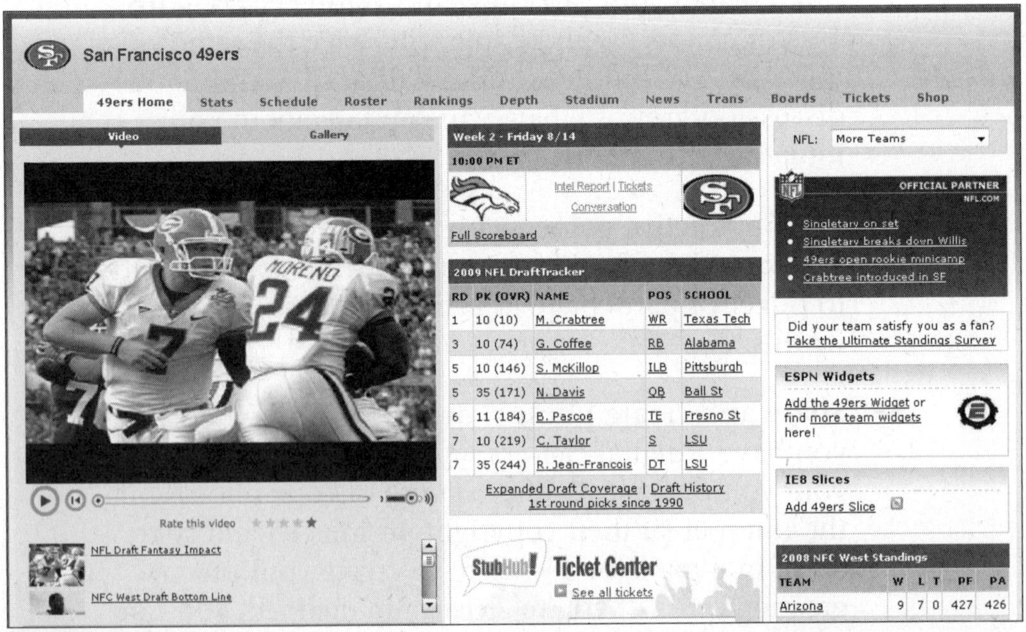

Figure 1-2

Understand Hardware and Software

Your computing experience is made up of interactions with hardware and software. The *hardware* is all the tangible computer equipment, such as the monitor, central processing unit, keyboard, and mouse. The *software* is what makes the hardware work or lets you get things done, such as writing documents with Microsoft Word or playing a game of solitaire. Think of the hardware as being like your television set and the shows that you watch as being like the software.

Your computer hardware consists of

➡ **A central processing unit (CPU),** which is the very small, very high-tech semiconductor *chip* that acts as the brains of your computer. The CPU is stored in a computer tower — or in all-in-one computer models, laptops, and tablets, in a single unit along with the monitor. The CPU also contains other nuts and bolts used to run your computer.

➡ **A monitor,** which displays images on its screen such as the Microsoft Windows desktop, a video you watch from an online entertainment site, or a document in a software program. Today, more and more computers sport touchscreen monitors, which allow you to use your finger on the screen to provide input to the computer.

➡ **A keyboard,** which is similar to a typewriter keyboard. In addition to typing words, you can use a keyboard to give the computer commands such as selecting, copying, and pasting text.

➡ **A mouse,** which you also use to give your computer commands, but this little device is based on a more free-flowing way of providing input than your keyboard. You move the mouse around your desk with your hand, which moves a pointer around onscreen. Using this pointer, you can click an item — an onscreen button, for example — that causes an action, or click on the screen and drag the mouse to select text or an object to perform an action on it (such as deleting the text or making it bold). A mouse can be a separate device that is mouselike in shape, or can be built into devices like laptops in the form of a touch button or touchpad.

➡ **Peripherals,** such as a printer, speakers, webcams, and headphones. These may or may not come with your computer when you buy it, but your computer does come with slots (called *ports*) where you plug in various peripherals.

Software (also known as *programs* or *applications*) is installed on your computer hard drive, which resides in the computer casing (either in your laptop or, for a desktop computer, in the computer tower or monitor in all-in-one PCs). Here are a few basics about software:

➡ **You use software to get your work done, run entertainment programs, and browse the Internet.** For example, Quicken is a financial management program you can use to balance your checkbook or keep track of your home inventory for insurance purposes.

➡ **Some programs come preinstalled on your computer; you can buy and install other programs as you need them.** For example, a computer always has an operating system because the operating system runs all the other programs. Also, some programs are included with your operating system, such as WordPad, a simple word- processing program, which comes with Windows 8.

Skype, a program with which you can make online phone calls using your computer, is an example of a popular program that you can find on the Internet and install on your computer for free.

➠ **You can uninstall programs you no longer need.** Uninstalling unwanted programs helps to free up some space on your computer, which helps it perform better.

➠ **Software programs called *utilities* exist to keep your computer in shape.** An *antivirus* program is an example of a utility used to spot and erase computer viruses from your system. Your *operating system* (such as Windows 8, which is the main focus of this book), also includes some utilities, such as the Windows Defender program. Windows Defender protects your computer from unwanted intrusion by malicious programs called *spyware*. See Part V for details about using utilities.

Explore Types of Computers

Just as there are many styles of shoes or mobile phones, you can find several styles of computers. Some are small and portable, some use different operating systems to make everything run, and some excel at certain functions such as working with graphics or playing games. This task explains some features you should consider when buying a computer.

➠ **Operating system:** An operating system is the software that allows you to start and shut down your computer and work with all the other software programs, manage files, and connect to the Internet. Windows is probably the most common computer operating system (OS), and this book mainly focuses on its features.

However, Macintosh computers from Apple are also very popular. These use Apple-specific software; however, many software applications written for Windows are also available for the Macintosh, and you can also set up your Mac to run the Windows operating system, which gives you the best of both worlds. Some computers run on a freely available operating system called Linux, which has similar functionality to Windows.

- A *laptop* is portable, weighing anywhere from 2 to 8 pounds. The monitor, keyboard, and mouse (touchpad) are built into the laptop. (Note that if the monitor is ever damaged, you have to pay quite a bit to have it repaired, or else hook the computer up to an external monitor.) **Figure 1-3** shows an example of a laptop, which is sometimes called a *notebook* computer. Choose a laptop if you want to use your computer mainly away from home or you have little space in your home for a larger computer.

Figure 1-3

- *Desktop* models typically have a large tower, such as the tower shown in **Figure 1-4**, that contains the computer's central processing unit (called a CPU). The keyboard, mouse, and monitor are separate. All-in-one models contain the CPU within the monitor. Desktop computers take up more space than laptops and aren't portable, but they're sometimes less expensive.

A computer's central processing unit (CPU)

Figure 1-4

➠ Tablets such as iPad and Kindle Fire and Windows-based tablets offer many computing capabilities, such as reading and working on simple documents, connecting to the Internet to send and receive e-mail, playing games, listening to music, and so on. However, they have relatively small touchscreens (with a touchscreen, you provide input with your finger or a stylus); onscreen keyboards, which can be a bit challenging to use; no mouse; and often less file-management capabilities.

If you just want to browse the web, read e-mail, and play games, a tablet could be a way to go. If you want a broader range of capabilities with a larger screen size and can live with less portability, a computer is the way to go. Many people have both a computer and a laptop or tablet. They do complement each other nicely if that approach fits your budget.

➠ **Pictures and sound:** If you work with a lot of *visual elements* (for example, photographs, home movies, or computer games), consider a computer that has a better graphics card. Games often involve sound, so a high-end sound card may also be useful.

Computers with more sophisticated sound and image capabilities are often referred to as *gaming* or *multimedia* models and they typically require a larger hard drive to handle these functions. Because the capabilities of these cards change all the time, I don't give you the specifications for what's high end; instead, ask the person you're buying the computer from whether the system can handle sophisticated sound and graphics.

Choose a Version of Windows

As mentioned in the previous task, choosing your computer's *operating system* (software that runs all the programs and organizes data on your computer) will be one of your first decisions. This book focuses on computers running the current version of Windows, which is called Windows 8. Windows 8 is a radical departure from previous Windows operating systems, so if you opt for an earlier version of Windows, such as Windows 7, you would need to buy the Windows 7 edition of this book. Windows 8 comes in two different versions for home and small business users:

➡ **Windows 8:** Includes entertainment tools such as Windows Media Center for playing music and movies. If you want to do more than look at photos, you'll find that this version of Windows 8 is good at working with design and image-manipulation programs such as Photoshop. Also, if you choose a laptop, be aware that Home includes great features for managing the battery power of your computer. If you consider yourself primarily a home user, you should consider this version of Windows 8

➡ **Windows 8 Pro:** Is great for small businesses or if you work from home. This version of Windows has ultimate security features and you can also use a Media Pack add-on with this version to get richer multimedia features.

Windows 8.1 offers Windows, Windows Pro, and Pro Student for the average user. Windows 8.1 Enterprise is for those using Windows in an organizational setting.

Choose a Price Range

You can buy a computer for anywhere from about $299 to $5,000 or more, depending on your budget and computing needs. You may start with a base model, but extras such as a larger monitor or higher-end graphics card can soon add hundreds to the base price.

You can shop in a retail store for a computer or shop online using a friend's computer (and perhaps get his or her help if you're brand new to using a computer). Consider researching different models and prices online and using that information to negotiate your purchase in the store if you prefer shopping at the mall. Be aware, however, that most retail stores have a small selection compared to all you can find online on a website such as NewEgg.com.

Buying a computer can be confusing, but here are some guidelines to help you find a computer at the price that's right for you:

➡ **Determine how often you will use your computer.** If you'll be working on it eight hours a day running a home business, you will need a better-quality computer to withstand the use and provide good performance. If you turn on the computer once or twice a week, it doesn't have to be the priciest model in the shop.

➡ **Consider the features that you need.** Do you want (or have room for) a 20-inch monitor? Do you need the computer to run very fast and run several programs at once, or do you need to store tons of data? (Computer speed and storage are covered later in this chapter.) Understand what you need before you buy. Each feature or upgrade adds dollars to your computer's price.

➠ **Shop wisely.** If you walk from store to store or do your shopping online, you'll find that the price for the same computer model can vary by hundreds of dollars at different stores. See if your memberships in organizations such as AAA, AARP, or Costco make you eligible for better deals. Consider shipping costs if you buy online, and keep in mind that many stores charge a restocking fee if you return a computer you aren't happy with. Some stores offer only a short time period, such as 14 days, in which you can return a computer.

➠ **Buying used or refurbished is an option, though new computers have reached such a low price point that this may not save you much.** In addition, technology gets out of date so quickly that you might be disappointed buying an older model, which might not support newer software or peripheral devices (such as Bluetooth headphones). Instead, consider going to a company that produces customized computers at lower prices — perhaps even your local computer repair shop. You might be surprised at the bargains you can find (but make sure you're dealing with reputable people before buying).

➠ **Online auctions are a source of new or slightly used computers at a low price.** However, be sure you're dealing with a reputable store or person by checking reviews others have posted about them or contacting the Better Business Bureau. Be careful not to pay by check (this gives a complete stranger your bank account number); instead use the auction site's tools to have a third party handle the money until the goods are delivered in the condition promised. Check the auction site for guidance on staying safe when buying auctioned goods.

Some websites, such as Epinions, allow you to compare several models of computers side by side, and others, such as Nextag, allow you to compare prices on a particular model from multiple stores.

Select a Monitor

Monitors are the window to your computer's contents. If you're buying a desktop computer, it may come with a monitor that suits your purposes, or you might upgrade to a better monitor. A good monitor can make your computing time easier on your eyes. The crisper the image, the more impressive your vacation photos or that video of your last golf game will be.

Consider these factors when choosing a monitor:

➠ **Size:** Monitors for the average computer user come in all sizes, from tiny 9-inch screens on smaller laptops to 28-inch desktop models. Larger screens are typically more expensive. Although a larger monitor can take up more space side to side and top to bottom, many don't have a bigger *footprint* (that is, how much space their base takes up on your desk) than a smaller monitor.

➠ **Image quality:** The image quality can vary greatly. You will see terms such as LCD (*liquid crystal display*, also referred to as *flat panels*), flat screen, brightness, and resolution.

Look for an LCD monitor, preferably with a flat screen (see **Figure 1-5**) that reduces glare.

➠ **Resolution:** A monitor's resolution represents the number of pixels that form the images you see on the screen. The higher the resolution, the crisper the image. You should look for a monitor that can provide at least a 1024-x-768 pixel resolution.

An LCD monitor with a flat screen
Figure 1-5

➠ **Cost:** The least-expensive monitor might be the one that comes with a computer package, and many of these are perfectly adequate. You can often upgrade your monitor when you buy if you customize a system from a company such as Dell or Gateway. Monitors purchased separately from a computer can range from around $100 to $3,000 or more. Check out monitors in person to really see whether their image quality and size are worth the money.

➠ **Touchscreen technology:** Windows 8 provides support for using a touchscreen interface, which allows you to use your fingers to provide input by tapping or swiping on the screen itself. If you opt for a touchscreen device you can still use your keyboard and mouse to provide input, but touchscreen technology can add a wow factor when performing tasks such as using painting software or browsing around the web or an electronic book (e-book).

Choose an Optical Drive

You've probably played a movie from a DVD from your local video store or from a service such as Netflix. Computers can also read data from or play music from DVDs. To make this possible, your computer comes with at least one *optical drive*, which is a small drawer that pops out, allowing you to place a DVD in a tray, push the drawer back into the computer, and view the contents of the DVD. If you buy a software program, it may come on a CD or DVD, so you also need this drive to install some software.

When you buy a computer, keep these things in mind about optical drives:

➡ **DVDs versus CDs:** DVDs have virtually replaced CDs as the computer storage medium of choice, but you might still find a CD floating around with music or data on it that you need to read. For that reason, you might want a DVD/CD combo drive.

➡ **DVD drives:** DVD drives are rated as Read (R), Write (W), or read-writable (RW). A *readable* DVD drive allows you to only look at data on it, but not save data to it. A *writeable* DVD drive allows you to save data (or images, or music) to it. A read-writeable, DVD drive lets you both read and write to DVDs.

➡ **DVD standards:** In the earliest days of DVDs, there were two different standards, + and –. Some drives could play DVDs formatted + but not those format-ted –, for example. Today, you should look for a DVD drive that is specified as +/– so it can deal with any DVD you throw at it.

➡ **Blu-ray discs:** If you want to play the latest optical discs, get a computer with a Blu-ray player. Blu-ray is a great medium for storing and playing back feature-length movies because it can store 50GB, the size of most movies.

One of the first things you should do when you buy a computer, if it doesn't come with recovery discs, is to burn recovery discs that you can use if you have to restore the computer to factory settings. You might need to do this, for example, if a virus corrupts your system data. Your computer should offer this as an option when you first start it, but if it doesn't, check your computer's help system or the manufacturer's website to find out how to burn recovery discs.

Some laptop computers come without DVD capabilities because you can download and install software or play videos and music from the *cloud* (that is, via the Internet), so it's possible to get along just fine without the ability to play DVDs. However, most desktop computers still come with a DVD drive.

Understand Processor Speed and Memory

Your computer contains a processor on a computer chip. The speed at which your computer runs programs or completes tasks is determined in great measure by your computer's processor speed, which is measured in *gigahertz* (GHz). The higher this measurement, the faster the processor. I won't quote the speed you should look for because these chips are constantly getting smaller and more powerful. However, when you shop, know that the higher numbers give the best performance, so factor that into your decision, depending on your needs.

In addition, computers have a certain amount of storage capacity for running programs and storing data. You'll see specifications for RAM and hard drive memory when you go computer shopping. Again, the specific numbers will change, so the rule of thumb is to look for computers with comparatively higher RAM numbers if you feel you need more storage capacity.

➡ **RAM is the memory needed to simply access and run programs.** RAM chips come in different types, including DRAM, SDRAM, and the latest version, DDR2. Look for a minimum of 1 gigabyte (GB) of RAM for everyday computing.

➠ **RAM chips are rated by** *access speed,* **which relates to how quickly a request for data from your system can be completed.** You might see RAM speed measured in megahertz (MHz). Today, 800 MHz could be considered good access speed. Also, note the two common RAM types: SRAM and DRAM. DRAM is more efficient.

➠ **Your hard drive has a certain capacity for data storage, measured in gigabytes (GB).** These days, you should probably look for a minimum of a 2500GB hard drive, but hard drives can come with a range of huge capacities, with the largest being measured in terabytes (TB, measured in thousands of gigabytes).

➠ **Your computer will require some RAM to run the operating system.** Windows 8 requires 1GB of main memory for a 32-bit system and 2GB for a 64-bit system. It also requires 16GB of hard drive space for a 32-bit system and 20GB for a 64-bit system. Check your computer user guide to find out which system you have.

➠ **Your processor has multiple cores.** Most processors today are multiple-core processors, such as the i3, i5, and i7 processor lines from Intel. *Multiple core* means that two or more processors are involved in reading and executing software instructions as you use your computer. Those with two processors are called *dual-core;* those with four processors are called *quad-core;* and processors with six cores are referred to as *hexa-core.* The bottom line with cores is that the more you have, the faster your computer can process instructions because all the cores can work at once. This is what makes multitasking possible. (*Multitasking* is when you're running several programs at once, as when you're playing music, downloading files from the Internet, running an antivirus scan, and working in a word processor —with all of these processes running at the same time.)

Determine How You'll Connect to the Internet

You have to decide how you'll connect to the Internet. You can use a dialup connection over a standard phone line or pay a fee to get a broadband connection such as DSL. (Check with AARP to find out if it offers discounted connections in your area.) However, if you want a wireless connection that picks up a signal in range of a wireless home network or have a laptop and want to access certain public networks called *hotspots*, you have to be sure to buy a computer with wireless capabilities. Here's how these work:

➡ **Broadband:** These connections typically come through a DSL (digital subscriber line) or cable modem in your home. In both cases, you pay a fee to a provider, which might be your phone or cable company. DSL works over your phone line but doesn't prohibit you from using the phone when you're online. Cable runs over your cable TV line and is a bit faster than DSL. Both are considered always-on connections, meaning that you don't have to dial up to a phone connection or connect to a wireless network — you're always connected.

➡ **Dialup:** If you intend to use a dialup connection (that is, connect over your phone line), your computer has to have a dialup modem either built in or external. Dialup connections can be very slow, and while you're using them, you can't use your phone to make or receive calls. I'd discourage you from using dialup unless you absolutely have to.

➡ **Wireless:** These connections require that you have a computer equipped with wireless capability. You can access the Internet wirelessly through a wireless network you set up in your home, or when you're near a wireless *hotspot* (a place that offers wireless service), and many hotspots are available at public places such as hotels, airports, and restaurants. You can also subscribe to a Wireless Wide Area Network (WWAN) service from a mobile phone provider to tap into its connection or use a technology called *tethering* to connect via your smartphone's 3G connection. Check the computer model you want to buy to be sure it's wireless enabled. There are various techy standards for wireless, such as 802.11a, b, or g. The very latest standard to look for is 802.11n, which delivers better wireless performance.

 See Chapter 11 for more about setting up your Internet connection.

Buy a Customized Computer

You can buy prepackaged computer systems online or in an electronics store. An alternative is to buy a customized computer. Companies such as Dell (see **Figure 1-6**) and Gateway offer customized computer systems. When you buy the computer in their online stores, you can pick and choose various features, and the provider will build the system for you.

Figure 1-6

Here are some of the variables you'll be asked about when you purchase a customized system, many of which are discussed in this chapter:

➠ Type and speed of processor

➠ Amount of RAM or hard drive capacity

➠ Installed software, such as a productivity suite like Microsoft Office or Microsoft Works, or a premium version of an operating system

➠ More sophisticated graphics or sound cards

➠ Peripherals such as a printer or an upgrade to a wireless mouse or keyboard

➠ Larger or higher-end monitor

➠ Wireless capability

➠ Warranty and technical support

These choices can add to your final price, so be sure you need an option before you select it. Most of these companies provide explanations of each item to help you decide.

Upgrading to Windows 8.1

To upgrade to Windows 8.1, click the Store tile on the Start screen. Click the image with an Upgrade to Windows 8.1 link on it. On the following screen, you can test whether your computer meets 8.1 requirements, run the Upgrade Assistant to check for hardware and software compatibility, or click the Download button to begin the upgrade. Windows tells you when to restart your computer, how to choose settings, and when to sign in with your Microsoft account.

Setting Up Your Computer

*O*nce you unpack your new computer, you may need help getting it set up. Here I cover the basics: connecting your computer to a monitor, keyboard, and mouse (if you bought a laptop computer, you can skip these tasks as the hardware is built in!); turning the computer on and off; mastering the basic use of your mouse, becoming familiar with some basic keystroke shortcuts, and, if you have a touchscreen, find out how to use it.

Next, you can set up the date and time in your computer's internal clock so they match your time zone and you can apply daylight saving time settings properly. Finally, you get to work with your user accounts. Windows allows you to create multiple user accounts; each account saves certain settings and allows you to control files and folders separately. When each user logs on with a particular user account, it's like accessing a unique personal computer.

Here, then, are the procedures that you can follow to get going with your computer.

Get ready to . . .

➡ Connect the Monitor, Keyboard, and Mouse......... 28

➡ Use the Mouse.................... 29

➡ Work with a Touchscreen 30

➡ Use Shortcuts...................... 31

➡ Log on to Windows 8 31

➡ Set the Date and Time 33

➡ Create a New User Account 35

➡ Switch User Accounts 38

➡ Change Your User Account Type 38

➡ Shut down Your Computer ... 40

Connect the Monitor, Keyboard, and Mouse

Your computer comes with a monitor, keyboard, and mouse. You should connect these before turning on the computer. Your computer will offer several types of connection ports, though USB ports are becoming the most common. For example, wireless keyboards and mice use a small transmitter that you insert into a USB port. Wired keyboards and mice plug into your computer using a USB cable.

The setup information provided by your computer's manufacturer should help you get things connected. Use the following table in conjunction with **Figure 2-1** to identify device-to-PC connector ports.

Connection	Location	What It's Good For
VGA port	1	Connect your monitor.
USB port	2	Connect various USB devices, such as a digital camera or wireless mouse.
Parallel port	3	Connect a non-USB printer.
Audio port	4	Connect speakers.

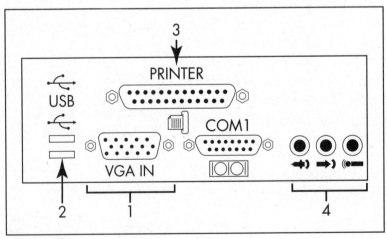

Figure 2-1

Use the Mouse

Unlike using a typewriter, which uses only a keyboard to enter text into documents, with a computer you use both a keyboard and a mouse to enter text and give commands to the computer. Though you might have used a keyboard of some type before, a mouse might be new to you, and frankly, it takes a little getting used to. In effect, when you move your mouse around on your desk (or in some models, roll a ball on top of the mouse), a corresponding mouse pointer moves around your computer screen. You control the actions of that pointer by using the right and left buttons on the mouse.

Here are the main functions of a mouse and how to control them:

➡ **Click.** When people say "click," they mean that you should press and release the left mouse button.

Clicking has a variety of uses. You can click while you're in a document to move the *insertion point*, a little line that indicates where your next action will take place. For example, in a letter you're writing, you might click in front of a word you already typed and then type another word to insert it. Clicking is also used in various windows to select check boxes or radio buttons (also called *option buttons*) to turn features on or off or to select an object such as a picture or table in your document.

➡ **Right-click.** If you click the right mouse button, Windows displays a shortcut menu that's specific to the item you clicked. For example, if you right-click a picture, the menu that appears gives you options for working with the picture. If you right-click the Windows desktop, the menu that appears lets you choose commands that display a different view or change desktop properties.

→ **Click and drag.** To click and drag, you press and continue to hold down the left mouse button and then move (drag) the mouse to another location. For instance, you can click in a document and drag your mouse up, down, right, or left to highlight contents of your document. This highlighted text is *selected*, meaning that any action you perform, such as pressing the Delete key on your keyboard or clicking a button for bold formatting, is performed on the selected text.

→ **Scroll.** Many mouse models have a wheel in the center that you can roll up or down to scroll through a document or website on your screen. Just roll the wheel down to move through pages going forward, or scroll up to move backward in your document.

Work with a Touchscreen

Though most people don't have touchscreen computers today, Windows 8 was designed to work with this form of input, so I want to give you an overview of how to use a touchscreen computer with Windows 8.

With a touchscreen computer or tablet device, your finger replaces a mouse click. You can tap the screen to select something, to activate features with buttons, and to make a field active so you can type content. Windows 8 also offers an onscreen keyboard that touchscreen users can work with to enter text with the tap of a finger.

You can also use your finger to swipe to the right, left, up, or down to move from one page to another (for example, from one web page to another or from one photo to the next in the Gallery app) or to move up or down on a page.

Windows 8 also offers some gestures you can make with your fingers, such as moving your fingers apart and then pinching them together to minimize elements on your screen, or swiping down from the top of the screen to close an app. If you do own a touchscreen and want to learn more, visit `http://windows.microsoft.com/en-us/windows7/using-touch-gestures` for more information.

Use Shortcuts

A *keyboard shortcut* refers to a key or combinations of keys that you press and hold to perform an action. Many shortcuts involve the Windows key (it's the one near the left-bottom corner of your keyboard that sports the Windows logo). For example, you can press and hold the Windows key plus C (Win+C) to display the Charms in Windows 8.

In Windows 8, keyboard shortcuts can be very helpful to those who don't have a touchscreen computer. Table 2-1 lists some handy shortcuts to know.

Table 2-1	Common Windows 8 Keyboard Shortcuts
Key(s)	**Result**
Windows key	Displays the Start screen.
Win+B	Displays the desktop.
Win+C	Displays the Charms bar.
Win+E	Displays File Explorer.
Win+F	Displays the Files search field.
Win+I	Displays the Settings panel.
Win+L	Displays the Lock screen.
Atl+D	Displays the Address field in Internet Explorer 10.
Win+Tab	Displays recently used apps.

Log on to Windows 8

1. With your computer set up, you're ready to turn it on. Start by pressing the power button on your computer to begin the Windows 8 start-up sequence.

2. In the resulting Windows 8 Welcome screen, click the bottom of the screen and drag upward to reveal the sign-in screen.

Enter your password or PIN, if you've set one, and then press Enter on your keyboard. (If you haven't set up the password-protection feature for more than one user, you're taken directly to the Windows 8 desktop when you turn on your computer. If you have more than one user you have to choose the one you want to log on as.) Windows 8 verifies your password and displays the Windows 8 Start screen.

 For more on adding and changing user passwords, see Chapter 22. After you set up more than one user, before you get to the password screen, you have to click the icon for the user you wish to log on as.

Log in directly to the desktop in Windows 8.1

By default, when you log in to a Windows 8 or 8.1 computer, the Start screen appears. If you prefer to use the desktop interface, which is more familiar to users of Windows 7 and before, you can set up your Windows 8.1 laptop to log in to the desktop.

1. Log in to Windows 8.1 and click the desktop tile to go to the desktop interface.

2. Right-click the taskbar and click Properties on the pop-up menu.

3. Click the Navigation tab.

4. Click the Go to the Desktop Instead of Start When I Sign In check box.

5. Click OK.

Set the Date and Time

1. The calendar and clock on your computer keep good time, but you might have to provide the correct date and time for your location. Place your mouse in the upper- or lower-right corner of the screen to display the Charms bar.

2. Click Settings (the bottom charm in the Charms bar that appears, as shown in **Figure 2-2**).

3. In the Settings panel, click Change PC Settings.

4. In the PC Settings panel, click General (see **Figure 2-3**).

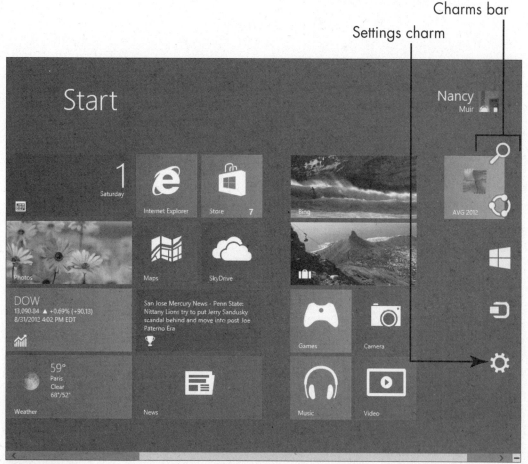

Figure 2-2

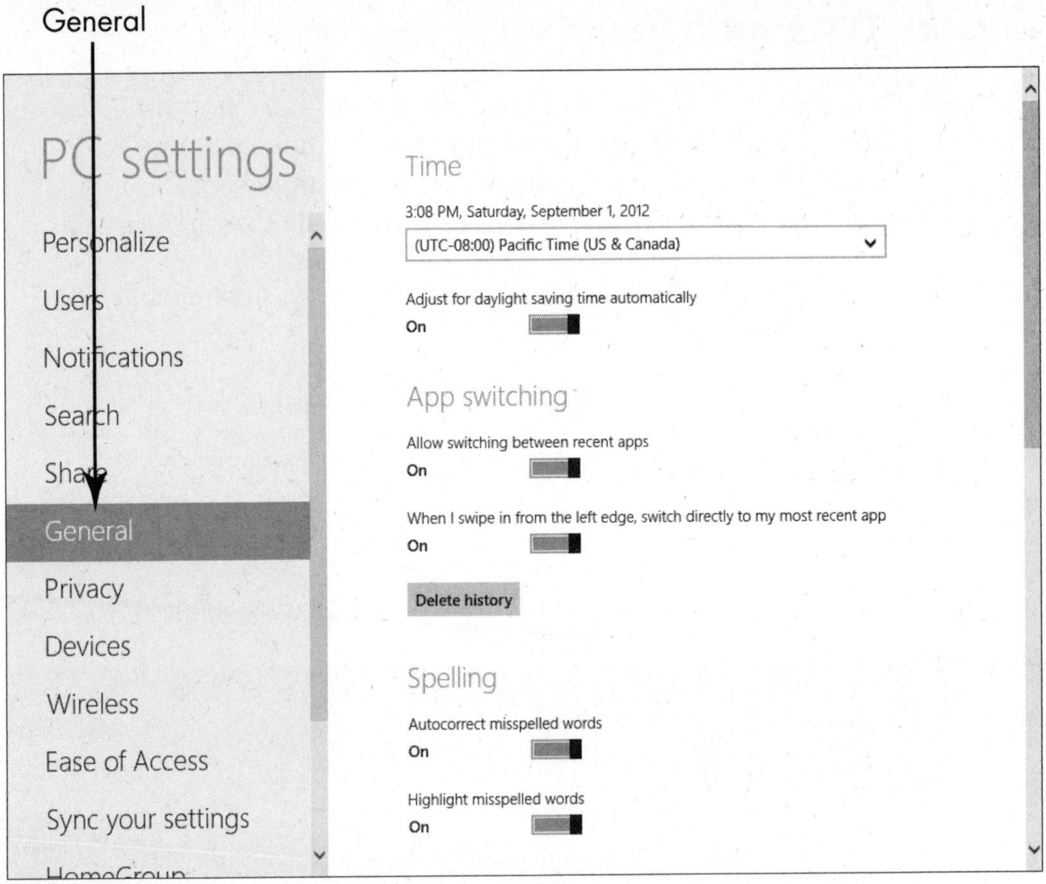

General

PC settings

Personalize

Users

Notifications

Search

Share

General

Privacy

Devices

Wireless

Ease of Access

Sync your settings

HomeGroup

Time

3:08 PM, Saturday, September 1, 2012

(UTC-08:00) Pacific Time (US & Canada)

Adjust for daylight saving time automatically

On

App switching

Allow switching between recent apps

On

When I swipe in from the left edge, switch directly to my most recent app

On

Delete history

Spelling

Autocorrect misspelled words

On

Highlight misspelled words

On

Figure 2-3

5. Click the Time field in the right panel and then choose a time zone.

6. If you want to, click the Adjust for Daylight Saving Time Automatically On/Off button to turn this feature on or off.

7. Press the Windows key on your keyboard to return to the Start screen.

 Another way to display the Charms bar is to press Win+C.

Windows 8.1 has different PC settings than Windows 8, so some procedures such as setting the date and time have different steps. PC Settings in Windows 8.1 include: PC & Devices, Accounts, SkyDrive, Search & Apps, Privacy, Network, Time & Language, Ease of Access, and Update & Recovery. In the case of Date and Time settings, you find them under Time & Language in 8.1 rather than under General.

Create a New User Account

1. You must have administrator status to create new users. This time, try a keyboard shortcut to get to the Settings panel. Press Win+I.

2. Click Change PC Settings.

3. In the PC Settings screen shown in **Figure 2-4,** click Users and then scroll down and click the Add a User button (it's about halfway down the right panel and has a plus sign on it).

4. In the next screen, shown in **Figure 2-5,** enter the user's Microsoft e-mail address (such as a Microsoft Hotmail account ending in @msn.com, @live.com, @hotmail.com, and accounts in the most recent version of Microsoft mail, Outlook.com). By providing this account information, you make it easy to sync settings, files, and apps (programs such as the Weather or Calendar app) among different devices.

   If the person doesn't have such an account, click the Sign Up For A New Email Address link at the bottom of the screen and follow the instructions to create an account; or if the person doesn't want to use such an account, click the Sign in without a Microsoft Account link and then click the Local Account button on the screen that appears and fill in the user information.

Click Users...

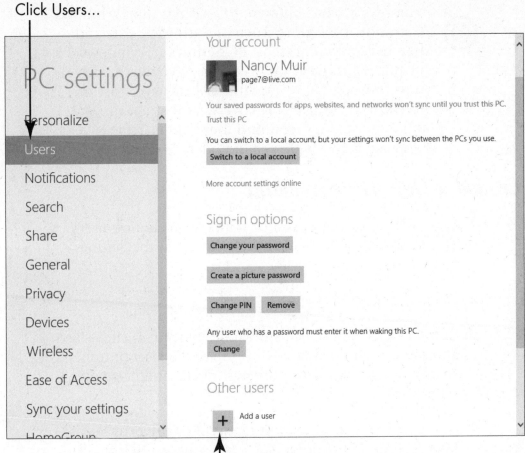

then click the Add a User button

Figure 2-4

5. Click Next.

6. On the next screen, click Finish.

 After you create an account, when a user with administrative privileges is logged in he or she can make changes to the user account in the Users panel of PC Settings, such as assigning a password. See Chapter 21 for information about setting and changing user passwords.

Enter the e-mail address here

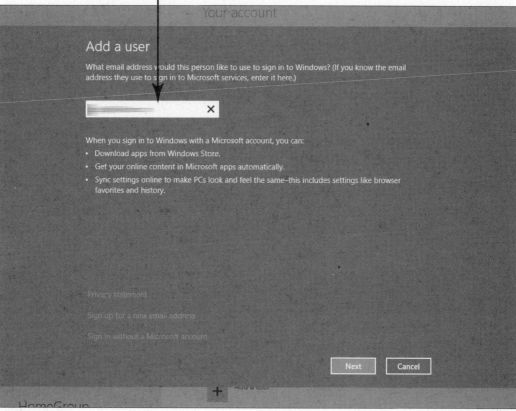

Figure 2-5

 If you prefer, you can log in with a four-digit PIN in place of a traditional password. This makes it quicker to sign in. When you've logged in as the user for which you want to set a PIN, follow the first two steps of the previous task and then in the Users section of PC Settings, just click Create a PIN, enter the current password, enter a four-digit PIN and verify it, and then click OK.

 You can set up several user accounts for your computer, which helps you save and access specific user settings and provides privacy for each user's files with passwords.

Switch User Accounts

1. To change to another user account after you've logged in, you can click the logged in user's name in the upper-right corner of the Start screen and choose Sign Out; or you can click the Power button in the Settings screen and then click Sleep (see **Figure 2-6**). Windows 8 logs off.

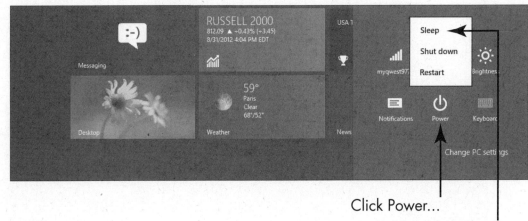

Click Power...

then click Sleep

Figure 2-6

2. Click your mouse to redisplay the welcome screen.

3. Click and drag the welcome screen upward.

4. Click the arrow to the left of the user picture to display a list of users.

5. Click the username, type the password, and press Enter to go to the Windows Start screen.

Change the User Account Type

1. Only users with administrator status can create and make changes to user accounts. You set the type of account (administrator or standard user) for the logged-in user in

the desktop Control Panel. From the Start screen, begin
to type **control panel** and then click the Control Panel
app that appears in the results.

2. Click User Accounts and Family Safety.

3. Click User Accounts (see **Figure 2-7**).

Click this option

Figure 2-7

4. Click Change Account Type and enter an administrator
password if requested.

5. Select the type of account you want to create in the
screen shown in **Figure 2-8**:

- **Administrator,** who can do things such as creating
and changing accounts and installing programs

- **Standard user,** who can access his or her own
account, but can't make the changes to user
account settings that an administrator can

6. Click the Change Account Type button and then close the
Control Panel.

Select the account type here

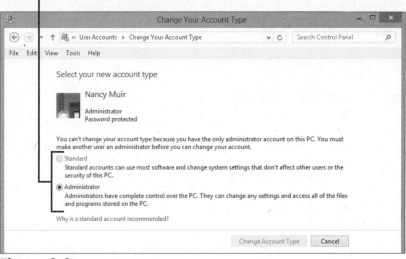

Figure 2-8

Shut down Your Computer

1. To turn off your computer when you're done, you need to initiate a shutdown sequence in your operating system instead of simply turning off the power. Press Win+I to open the Settings panel.

2. Click the Power button (refer to **Figure 2-6**). If you prefer to stop your computer running but not turn the power off, click Sleep (or simply close the lid of your laptop). If you want to reboot (turn off and turn back on) your computer, choose Restart. To shut off the power, click Shut Down.

 If your computer freezes up for some reason, you can turn it off in a couple of ways. Press Ctrl+Alt+Delete twice in a row, or press the power button on your CPU and hold it until the computer shuts down.

 Don't simply turn off your computer at the power source unless you have to because of a computer dysfunction. Windows might not start up properly the next time you turn it on if you don't follow the proper shutdown procedure.

Getting around Windows 8

Chapter 3

Windows has always used a desktop metaphor for the main Windows screen, a place where you can access all the tools you use to get your work done. However, in Windows 8, you have both a desktop and a Start screen interface (the *interface* is simply what you see on the screen), and you can use either one to complete most of the tasks you need to do. This dual interface helps users of earlier versions of Windows to fall back on the more familiar desktop as they learn their way around the Start screen, and the desktop actually provides the only access to some settings and features.

This chapter is an introduction to the things you can do from the desktop and Start screen and how these two interfaces differ. Along the way, you discover the Charms bar, accessible from either interface and used for accessing various settings. You discover how to work with the new integrated Search feature from the Start screen. You also encounter the Recycle Bin accessed through the desktop; this is where you place deleted files and folders. Finally, you find out how to work with desktop windows, create a desktop shortcut, and close a desktop program window.

Get ready to . . .

➡ Understand Changes in Windows 8 42

➡ Work with the Start Screen ... 43

➡ Display the Charms Bar 46

➡ Search for Files, Apps, and Settings 47

➡ View Recent Apps 49

➡ Work with Windows 8 Using a Touchscreen Device... 50

➡ Explore the Desktop 50

➡ Work with Frequently Used Programs 52

➡ Arrange Icons on the Desktop 54

➡ Empty the Recycle Bin.......... 55

➡ Find a File or Open an Application with File Explorer 56

➡ Create a Shortcut to a File or Folder 57

➡ Switch between Programs 58

➡ Resize Windows 59

Understand Changes in Windows 8

The Start screen (see **Figure 3-1**) is made up of small boxes called *tiles* that represent apps such as Weather, Music, and Mail. The Start screen is a command center for organizing your computer work. You can add or remove tiles to access the apps you use most often.

The Start screen is also designed to work well with touchscreen devices, such as touchscreen computers and tablets, because it's graphical in nature. You tap a tile, and an app opens without you having to select from a menu or list. But you can also easily use a mouse and keyboard to get things done on the Start screen.

Figure 3-1

You can toggle back and forth from the Start screen to the desktop (see **Figure 3-2**). On the desktop, a taskbar offers settings for items such as your computer's date and time, as well as shortcuts to currently active programs. If you've used previous versions of Windows, you're familiar with the desktop.

Figure 3-2

You can move back and forth between the Start screen and desktop at any time by pressing the Windows key on your keyboard. If you press this key from within an app, you go to the Start screen.

Work with the Start Screen

1. If the Start screen isn't displayed, press the Windows key on your keyboard to display it.

2. Click the Weather tile (see **Figure 3-3**); the Weather app opens.

3. Press the Windows key to return to the Start screen.

4. Click the right arrow along the bottom of the screen to scroll to the right and view more apps (see **Figure 3-4**).

5. Click the left arrow at the bottom of the screen to scroll to the left.

6. Move your mouse over the top-left corner of the screen to see thumbnails of recently used apps (see **Figure 3-5**).

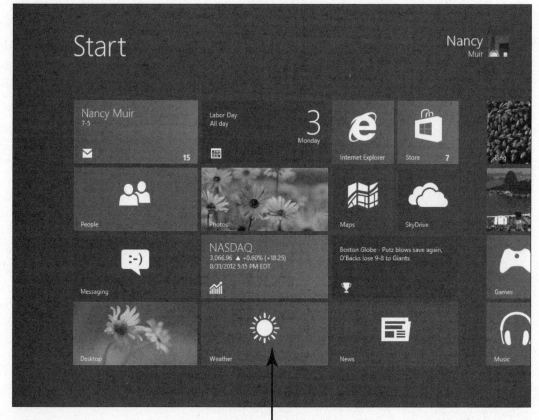

Click this tile

Figure 3-3

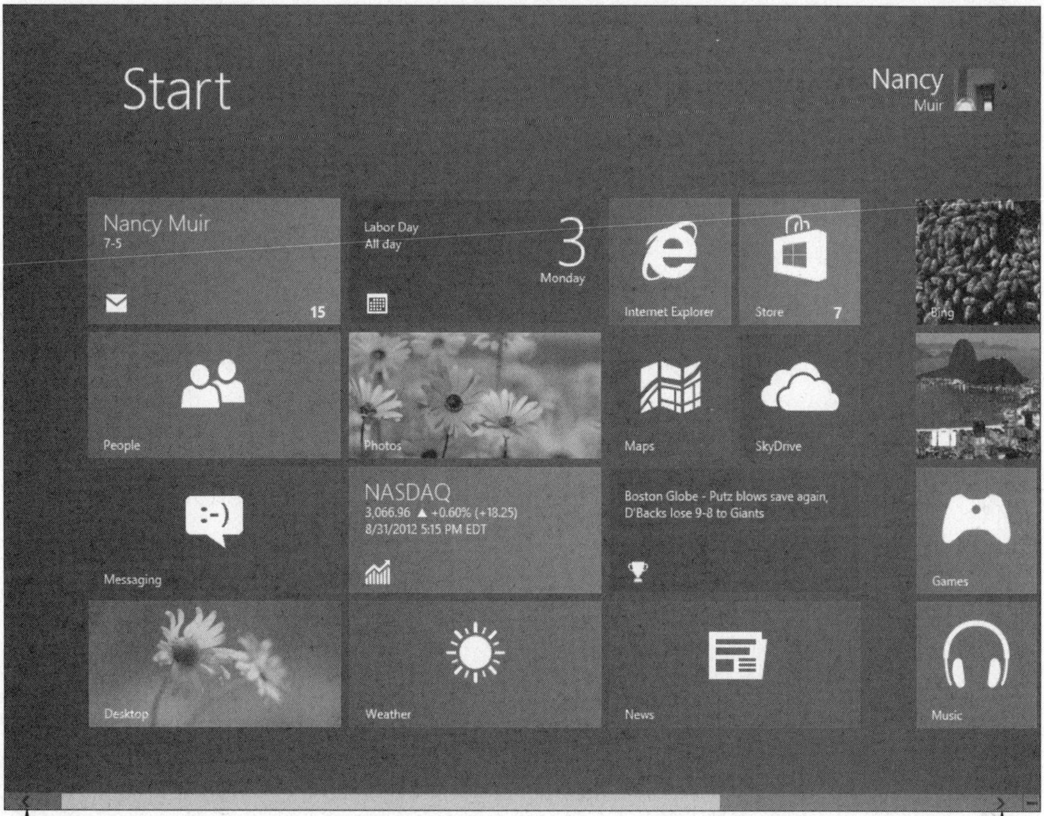

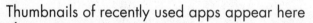

Scroll left   Scroll right

Figure 3-4

Thumbnails of recently used apps appear here

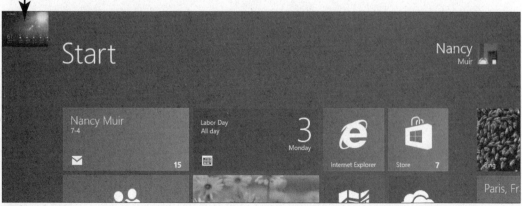

Figure 3-5

Display the Charms Bar

1. The Charms bar provides another way to go to the Start screen, the integrated Search feature, and various settings for your computer. Move your mouse to the top- or bottom-right corner of the screen to display the Charms bar (see **Figure 3-6**).

2. Move your mouse to the Settings charm to display some of the most commonly accessed settings such as Volume and Power (see **Figure 3-7).**

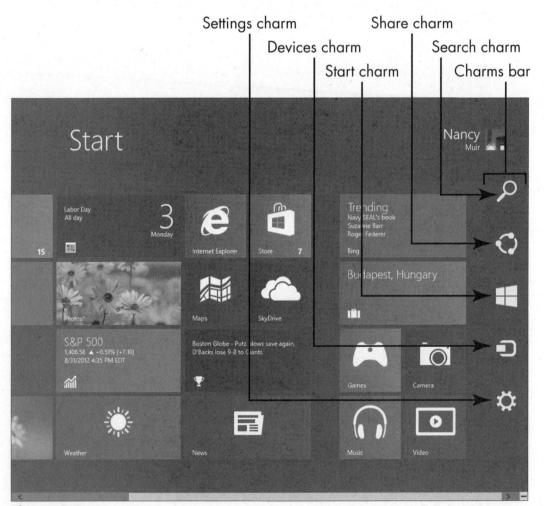

Figure 3-6

Figure 3-7

3. Move your mouse to the top- or bottom-right corner of the screen again and click the Start charm to display the Start screen.

A quick way to display the Charms bar from the desktop or Start screen is to press the Windows key and, while keeping it held down, press C.

Search for Files, Settings, and Apps

1. Windows 8 has an integrated search feature that you access by simply typing on the Start screen. Typing part of the name of any file, setting, or app brings up the Search screen and any search results. This is the easiest way to open an app that doesn't have a dedicated tile on the Start screen. With the Start screen displayed, begin to type **print**.

2. On the Search screen that appears (see **Figure 3-8**), click the Files category in the panel on the right if it's not already selected to view files containing the search term.

Click this category

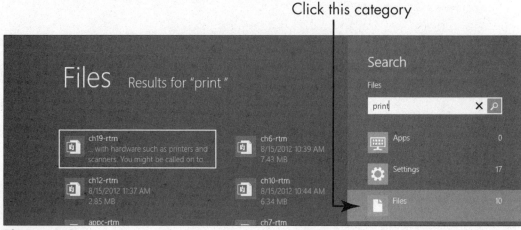

Figure 3-8

3. Click Settings (see **Figure 3-9**) to view search results for settings related to the search term.

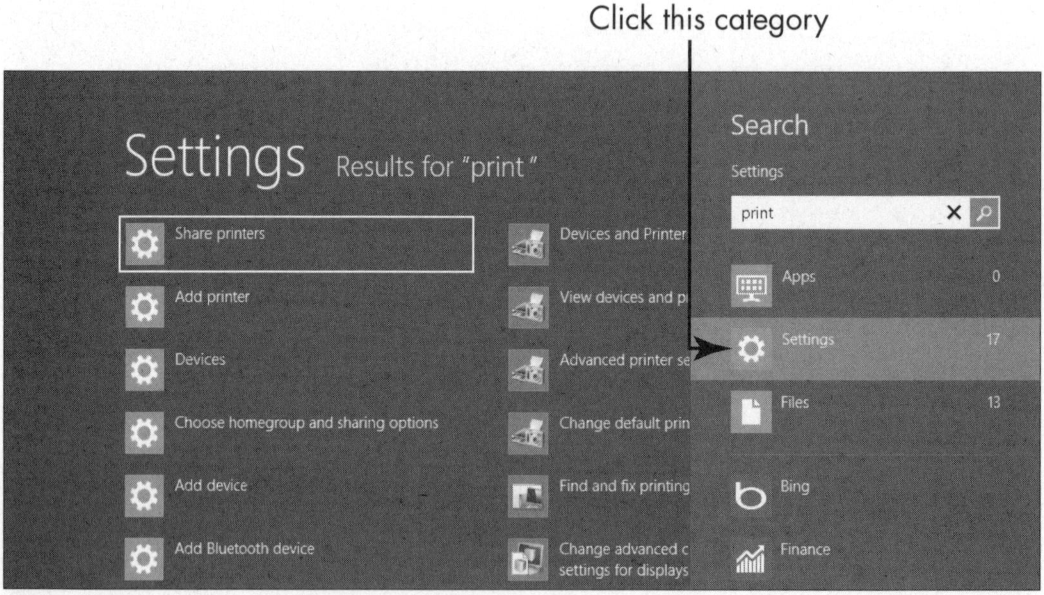

Click this category

Figure 3-9

4. Click the Apps category in the panel on the right to view results for apps related to the search term.

5. Press the Windows key on your keyboard to return to the Start screen.

 Desktop apps open in the desktop, and Windows 8 apps (those designed to be accessed through tiles on the Start screen) open full screen. To test this out, type **video** from the Start screen and then click the Video app in the search results.

View Recent Apps

1. Move your mouse to the upper-left corner of the Start screen until a thumbnail of an app appears.

2. Drag your mouse down the left edge of the screen to see all recently opened apps and settings (see **Figure** 3-10).

Recently opened apps and settings

Figure 3-10

3. Click to open the item whose thumbnail appears to the right of the mouse cursor. The app opens.

 The Recent Apps feature also works from the desktop. When you display recently opened apps from the desktop, you see a Start screen thumbnail at the

bottom of the display that you can click to go to the
Start screen.

Work with Windows 8 Using a Touchscreen Device

If you have a touchscreen device, either a computer, laptop, or tablet,
you'll be glad to hear that Windows 8 is designed, to a great degree, to
be used with a touchscreen. Table 3-1 lists several of the ways you can
interact with your touchscreen computing device.

Table 3-1	Touchscreen Gestures for Windows 8
Gesture	**Result**
Swipe up or down.	Move up or down on a web page; swipe down from the top edge to close an app; swipe up from the bottom of a screen to display tools.
Swipe left or right.	Move to the right or left; for example, you can swipe left or right on the Start screen to display more app tiles.
Swipe the right edge of the screen.	Display the Charms bar.
Pinch to zoom in or out.	Zoom in or out on a page or the Start screen.
Tap.	Select an item.
Right-click.	Hold the screen until a small pop-up appears and then lift your finger to reveal the context-specific menu.

Explore the Desktop

You can use various elements of the desktop to open or manage files,
access Windows settings, go online, and more. **Figure 3-11** shows the
desktop and some of the elements on it, including the following:

➠ The **taskbar** displays frequently used programs such
as Internet Explorer and File Explorer. It also shows
currently open programs; you can click an icon to
switch programs.

➡ The right end of the taskbar, which is called the **noti-fication area,** contains many commonly used functions such as the computer date and time settings, the network connections icons, and the icon to control system volume.

➡ The **Recycle Bin** holds recently deleted items. It will empty itself when it reaches its maximum size (which you can modify by right-clicking the Recycle Bin and choosing Properties), or you empty it manually. Check out the task "Empty the Recycle Bin" later in this chapter for more about this.

➡ **Desktop shortcuts** are icons that reside on the desktop and provide a shortcut to opening a software program or file, much like tiles on the Start screen. Your computer usually comes with some shortcuts, such as the Recycle Bin and a browser shortcut, but you can also add or delete shortcuts. Double-click a desktop shortcut to launch the associated program. See the "Create a Shortcut to a File or Folder" task later in this chapter.

You might be familiar with a set of apps called Gadgets (available in earlier versions of Windows) that you can access from the desktop. Unfortunately Gadgets are gone, giving way to the brave new world of apps.

The desktop is always there as you open desktop program windows to get your work done. If you make a program window as big as it can be (maximize it by clicking the Maximize button in the top-right corner, to the left of the Close button), you won't see the desktop, but you can go back to the desktop at any time by shrinking a window (minimizing it by clicking the Minimize button in the top-right corner) or closing the window (clicking the X button in the top-right corner). You can also press Alt+Tab simultaneously and choose the desktop from the open programs icons in the window that appears.

Recycle Bin   Desktop shortcuts

Taskbar   Notification area

Figure 3-11

Work with Frequently Used Programs

1. If you use certain programs often, you might want to pin them to the jump list area, which is on the left end of the taskbar (see **Figure 3-12**), for easy access. To open any of these items, click its icon.

Jump list area

Figure 3-12

2. The window for that program opens (see **Figure** 3-13). To close the window, click the Close button in the top-right corner (with an X on it).

Figure 3-13

3. To pin additional items to the taskbar, right-click an application on the desktop and then choose Pin This Program to Taskbar. You can also drag a desktop icon to the taskbar.

 If you want help creating a desktop shortcut, see the task, "Create a Shortcut to a File or Folder," later in this chapter.

 You can add other functions to the taskbar. Right-click a blank area of the taskbar and choose Properties. Click the Toolbars tab to display it. Click the check box for any of the additional items listed there, such as a browser address bar or links.

Arrange Icons on the Desktop

1. Right-click the desktop and choose View from the result-ing shortcut menu; be sure that Auto Arrange Icons isn't selected, as shown in **Figure 3-14.** If it is selected, dese-lect it before proceeding to the next step.

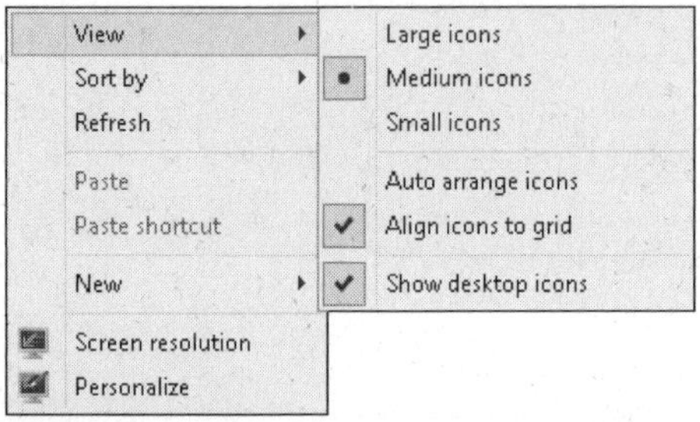

Figure 3-14

2. Right-click the Windows desktop. From the resulting shortcut menu, choose Sort By, and then click the criteria for sorting your desktop shortcuts (see **Figure 3-15**).

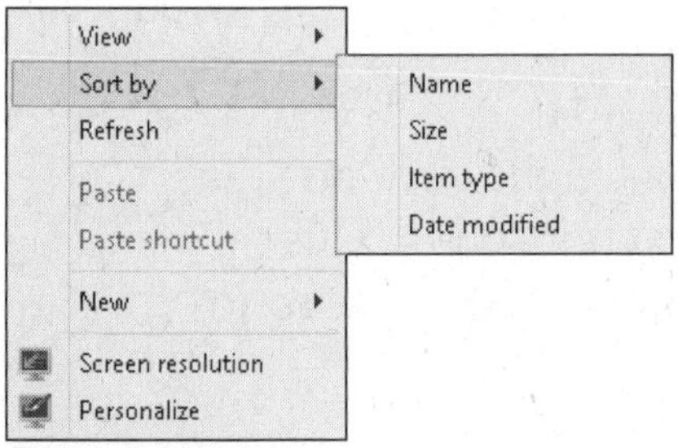

Figure 3-15

3. You can also click any icon and drag it to another loca-tion on the desktop — for example, to separate it from other desktop icons so you can find it easily.

If you've rearranged your desktop by moving items hither, thither, and yon and you want your icons in orderly rows along the left side of your desktop, snap them into place with the Auto Arrange feature.

Right-click the desktop and then choose View➪Auto Arrange Icons.

 Use the shortcut menu in Step 1 and choose Large Icons, Medium Icons, or Small Icons in the View sub-menu to change the size of desktop icons.

Empty the Recycle Bin

1. When you throw away junk mail, it's still in the house — it's just in the Recycle Bin instead of on your desk. That's the idea behind the Windows Recycle Bin. Your old files sit there, and you can retrieve them until you empty it — or until it reaches its size limit and Windows dumps a few files. Right-click the Recycle Bin icon on the Windows desktop and choose Empty Recycle Bin from the menu that appears (see **Figure 3-16**).

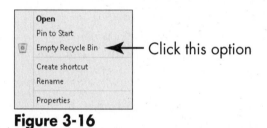

Figure 3-16

2. In the confirmation dialog box that appears (see **Figure 3-17**), click Yes. A progress dialog box appears, indicating the contents are being deleted. *Remember:* After you empty the Recycle Bin, all files that were in it are unavailable to you.

Figure 3-17

Up until the moment you permanently delete items by performing the preceding steps, you can retrieve them from the Recycle Bin by double-clicking the Recycle Bin desktop icon. Select the item you want to retrieve and then click the Restore the Selected Items link on the Manage tab of the Recycle Bin ribbon.

 You can modify the Recycle Bin properties by right-clicking it and choosing Properties. In the dialog box that appears, you can change the maximum size for the Recycle Bin and whether to immediately delete files you move to the Recycle Bin. You can also dese-lect the option of having a confirmation dialog box appear when you delete Recycle Bin contents.

Find a File or Open an Application with File Explorer

1. File Explorer is a program you can use to find a file or folder by navigating through an outline of folders and subfolders. It's a great way to look for files on your com-puter. From the desktop, click the File Explorer button on the taskbar (it looks like a set of folders.)

2. In the resulting File Explorer window (shown in **Figure 3-18**), double-click a folder in the main window or in the list along the left side to open the folder.

3. The folder's contents are displayed. If necessary, open a series of folders in this manner until you locate the file you want.

4. When you find the file you want, double-click it to open it.

 To see different perspectives and information about files in File Explorer, click the View tab and choose one of the following options: Extra Large Icons, Large Icons, Medium Icons, or Small Icons for graphical displays, or choose Details to show details such as the last date files were modified.

Double-click a folder to open it

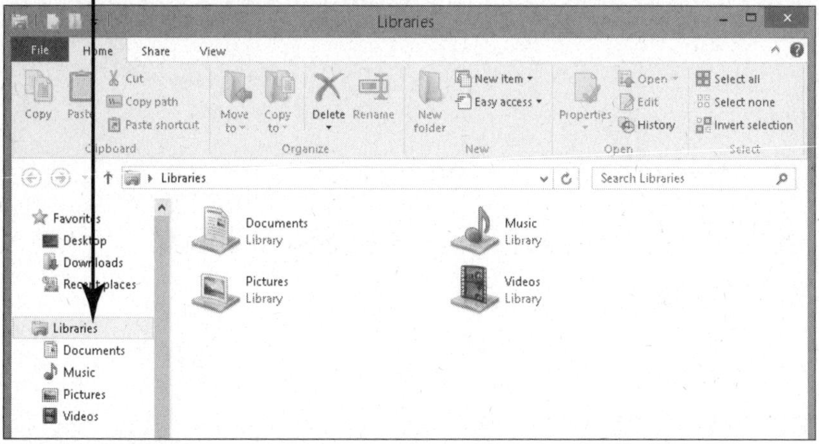

Figure 3-18

Create a Shortcut to a File or Folder

1. Shortcuts are handy little icons you can put on the desktop for quick access to items you use on a frequent basis. (See the earlier task, "Explore the Desktop," for an introduction to shortcuts.) To create a new shortcut, first click the File Explorer icon on the taskbar.

2. Locate a file or folder and then right-click and choose Create Shortcut, as shown in **Figure 3-19**.

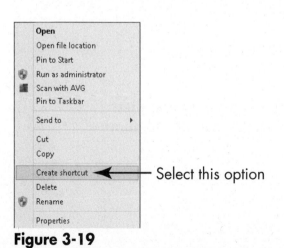 ——— Select this option

Figure 3-19

3. Click and drag the shortcut that appears to the desktop (see **Figure 3-20**). Double-click the icon to open the file or folder.

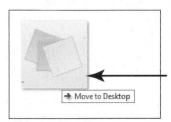

Double-click to use the new shortcut

Figure 3-20

 To restore your desktop to its original shortcuts, right-click the desktop and choose Personalize. Click the Change Desktop Icons link to the left. In the Desktop Icon Setting dialog box that appears, click the Restore Default button, which returns to the original desktop shortcuts set up on your computer.

 You can create a shortcut for a brand-new item by right-clicking the desktop, choosing New, and then choosing an item to place there, such as a text document, bitmap image, or contact. Then double-click the shortcut that appears and begin working on the file in the associated application.

Switch between Programs

1. Open two or more programs. The last program that you open is the active program.

2. Press Alt+Tab to reveal all open programs and press Tab to cycle from one open application window to another, as shown in **Figure 3-21**.

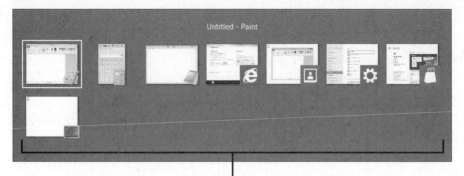

Press the Tab key to select another open application in this list

Figure 3-21

3. Release the Alt key, and Windows 8 switches to whichever program is selected. To switch back to the last program that was active, simply press Alt+Tab, and that
program becomes the active program once again.

 All open programs also appear as items on the
Windows 8 desktop taskbar. Just click any running
program on the taskbar to display that window and
make it the active program. If the taskbar isn't visible,
press the Windows key on your keyboard to display it.

Resize Windows

1. When you open an application window, it can be maximized to fill the whole screen, restored down to a smaller
window, or minimized to an icon on the taskbar. With
an application open and maximized, click the Restore
Down button (the icon showing two overlapping windows) in the top-right corner of the program window
(see **Figure 3-22**). The window reduces in size.

 The Restore Down button

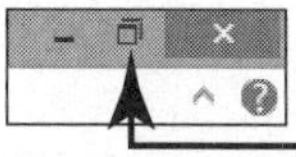

Figure 3-22

2. To enlarge a window that has been restored down, to again fill the screen, click the Maximize button. (*Note:* This button is in the same location as the Restore Down button; this button changes its name to one or the other, depending on whether you have the screen reduced in size or maximized. A ScreenTip identifies the button when you rest your mouse pointer on it.)

3. Click the Minimize button (it's to the left of the Restore Down/Maximize button and looks like a dash or underline) to minimize the window to an icon on the taskbar. To open the window again, just click the taskbar icon.

 With a window maximized, you can't move the window. If you reduce a window in size, you can then click and hold the title bar to drag the window around the desktop, which is one way to view more than one window on your screen at the same time. You can also click and drag the corners of a reduced window to resize it to any size you want.

What's new in Windows 8.1?

Windows 8.1 added a Start button to the desktop. Clicking this takes you to the Start screen; right-clicking it produces a menu of commands that allow you to go to the Control Panel and Task Manager, manage devices and network connections, and much more. You can also log in directly to the desktop or the Start screen (Windows 8 logs in only to the Start screen) and customize backgrounds so your desktop and Start screen use the same background. In addition, PC Settings offer different options in 8.1 — it may take you a few moments to figure out how to get some tasks done.

Setting Up Your Display

*Y*ou chose your designer Day Planner, paper clip holder, and solid maple inbox for your real-world desktop, right? Why shouldn't the Windows desktop and Start screen give you the same flexibility to make things look the way you like? After all, these are the main work areas of Windows, spaces that you traverse many, many times in a typical day. Take it from somebody who spends many hours in front of a computer: Customizing your computer interface pays off in increased productivity as well as decreased eyestrain.

The desktop and Start screen each offer their own customization options. To customize their appearance, you can do the following:

➠ Set up the desktop, Start screen, and lock screen to display background images and colors.

➠ Use screen saver settings to switch from the tasks you work on every day to a pretty animation when you've stopped working for a time.

➠ You can modify your *screen resolution* setting, which controls the visual crispness of the images your screen displays. (See Chapter 5 for more about resolution settings that help those with visual challenges.)

Get ready to . . .

➠ Customize Windows's Appearance 62

➠ Set Your Screen's Resolution 63

➠ Change the Start Screen Background and Color 65

➠ Change the Lock Screen Picture 66

➠ Change Your Account Picture 67

➠ Change the Desktop Background 70

➠ Choose a Desktop Theme 72

➠ Set Up a Screen Saver 73

➠ Modify Windows transparency. Windows Aero Glass is an effect that makes the borders of your windows transparent so you can see other windows layered underneath the active window. You might love it or hate it, but you should know how to turn the effect on or off.

Customize Windows's Appearance

When you take your computer out of the box, Windows comes with certain preset, or default, settings such as the appearance of the desktop and a color scheme for items you see on your screen. Here are some of the things you can change about the Windows environment and why you might want to change them:

➠ Desktop and Start screen backgrounds: As you work with your computer, you might find that changing the appearance of various elements on your screen not only makes them more pleasant to look at, but also helps you see the text and images more easily. You can change the graphic that's shown as the desktop background, even displaying your own picture there, or choose from several preset background patterns for the Start screen.

➠ Screen resolution: You can adjust your screen resolution to not only affect the crispness of images on your screen but also cause the items on your screen to appear larger, which could help you if you have visual challenges. (See Chapter 5 for more about Windows features that help people with visual, hearing, or dexterity challenges.)

➠ Themes: Windows has built-in desktop *themes* that you can apply quickly. Themes save sets of elements that include menu appearance, background colors or patterns, screen savers, and even mouse cursors and system sounds. If you choose a theme and then modify the way your computer looks in some way — for example, by changing the color scheme — that change overrides the setting in the theme you last applied.

➠ Screen **savers:** These animations appear after your computer remains inactive for a specified time. In the early days of personal computers, screen savers helped to keep monitors from burning out from constant use. Today, people use screen savers to automatically conceal what they're doing from pass-ersby or just to enjoy the pretty picture when they take a break.

Set Your Screen's Resolution

1. Changing screen resolution can make items onscreen eas-ier to see. From the Start screen, begin to type **control panel** and then click the Control Panel app in the results.

2. Click the Adjust Screen Resolution link under Appearance and Personalization.

3. In the resulting Screen Resolution window, click the arrow to the right of the Resolution field.

4. Use the slider (as shown in **Figure 4-1**) to select a higher or lower resolution. You can also change the orientation of your display by making a choice in the Orientation drop-down list.

5. Click OK to accept the new screen resolution and then click the Close button to close the window.

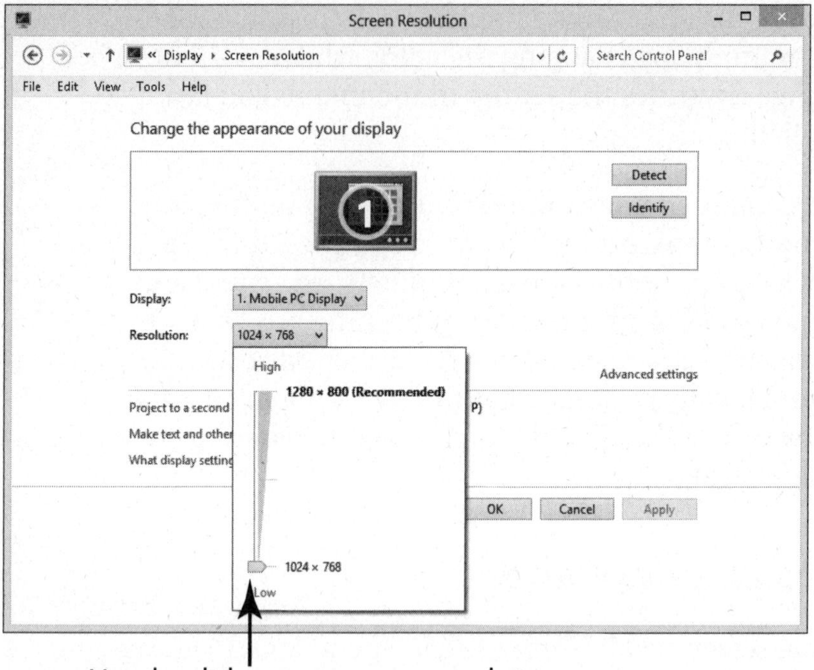

	Screen Resolution	– ▢ ✕

⊙ ⊙ ▾ ↑ | ‹‹ Display ▸ Screen Resolution   ∨ ↻   Search Control Panel   🔍

File Edit View Tools Help

Change the appearance of your display

> [①]   Detect
>   Identify

Display: 1. Mobile PC Display ∨

Resolution: 1024 × 768 ∨

High
       1280 × 800 (Recommended)   Advanced settings

Project to a second   P)
Make text and other
What display setting

                                          OK   Cancel   Apply

              1024 × 768

    Low

Use the slider to set screen resolution

Figure 4-1

 Higher resolutions, such as 1400 x 1250, produce smaller, crisper images. Lower resolutions, such as 800 x 600, produce larger, somewhat jagged images. The upside of higher resolution is that more fits on your screen; the downside is that words and graphics can be hard to see.

 The Advanced Settings link in the Screen Resolution window displays another dialog box where you can work with color management and monitor settings.

 Remember that you can also use your View settings in most software programs to get a larger or smaller view of your documents without having to change your screen's resolution.

Change the Start Screen Background and Color

1. Windows 8 offers several preset background patterns and color sets you can choose from the PC Settings. Press Win+I and then click the Change PC Settings link.

2. Click Personalize and then click the Start Screen tab in the right panel (see **Figure** 4-2).

3. Click a background.

4. Click a background color.

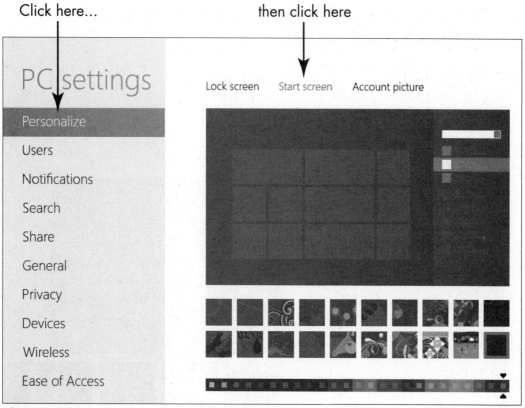

Figure 4-2

Some colors are easier on the eyes than others. For example, green is more restful to look at than purple. Choose a color scheme that's pleasant to look at and easy on the eyes!

Change the Lock Screen Picture

1. You can choose a Windows 8 picture for your lock screen (the screen that appears when your computer goes to sleep) or use one of your own pictures for the lock screen background. Press Win+I and then click the Change PC Settings link.

2. Click Personalize and then click the Lock Screen tab in the right panel (see **Figure 4-3**).

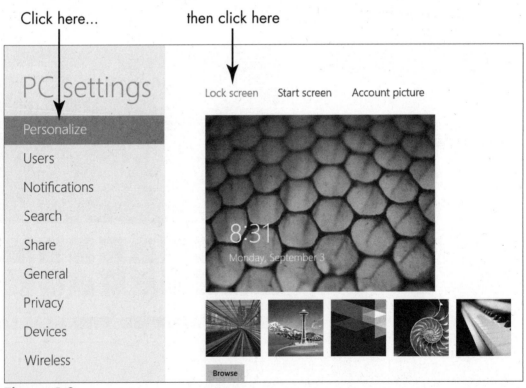

Figure 4-3

3. Click one of the pictures displayed, or click Browse to choose another picture.

4. If you chose to browse for one of your own pictures, from the Pictures folder that's displayed click a picture to use. If the picture is located in another folder, click the Go Up link to browse other folders.

5. Click the Choose Picture button.

 You can also choose a few apps that you want to keep running when your lock screen appears. On the Lock Screen tab shown in Figure 4-3, just click one of the plus signs to display the apps that are available to display, such as Weather or Mail.

Change Your Account Picture

1. Windows 8 allows you to assign a unique picture to each user account you create. When you perform these steps, you should be logged in as the user for whom you want to change the account picture; see Chapter 2 for more about this procedure. Press Win+I and then click the Change PC Settings link.

2. Click Personalize and then click the Account Picture tab in the right panel (see **Figure 4-4**).

3. At this point, you can do one of two things:

 • **Click the Browse button** and choose a picture from the files that appear (see **Figure 4-5**); click the Go Up link to explore other folders on your computer. Click the picture and then click the Choose Image button to apply it to the active account.

Click here...   then click here

Figure 4-4

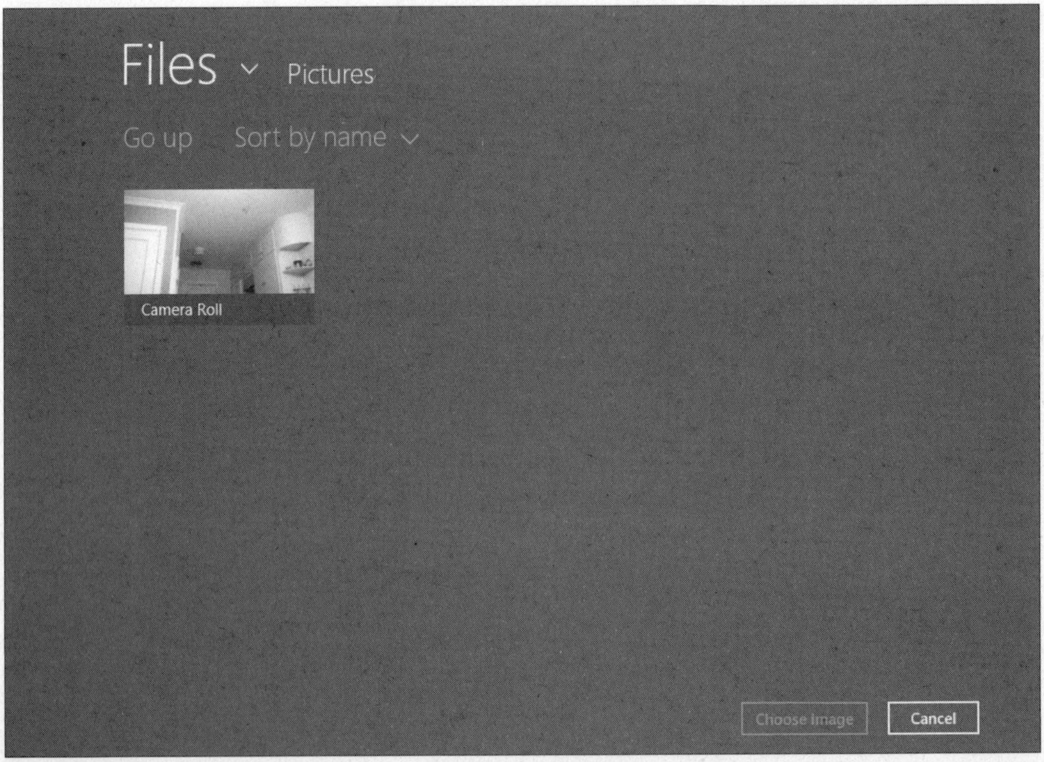

Figure 4-5

- **Click the Camera button** and in the Camera app that opens (see **Figure** 4-6) snap a picture of a person or object near your computer's *webcam* (a built-in camera device). Click the screen to take the picture, and then click the OK button to apply it to the active account.

 Many computers allow you to switch between a front- and a rear-facing camera to give you more options for taking pictures of objects around you. While in the Camera app, just click the Change Camera button to do this, if your computer has two cameras.

Camera options   Timer   Video mode

Figure 4-6

Change the Desktop Background

1. You can display a picture or color that appeals to you on your desktop. Right-click the desktop and choose Personalize from the shortcut menu.

2. In the resulting Personalization window (see Figure 4-7), click the Desktop Background link to display the Desktop Background dialog box.

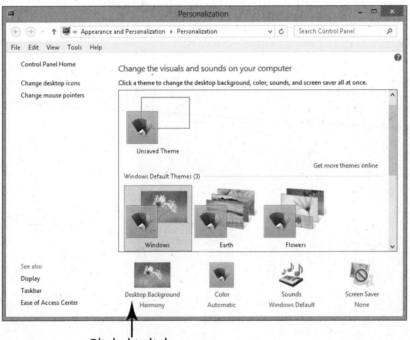

Click this link

Figure 4-7

3. Select a category of desktop background options from the Picture Location drop-down menu (see **Figure** 4-8) and then click the image that you want to use from the background preview list. The background is previewed on your desktop.

Select a category option here

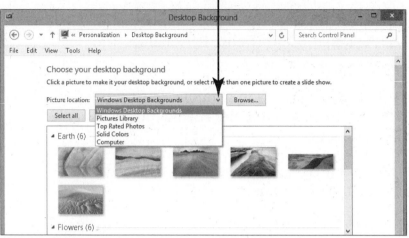

Figure 4-8

4. Click the arrow on the Picture Position list and choose a position for the picture from the thumbnails displayed there. For example, you can have the image fill the entire screen or you can tile multiple copies of the image across the screen.

5. Click the Change Picture Every setting to have the desktop background change at regular intervals.

6. Click Save Changes to apply the settings and close the dialog box, and then close the Personalization window.

 If you apply a desktop theme (see the next task), you overwrite whatever desktop settings you've made in this task. If you apply a desktop theme and then go back and make desktop settings, you replace the theme's settings. However, making changes is easy and keeps your desktop interesting, so play around with themes and desktop backgrounds all you like!

Choose a Desktop Theme

1. Themes apply several color and image settings at once. Right-click the desktop and choose Personalize. The Personalization window opens.

2. In the resulting Personalization window, shown in **Figure 4-9,** click to select a theme. Theme categories include the following:

- **My Themes:** Uses whatever settings you have and save them with that name.

- **Windows Default Themes:** Offers you the default Windows theme and themes related to Nature, Landscapes, Light Auras, and your country of residence.

- **Basic and High Contrast Themes** offers the Windows Basic theme as well as a variety of easy-to-read contrast settings in a variety of themes.

Select a desktop theme

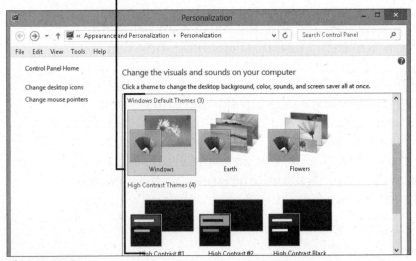

Figure 4-9

3. Click the Close button to close the dialog box.

 Themes save sets of elements that include menu appearance, background colors or patterns, screen savers, and even mouse cursors and sounds. If you modify any of these individually — for example, by changing the screen saver to another one — that change overrides the setting in the theme you last applied.

 You can save custom themes. Simply apply a theme, make any changes to it you like using the various Appearance and Personalization settings options, and then in the Personalization dialog box, right-click the Unsaved Theme and then click Save Theme from the menu that appears. In the resulting dialog box, give your new theme a name and click Save. It will now appear on the Theme list with that name.

Set Up a Screen Saver

1. If you want an animated sequence to appear when your computer isn't in use for a period of time, set up a screen saver. Right-click the desktop and choose Personalize. In the resulting Personalization window, click the Screen Saver button to display the Screen Saver Settings dialog box, as shown in **Figure 4-10.**

2. From the Screen Saver drop-down list, choose a screen saver.

3. Use the arrows in the Wait *xx* Minutes text box to set the number of inactivity minutes that Windows 8 waits before displaying the screen saver.

4. Click the Preview button to take a peek at your screen saver of choice. When you're happy with your settings, click to stop the preview, and then click OK.

5. Click the Close button in the Personalization window to close it.

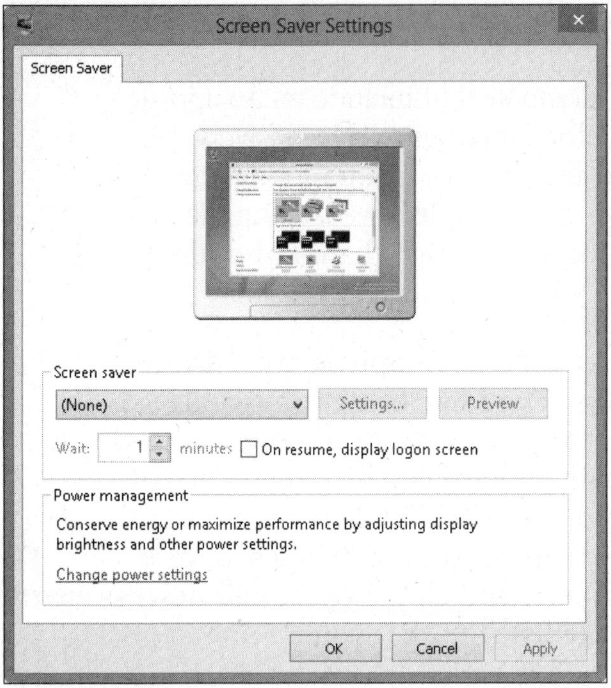

Figure 4-10

Windows 8.1 desktop background on the Start screen

If you want a more cohesive look in your computing environment, consider using the desktop background on the Start screen feature of Windows 8.1. After you make this setting, if you change the desktop background the change is reflected on the Start screen.

1. From the desktop, right-click the taskbar and choose Properties.

2. Click the Navigation tab.

3. Click the Show My Desktop Background on Start check box.

4. Click OK.

Getting Help with Vision, Hearing, and Dexterity Challenges

Chapter 5

People don't always know right off the bat how to get along when they meet someone new. Similarly, sometimes Windows has to be taught how to behave. For example, it doesn't know that somebody using it has a vision challenge that requires special help, or that a user prefers a certain mouse cursor or has difficulty using a keyboard.

Somebody taught you manners, but Windows depends on you to make settings that customize its behavior. This is good news for you because the ability to customize Windows gives you a lot of flexibility in how you interact with it.

Here's what you can do to customize Windows to work with physical challenges:

➡ Control features that help visually challenged users to work with a computer, such as setting a higher contrast, using Narrator to read the onscreen text aloud, or increasing the size of text onscreen.

Get ready to . . .

➡ Use Tools for the Visually Challenged 76

➡ Replace Sounds with Visual Cues 78

➡ Make Text Larger or Smaller 79

➡ Set Up Speech Recognition ... 81

➡ Modify How Your Keyboard Works 84

➡ Use the Onscreen Keyboard Feature 86

➡ Set Up Keyboard Repeat Rates 88

➡ Customize Mouse Behavior ... 89

➡ Change the Cursor.............. 91

➡ Work with the Speech Recognition feature, which allows you to input data into a document using speech rather than a keyboard or mouse.

➡ Modify the mouse functionality for left-handed use, change the cursor to sport a certain look, or make viewing the cursor as it moves around your screen easier.

➡ Work with keyboard settings that make input easier for those who are challenged by physical conditions, such as carpal tunnel syndrome or arthritis.

Use Tools for the Visually Challenged

1. You can set up Windows to use higher screen contrast to make things easier to see, read descriptions to you rather than make you read text, and more. Begin to type **control panel** from the Start screen and then click the Control Panel app in the search results.

2. In the Control Panel window, click the Optimize Visual Display link under the Ease of Access tools.

3. In the Make the Computer Easier to See dialog box (as shown in **Figure 5-1**), select the check boxes for features you want to use:

   • **High Contrast:** This is a color scheme that makes your screen easier to read. You can activate a keyboard shortcut to this feature by selecting the Turn On Higher Contrast When Left Alt+Left Shift+Print Screen Is Pressed check box. You can also choose to have a warning message display when you turn this setting on, or have a sound play when it's turned off or on.

   • **Hear Text and Descriptions Read Aloud:** You can turn on the Narrator feature, which reads onscreen text, and the Audio Description feature to describe what's happening in video programs that support closed-captioning features.

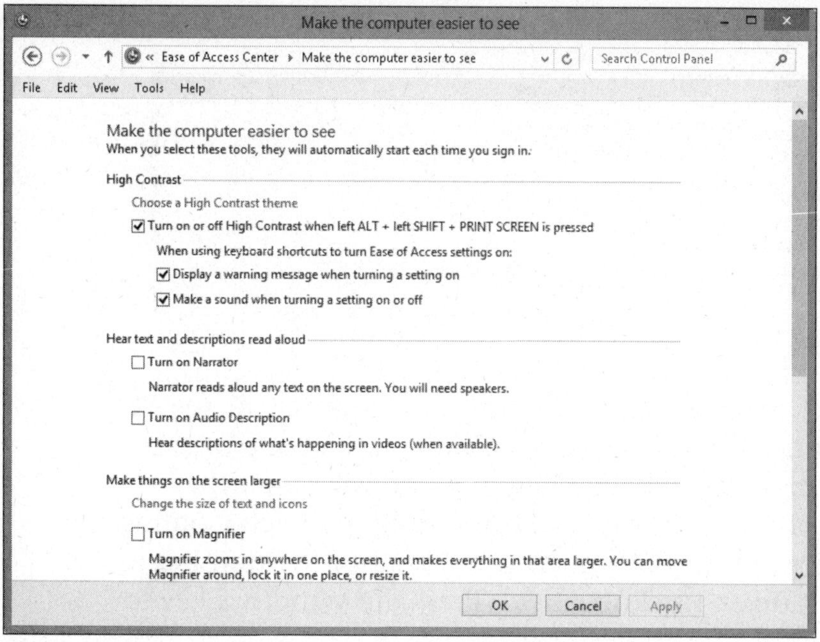

Figure 5-1

- **Make Things on the Screen Larger:** If you click Turn On Magnifier (see **Figure 5-2**), two cursors appear onscreen. One cursor appears in the Magnifier window where everything is shown enlarged, and one appears in whatever is showing on your computer (for example, your desktop or an open application). You can maneuver either cursor to work in your document. (They're both active, so it does take some getting used to.)

- **Make Things on the Screen Easier to See:** Here's where you make settings that adjust onscreen contrast to make things easier to see, set the thickness of the blinking mouse cursor, and get rid of distracting animations and backgrounds.

4. When you finish making settings, click OK to apply them and then click the Close button to close the dialog box.

Click here to turn the Magnifier on

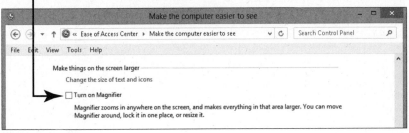

Figure 5-2

 Click Settings on the Charms bar, choose Change PC Settings⇨Ease of Access, and then make one of these settings that will also help you see what's on the screen more clearly: Click and drag the High Contrast slider to turn the feature on or change the number in the Cursor Thickness field. Press the Windows key to return to the Start screen.

Replace Sounds with Visual Cues

1. Sometimes Windows alerts you to events with sounds. If you have hearing challenges, you might prefer to get visual cues. From the Control Panel, click Ease of Access and then click the Replace Sounds with Visual Cues link.

2. In the resulting Use Text or Visual Alternatives for Sounds dialog box (see **Figure 5-3**), make any of the following settings:

- **Turn On Visual Notifications for Sounds (Sound Sentry).** If you select this check box, Windows will give a visual alert when a sound plays.

- **Choose Visual Warning.** These warnings essentially flash a portion of your screen to alert you to an event. Choose one option.

- **Turn On Text Captions for Spoken Dialog (When Available).** Select this check box to control text captions for any spoken words. *Note:* This isn't available with every application you use.

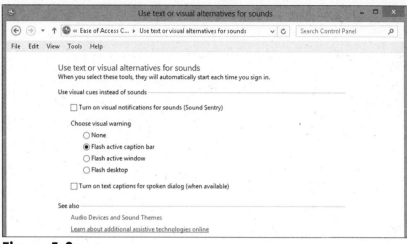

Figure 5-3

3. To save the new settings, click OK, and then click the Close button to close the dialog box.

 Visual cues are useful if you're hard of hearing and don't always pick up system sounds alerting you to error messages or a device disconnect. After the setting is turned on, it's active until you go back to the Use Text or Visual Alternatives for Sounds dialog box and turn it off.

 This may seem obvious, but if you're hard of hearing, you may want to simply increase the volume for your speakers. You can do this by using the volume adjustment in a program such as Windows Media Player (see Chapter 18) or by modifying your system volume by choosing Hardware and Sound in the Control Panel and then clicking the Adjust System Volume link.

Make Text Larger or Smaller

1. Press Win+I.

2. Click Change PC Settings and then click Ease of Access (see **Figure 5-4**).

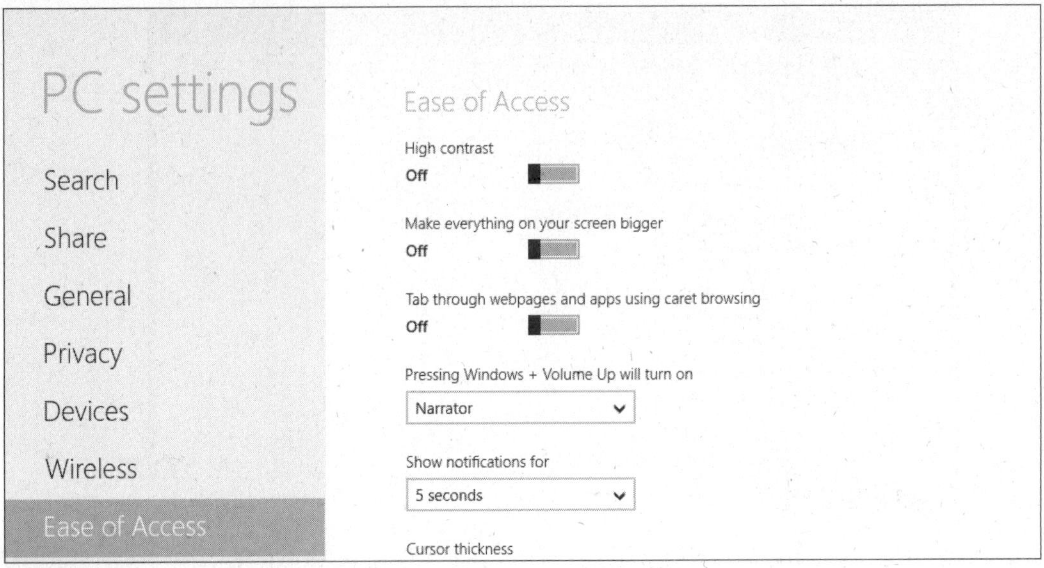

PC settings   Ease of Access

Search

Share

General

Privacy

Devices

Wireless

Ease of Access

High contrast
Off

Make everything on your screen bigger
Off

Tab through webpages and apps using caret browsing
Off

Pressing Windows + Volume Up will turn on
Narrator

Show notifications for
5 seconds

Cursor thickness

Figure 5-4

3. Click the On/Off slider for the Make Everything On Your Screen Bigger setting. You'll see the results immediately (see **Figure 5-5**, which shows the Larger setting applied).

Getting text larger with Windows 8.1

In Windows 8.1, steps for larger text are different than in the above task:

1. From Control Panel, choose Appearance and Personalization. In the next window under the Display options, click Make Text and Other Items Larger or Smaller.

2. In the resulting Display window, under Change the Size of All Items, click and drag the slider to set the size of text. Smaller is the default, but you can expand text size to 125 percent with the Medium setting and 200 percent using the Larger setting.

3. Click Apply and then click the Close button to close the window.

Figure 5-5

Set Up Speech Recognition

1. If you have dexterity challenges from a condition such as arthritis, you might prefer to speak commands, using a technology called *speech recognition*, rather than type them. Attach a desktop microphone or headset to your computer, begin to type **control panel** from the Start screen, and then click Control Panel in the search results.

2. Click Ease of Access⇨Start Speech Recognition.

3. The Welcome to Speech Recognition message appears; click Next to continue. (*Note:* If you've used Speech Recognition before, this message won't appear.)

4. In the resulting Microphone Setup Wizard (shown in **Figure 5-6**), select the type of microphone that you're using and then click Next. The next screen tells you how to place and use the microphone for optimum results. Click Next.

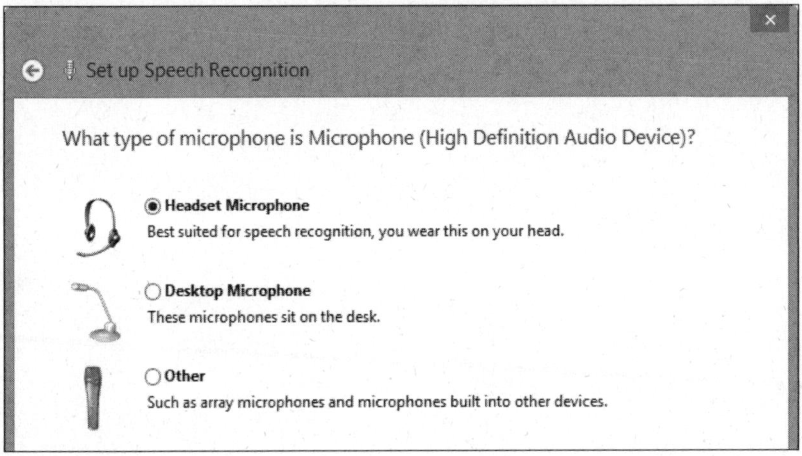

> **Set up Speech Recognition**
>
> What type of microphone is Microphone (High Definition Audio Device)?
>
> ◉ **Headset Microphone**
> Best suited for speech recognition, you wear this on your head.
>
> ○ **Desktop Microphone**
> These microphones sit on the desk.
>
> ○ **Other**
> Such as array microphones and microphones built into other devices.

Figure 5-6

5. In the following window (see **Figure 5-7**), read the sample sentence aloud. When you're done, click Next. A dialog box appears telling you that your microphone is now set up. Click Next.

> During the Speech Recognition setup procedure, you're given the option of printing out commonly used commands. It's a good idea to do this, as speech commands aren't always second nature!

6. A dialog box confirms that your microphone is set up. Click Next. In the resulting dialog box, choose whether to enable or disable *document review,* in which Windows examines your documents and e-mail to help it recognize your speech patterns. Click Next.

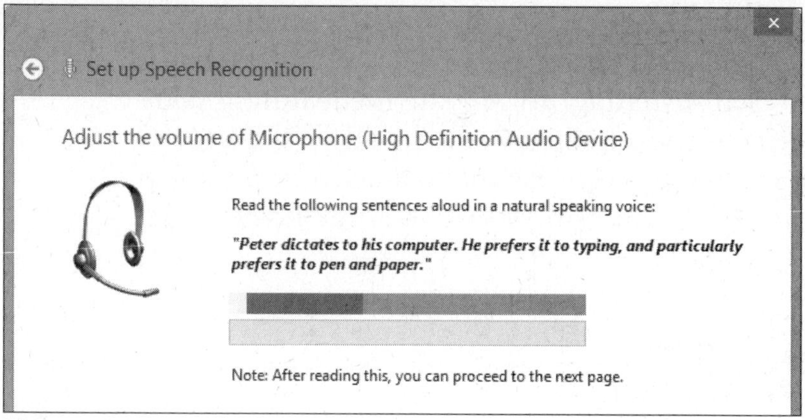

Set up Speech Recognition

Adjust the volume of Microphone (High Definition Audio Device)

Read the following sentences aloud in a natural speaking voice:

"Peter dictates to his computer. He prefers it to typing, and particularly prefers it to pen and paper."

Note: After reading this, you can proceed to the next page.

Figure 5-7

7. In the resulting dialog box, choose either manual activation mode, where you can use a mouse, pen, or keyboard to turn the feature on, or voice activation, which is useful if you have difficulty manipulating devices because of arthritis or a hand injury. Click Next.

8. In the resulting screen, if you wish to view and/or print a list of Speech Recognition commands, click the View Reference Sheet button and read or print the reference information, and then click the Close button to close that window. Click Next to proceed.

9. In the resulting dialog box, either click the Run Speech Recognition at Startup checkbox to automatically turn on Speech Recognition when you start your computer or leave the default setting to turn it on manually each time you need it. Click Next.

10. The final dialog box informs you that you can now control the computer by voice, and offers you a Start Tutorial button to help you practice voice commands. Click that button and follow the instructions to move through it, or click Skip Tutorial to skip the tutorial and leave the Speech Recognition setup.

11. When you leave the Speech Recognition setup, the Speech Recognition control panel appears (see **Figure 5-8**). Say, "Start listening" to activate the feature if you used voice activation in Step 7, or click the Start Speech Recognition link if you chose manual activation in Step 7. You can now begin using spoken commands to work with your computer.

 ——— The Speech Recognition control panel

Figure 5-8

 To stop Speech Recognition, click the Close button on the Speech Recognition control panel. To start the Speech Recognition feature again, click the Start Speech Recognition link in the Ease of Access area of the Control Panel. To learn more about Speech Recognition commands, click the Take Speech Tutorial link in the Speech Recognition Options window accessed from the Ease of Access window of the Control Panel.

Modify How Your Keyboard Works

1. If your hands are a bit stiff with age or you have carpal tunnel problems, you might look into changing how your keyboard works. From the Control Panel, click Ease of Access and then click the Change How Your Keyboard Works link.

2. In the resulting Make the Keyboard Easier to Use dialog box (see **Figure 5-9**), make any of these settings:

- **Turn On Mouse Keys.** Use this option to control your mouse pointer with keyboard commands. If you turn on this setting, click the Set Up Mouse Keys link to specify settings for this feature.

- **Turn On Sticky Keys.** Enable this setting if you'd like to press keys in keystroke combinations one at a time, rather than in combination.

- **Turn On Toggle Keys.** You can set up Windows to play a sound when you press Caps Lock, Num Lock, or Scroll Lock (which I do all the time by mistake!).

- **Turn On Filter Keys.** If you sometimes press a key very lightly or press it so hard it activates twice, you can use the **Turn On Filter Keys** setting to change repeat rates to adjust for that. Use the Set Up Filter Keys link to fine-tune settings if you make this choice.

- **Underline Keyboard Shortcuts and Access Keys.** To have Windows highlight keyboard shortcuts and access keys with an underline wherever these shortcuts appear, select this setting.

- **Make It Easier to Manage Windows.** If you want to avoid windows shifting automatically when you move them to the edge of your screen, select this setting.

- **Make It Easier to Move In Content.** To turn on caret browsing if it's available, click this check box.

3. To save the new settings, click OK, and then click the Close button to close the Ease of Access Center.

 You can click the Learn about Additional Assistive Technologies Online link to go the Microsoft website and discover add-on and third-party programs that might help you if you have a visual, hearing, or input-related disability.

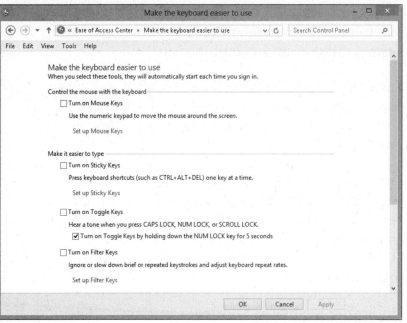

Figure 5-9

Every keyboard has its own unique feel. If your keyboard isn't responsive and you have a keyboard-challenging condition, you might also try different keyboards to see if one works better for you than another.

Use the Onscreen Keyboard Feature

1. Clicking keys with your mouse may be easier than using a regular keyboard. To use the onscreen keyboard, from the Control Panel click the Ease of Access category.

2. In the resulting window, click the Ease of Access Center link to open the Ease of Access Center dialog box (see **Figure 5-10**), and then click Start On-Screen Keyboard. The onscreen keyboard appears (see **Figure 5-11**).

The Ease of Access setting under PC Settings in Windows 8.1 offers many more options including settings for the mouse, keyboard, and magnifier.

Click this option

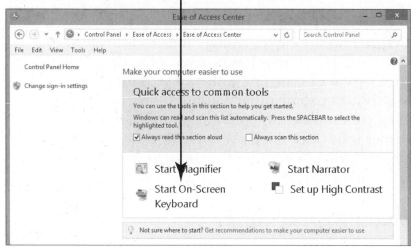

Figure 5-10

Figure 5-11

3. Open a document in any application where you can enter text, and then click the keys on the onscreen keyboard to make entries.

 To use keystroke combinations (such as Ctrl+Z), click the first key (in this case, Ctrl), and then click the second key (Z). You don't have to hold down the first key as you do with a regular keyboard.

4. To change settings, such as turning on the numeric keypad or hearing a click sound when you press a key, click the Options key on the onscreen keyboard, choose one of the options shown in the Options dialog box, and then click OK.

5. Click the Close button on the onscreen keyboard to stop using it.

 You can set up the Hover typing mode to activate a key after you hover your mouse over it for a pre-defined period of time (*x* number of seconds). If you have arthritis or some other condition that makes clicking your mouse difficult, this option can help you enter text. Click the Hover over Keys item in the Options dialog box and use the slider to set how long you have to hover before activating the key.

Set Up Keyboard Repeat Rates

1. Adjusting your keyboard settings might make it easier for you to type, and it can be helpful to people with dexterity challenges. To see your options, from the Control Panel type **keyboard** in the Search field. In the resulting window, click the Keyboard link.

2. In the Keyboard Properties dialog box that appears, click the Speed tab (see **Figure 5-12**) and drag the sliders to adjust the two Character Repeat settings, which do the following:

- **Repeat Delay:** Affects the amount of time it takes before a typed character is typed again when you hold down a key.

- **Repeat Rate:** Adjusts how quickly a character repeats when you hold down a key after the first repeat character appears.

 If you want to see how the Character Repeat settings work in action, click in the text box below the two settings and hold down a key to see a demonstration.

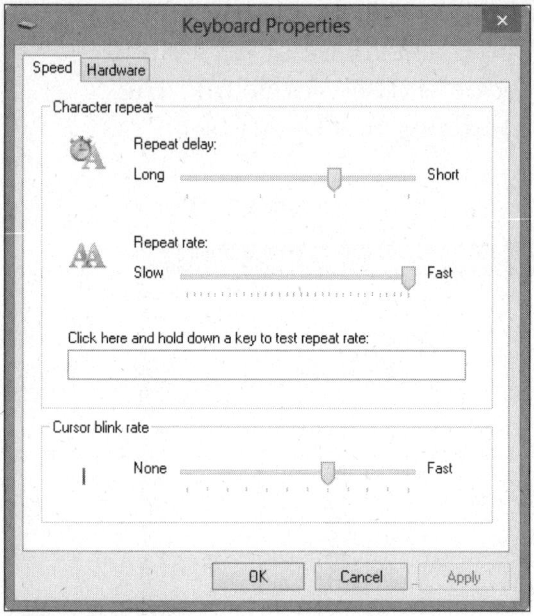

Figure 5-12

3. Drag the slider in the Cursor Blink Rate section. This affects cursors, such as the insertion line that appears in text.

4. Click OK to save and apply changes and close the dialog box. Click the Close button to close the Control Panel window.

If you have trouble with motion (for example, because of arthritis or carpal tunnel syndrome), you might find that you can adjust these settings to make it easier for you to get your work done. For example, if you can't pick up your finger quickly from a key, a slower repeat rate might save you from typing more instances of a character than you'd intended.

Customize Mouse Behavior

1. To avoid having to click your mouse too often, instead of moving your mouse with your hand, you can use your keyboard to move the cursor, or you can activate a window by hovering your mouse over it rather than clicking. From the Control Panel, click Ease of Access and then click the Change How Your Mouse Works link. The Make the Mouse Easier to Use dialog box opens (see **Figure 5-13**).

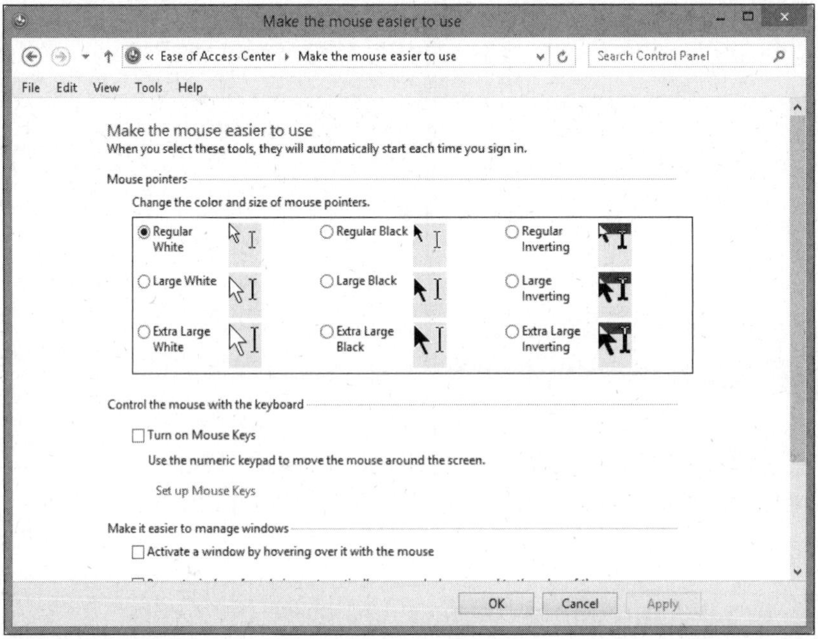

Figure 5-13

2. To use the numeric keypad to move your mouse cursor on your screen, choose the Turn On Mouse Keys setting. If you turn this feature on, click Set Up Mouse Keys to fine-tune its behavior.

3. Select the Activate a Window by Hovering Over It with the Mouse check box to enable this (pretty self-explanatory!) feature.

4. Click OK to save the new settings, and then click the Close button to close the Ease of Access Center.

If you're left-handed, click the Mouse Settings link in the Make the Mouse Easier to Use dialog box; then on the Buttons tab, use the Switch Primary and

Secondary Buttons feature to make the right mouse button handle all the usual left-button functions, such as clicking and dragging, and the left button handle the typical right-hand functions, such as displaying shortcut menus. This helps left-handed people use the mouse more easily.

 If you want to modify the behavior of the mouse pointer, in the Mouse Properties dialog box, click the Pointer Options tab to set the *pointer speed* (how quickly you can drag the mouse pointer around your screen), activate the Snap To feature that automatically moves the mouse cursor to the default choice in a dialog box, or modify the little trails that appear when you drag the pointer.

 If you have difficulty seeing the cursor onscreen, experiment with the Windows 8 color schemes to see if another setting makes your cursor stand out better against the background. See Chapter 4 for information on setting up the color scheme for your computer.

Change the Cursor

1. Having trouble finding the mouse cursor on your screen? You might want to enlarge it or change its shape. From the Control Panel, click Ease of Access and then click Change How Your Mouse Works. In the resulting Make the Mouse Easier to Use dialog box, click the Mouse Settings link.

2. In the resulting Mouse Properties dialog box, on the Pointers tab, as shown in **Figure 5-14,** click to select a pointer such as Normal Select and then click the Browse button. (**Note:** This dialog box may have slightly different tabs depending on your mouse model's features.) In the Browse dialog box that appears, click an alternate cursor and then click Open.

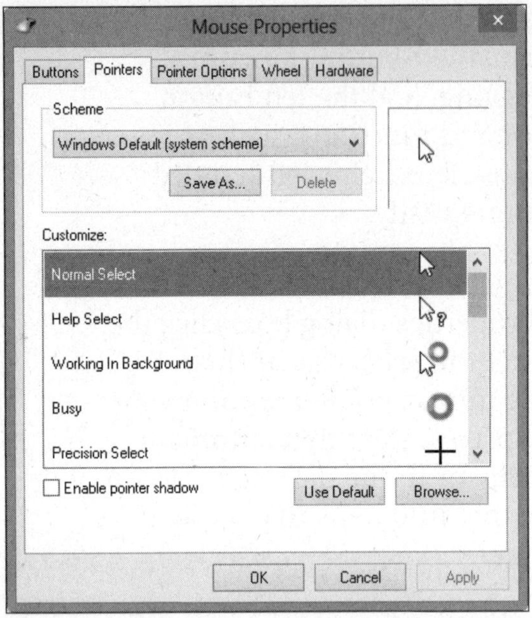

Figure 5-14

3. Click Apply to use the new pointer setting, and then click the Close button to close the Mouse Properties dialog box.

 Be careful not to change the cursor to another standard cursor (for example, changing the Normal Select cursor to the Busy hourglass cursor). This could prove slightly confusing for you and completely baffling to anybody else who works on your computer. If you make a choice and decide it was a mistake, return to the Pointers tab in the Mouse Properties dialog box and click the Use Default button to return a selected cursor to its default choice.

 You can also choose the color and size of mouse pointers in the Make the Mouse Easier to Use dialog box. A large white or extra-large black cursor might be more visible to you, depending on the color scheme you've applied to Windows 8.

Setting Up Printers and Scanners

Chapter 6

A computer is a great storehouse for data, images, and other digital information, but sometimes you need ways to turn printed documents into electronic files you can work with on your computer by scanning them, or sometimes you need to print *hard copies* (a fancy term for paper printouts) of electronic documents and images. Here are a few key ways to do just that:

➡ **Printers** allow you to create hard copies of your files on paper, transparencies, or whatever materials your printer can accommodate. To use a printer, you have to install software called a *printer driver* and use certain settings to tell your computer how to identify your printer and what to print.

➡ You use a **scanner** to create electronic files — pictures, essentially — from hard copies such as newspaper clippings, your birth certificate or driver's license, photos, or whatever will fit into/onto your scanner. You can then work with the electronic files, send them to others as an e-mail attachment, and modify and print

Get ready to . . .

➡ Install a Printer 94

➡ Add a Printer Manually 95

➡ Set a Default Printer 98

➡ Set Printer Preferences 100

➡ View Currently Installed
   Printers 103

➡ Remove a Printer 104

➡ Install a Plug-and-Play
   Scanner 105

➡ Install a Scanner
   Manually 105

➡ Modify Scanner Settings 106

them. Scanners also require that you install a driver, which is typically provided by your scanner's manufacturer. Note that several combination models feature both a printer and a scanner in one.

Install a Printer

1. Read the instructions that came with the printer. Some printers require that you install software before connecting them, but others can be connected right away.

2. Turn on your computer and then follow the option that fits your needs:

   • If your printer is a plug-and-play device (most are these days), you can connect it and power it on; Windows installs any required drivers automatically. If you have a printer that can connect to your computer using a wireless signal over a network (no wires required), be sure your wireless printer is turned on and available.

   • Connect your printer as instructed in the accompanying materials, insert the disc that came with the device, and follow the onscreen instructions.

3. If neither of these procedures works, you can try adding a printer. Begin by typing **control panel** from the Start screen and then click the Control Panel item in the results.

4. Click Hardware and Sound⇨Add A Device and let Windows 8 search for any available devices (see **Figure 6-1**).

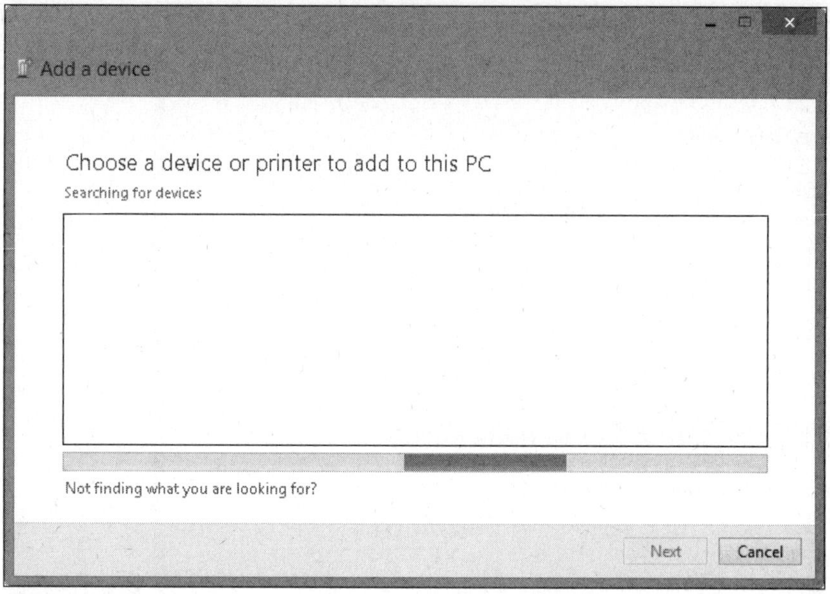

Figure 6-1

5. When it discovers your printer, click Next and follow the instructions.

Add a Printer Manually

1. If the previous procedure doesn't work, go to the Control Panel and, Click Hardware & Sound⇨Devices and Printers. In the Devices and Printers window that appears, click the Advanced Printer Setup link near the top.

2. In the resulting Add Printer wizard shown in **Figure 6-2**, if Windows 8 again doesn't find your printer, click the The Printer That I Want Isn't Listed link and click Next.

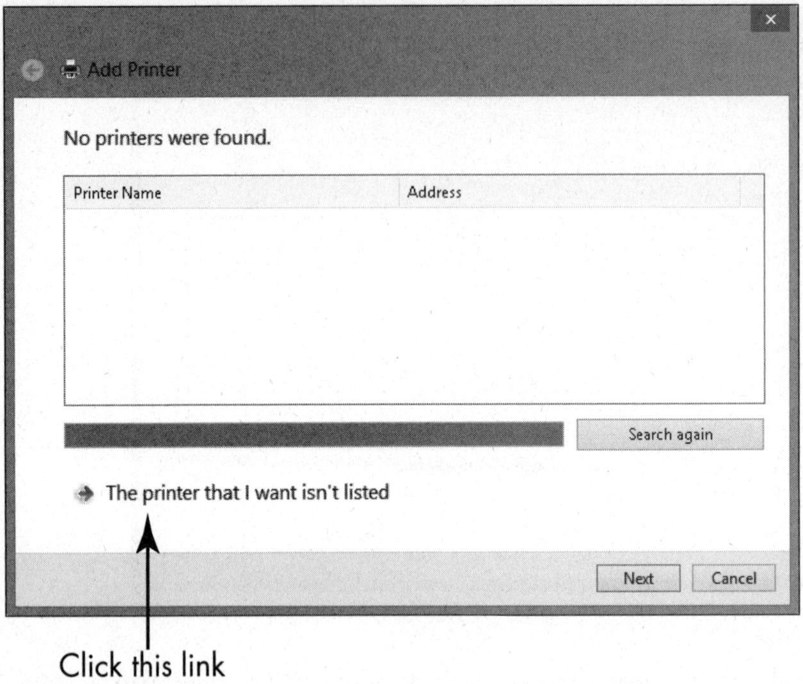

Click this link

Figure 6-2

3. In the following window, click the Add a Local Printer or Network Printer with Manual Settings option and then click Next.

4. In the following dialog box, shown in **Figure 6-3**, click the down arrow on the Use an Existing Port field and select a port, or just use the recommended port setting that Windows selects for you. Click Next.

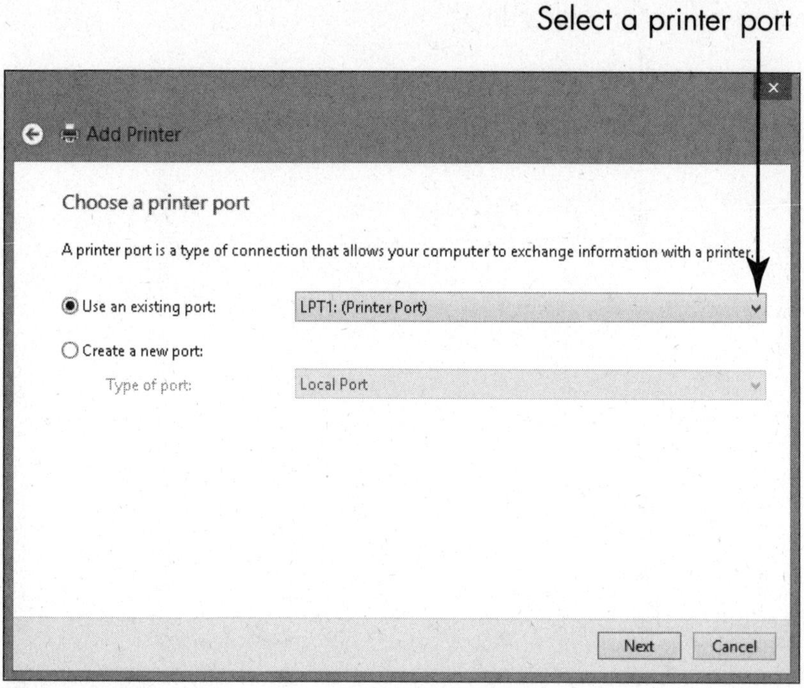

Select a printer port

Add Printer

Choose a printer port

A printer port is a type of connection that allows your computer to exchange information with a printer.

◉ Use an existing port: LPT1: (Printer Port)

○ Create a new port:

   Type of port: Local Port

Next   Cancel

Figure 6-3

5. In the next wizard window, choose a manufacturer in the list on the left and then choose a printer model in the list on the right. You then have two options:

- If you have the manufacturer's disc, insert it in the appropriate CD drive now and click the Have Disk button. Click Next.

- If you don't have the manufacturer's disc, click the Windows Update button to see a list of printer drivers that you can download from the Microsoft website. Click Next.

6. In the resulting Type a Printer Name dialog box (see **Figure** 6-4), enter a printer name. Click Next.

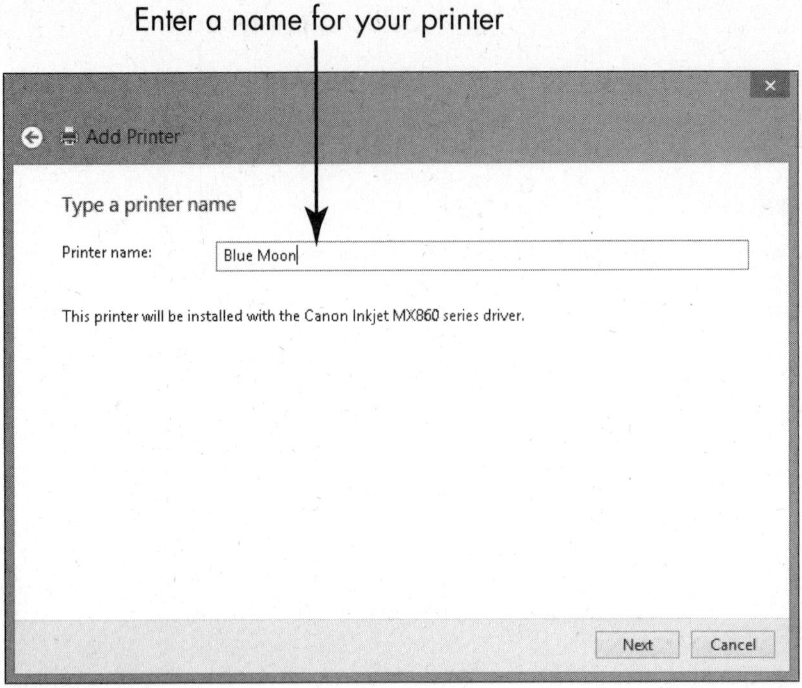

Enter a name for your printer

Add Printer

Type a printer name

Printer name: | Blue Moon |

This printer will be installed with the Canon Inkjet MX860 series driver.

Next   Cancel

Figure 6-4

7. In the resulting dialog box, click the Print a Test Page button and, if the test works, click Finish to complete the Add Printer Wizard.

 If your computer is on a network, after Step 6, you get additional dialog boxes in the wizard, including one that allows you to share the printer on your network. Select the Do Not Share This Printer option to stop others from using the printer, or select the Share Name option and enter a printer name to share the printer on your network. This means that others can see and select this printer to print to.

Set a Default Printer

1. You can set up a default printer that will be used every time you print, so you don't have to select a printer each time. From the Start screen, begin typing **control panel** and click Control Panel in the search results. Click the View Devices and Printers link.

2. In the resulting Devices and Printers window (shown in **Figure** 6-5), the current default printer is indicated by a check mark.

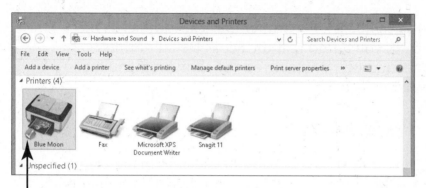

The default printer is checked

Figure 6-5

3. Right-click any printer that isn't set as the default and choose Set as Default Printer from the shortcut menu, as shown in **Figure 6-6**.

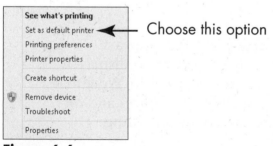 Choose this option

Figure 6-6

4. Click the Close button in the Devices and Printers window.

 To modify printing properties that are available for your particular printer model (for example, whether the printer prints in draft or high-quality mode, or whether it uses color or only black and white), right-click a printer in the Devices and Printers window and choose Printing Preferences (refer to **Figure 6-6**).

This same dialog box is available from most common Windows-based software programs, such as Microsoft Word or Excel, by clicking the Properties button in the Print dialog box.

 If you right-click the printer that's already set as the default, you'll find that the Set as Default Printer command isn't available on the shortcut menu mentioned in Step 3.

Set Printer Preferences

1. Your printer might have capabilities such as being able to print in color or black and white, or print in draft quality (which uses less ink) or high quality (which produces a darker, crisper image). To modify these settings for all documents you print, choose Devices and Printers in the Hardware and Sound group of the Control Panel.

2. In the resulting Devices and Printers window, any printers you've installed are listed. Right-click a printer and then choose Printing Preferences.

3. In the Printing Preferences dialog box that appears (shown in **Figure 6-7**), click any of the tabs to display various settings, such as Color (see **Figure 6-8**). Note that different printers might display different choices and different tabs in this dialog box, but common settings include

- **Color/Grayscale:** If you have a color printer, you have the option of printing in color. The grayscale option uses only black ink. When printing a draft of a color document, you can save colored ink by printing in grayscale, for example.

- **Quality:** If you want, you can print in fast or draft quality (these settings may have different names depending on your printer's manufacturer) to save ink, or you can print in a higher or best quality for your finished documents. Some printers offer a dpi (dots-per-inch) setting for quality — the higher the dpi setting, the better the quality.

- **Paper Source:** If you have a printer with more than one paper tray, you can select which tray to use for printing. For example, you might have 8-x-11-inch paper (letter sized) in one tray and 8-x-14-inch (legal sized) in another.

- **Paper Size:** Choose the size of paper or envelope you're printing to. In many cases, this option displays a preview that shows you which way to insert the paper. A preview can be especially handy if you're printing to envelopes and need help figuring out how to insert them in your printer.

Click a tab to see different settings

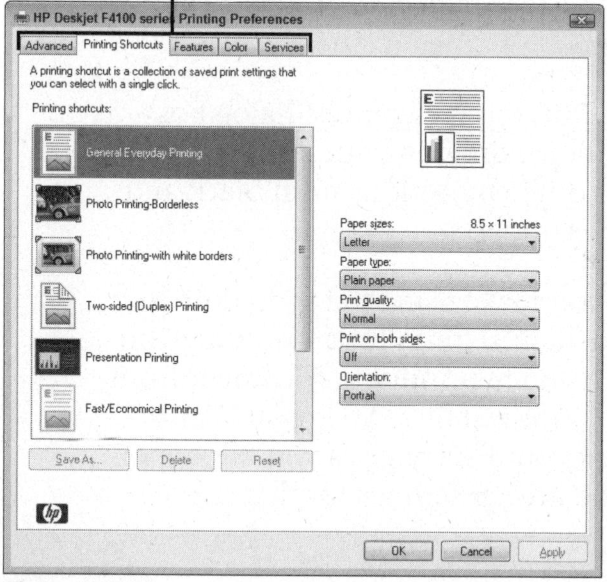

Figure 6-7

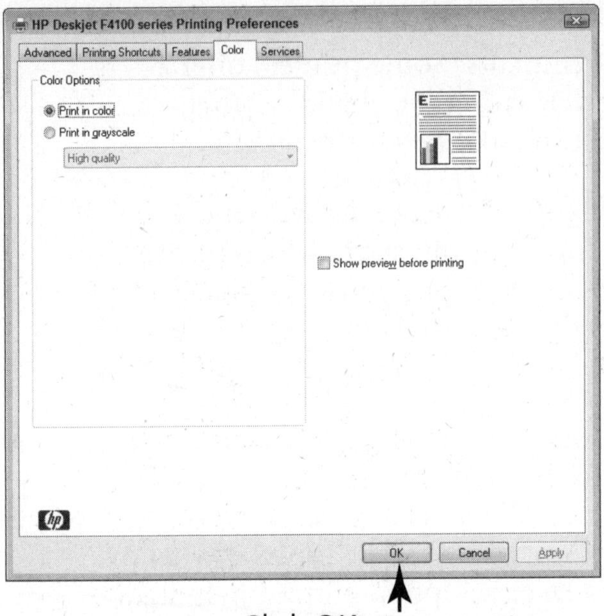

HP Deskjet F4100 series Printing Preferences

| Advanced | Printing Shortcuts | Features | Color | Services |

Color Options

⦿ Print in color

◯ Print in grayscale

High quality

☐ Show preview before printing

[OK] [Cancel] [Apply]

↑ Click OK to save settings

Figure 6-8

4. Click the OK button to close the dialog box and save settings, and then click the Close button to close other open
Control Panel windows.

The settings in the Printing Preferences dialog box
may differ slightly depending on your printer model;
color printers offer different options from black-and-
white printers, for example.

Whatever settings you make using the procedure in
this task are your default settings for all printing you
do. However, when you're printing a document from
within a program — for instance, Microsoft Works —
the Print dialog box you display gives you the opportunity to change the printer settings for that
document only.

View Currently Installed Printers

1. Over time, you might install multiple printers, in which case you may want to remind yourself of the capabilities of each or view the documents you've sent to be printed. To view the printers you've installed and view any documents currently in line for printing, click View Devices and Printers in the Control Panel.

2. In the resulting Devices and Printers window (see **Figure 6-9**), a list of installed printers and fax machines appears. If a printer has documents in its print queue, the number of documents is listed at the bottom of the window. If you want more detail about the documents or want to cancel a print job, select the printer and click the See What's Printing button at the top of the window. In the window that appears, click a document and choose Document⇨ Cancel to stop the printing, if you want. Click the Close button to return to the Devices and Printers window.

The number of documents in queue to print

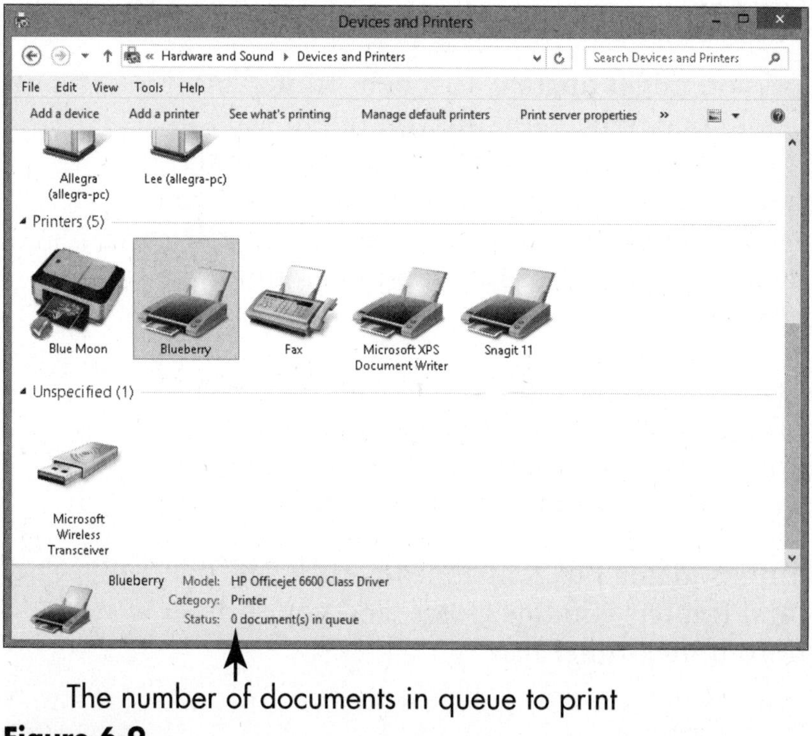

Figure 6-9

3. You can right-click any printer and then choose Properties (see **Figure 6-10**) to see details about it, such as which port it's plugged into or whether it can scan as well as print.

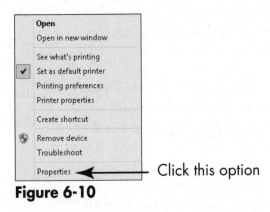

Click this option

Figure 6-10

4. Click the Close button (the red X in the upper right) to close the Devices and Printers window.

Remove a Printer

1. Over time, you might upgrade to a new printer and chuck the old one. When you do, you might want to also remove the older printer driver from your computer so your Printers window isn't cluttered with printers you don't need anymore. To remove a printer, choose Devices and Printers in the Hardware and Sound group of the Control Panel.

2. In the resulting Devices and Printers window (refer to **Figure 6-5**), right-click a printer and choose Remove Device. (**Note:** You can also select the printer and click the Remove Device button at the top of the window.)

3. In the Printers dialog box that appears, click Yes; the Devices and Printers window closes, and your printer is removed from the printer list.

If you remove a printer, it's removed from the list of installed printers, and if it was the default printer, Windows assigns default status to another printer you've installed. You can no longer print to it unless you install it again. See the earlier task, "Install a Printer," if you decide you want to print to that printer again.

Install a Plug-and-Play Scanner

1. Before you can scan documents into your computer with a scanner, you need to install the scanner driver so your scanner and computer can communicate. Start by connecting the scanner to your computer's USB port (see your scanner manual for information about how it connects to your computer).

2. Turn on the scanner. Some scanners use *plug-and-play*, a technology that Windows uses to recognize equipment and automatically install and set it up. If your scanner is plug-and-play enabled, Windows 8 shows a Found New Hardware message in the taskbar notification area (in the lower-right corner). Most plug-and-play devices will then automatically install, the message will change to verify the installation is complete, and that's all you have to do.

3. If that doesn't happen, either you're not using a plug-and-play device or Windows doesn't have the driver for that device, so you should click the Found New Hardware message and follow the Found New Hardware Wizard steps, or follow the steps in the next task to proceed.

Install a Scanner Manually

1. If you have a CD for the scanner, insert it in your CD drive and click Next. Windows 8 searches for your scanner driver software and installs it.

2. In the Control Panel Search box, type **scanners.** Windows returns a set of links. Click the View Scanners and Cameras link. In the resulting Scanners and Cameras window, click the Add Device button.

3. In the resulting Scanner and Camera Installation Wizard window, click Next.

4. In the next screen of the wizard (see **Figure 6-11**), follow the wizard directions by either choosing the model of scanner you have. If you don't have a disc, Windows will help you download software from the Internet. When you reach the end of the wizard, click Finish to complete the installation.

Select a manufacturer...   then select a model

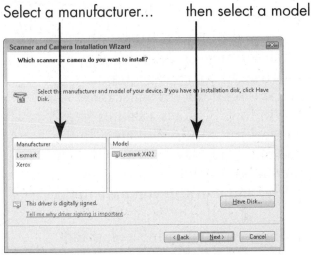

Figure 6-11

Modify Scanner Settings

1. After you install a scanner, you might want to take a look at or change its default settings. To do so, type **scanners** in the Control Panel search field.

2. In the resulting Control Panel window, click View Scanners and Cameras.

3. In the resulting Scanners and Cameras dialog box, a list of installed scanners appears (see **Figure 6-12**). Click any scanner in the Scanners and Cameras area, and then click the Scan Profiles button.

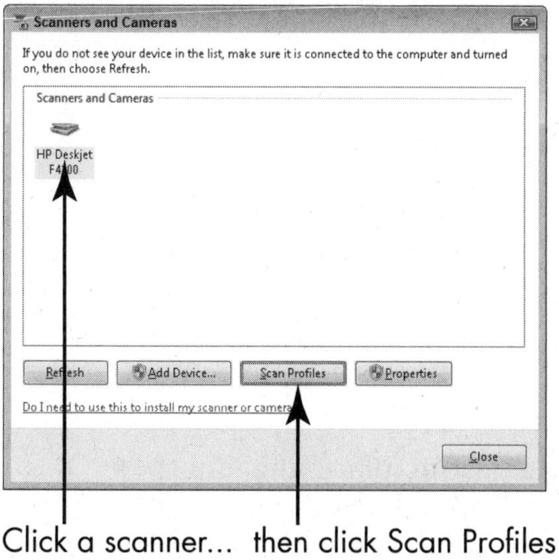

Click a scanner... then click Scan Profiles

Figure 6-12

4. In the resulting Profiles dialog box, select a scanner and click Edit. In the Edit Default Profile dialog box (see **Figure 6-13**), review the settings, which may include (depending on your scanner model) color management for fine-tuning the way colors are scanned and resolution settings that control how detailed a scan is performed (the higher the resolution, the crisper and cleaner your electronic document, but the more time it may take to scan).

5. Click Save Profile to return to the Properties dialog box, and then click the Close button twice to close the Scan Profiles and Scanners and Cameras windows.

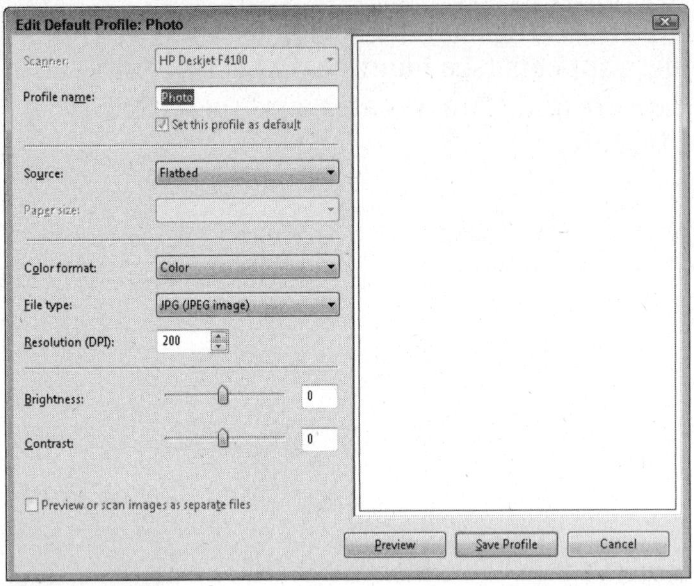

Edit Default Profile: Photo

Scanner:	HP Deskjet F4100 ▼
Profile name:	Photo
	☑ Set this profile as default
Source:	Flatbed ▼
Paper size:	▼
Color format:	Color ▼
File type:	JPG (JPEG image) ▼
Resolution (DPI):	200
Brightness:	0
Contrast:	0

☐ Preview or scan images as separate files

[Preview] [Save Profile] [Cancel]

Figure 6-13

 When you're ready to run a scan, place the item to be scanned in your scanner. Depending on your model, the item may be placed on a flat bed with a hinged cover or fed through a tray. Check your scanner's manual for the specific procedure to initiate a scan (for example, pressing a Scan or Start button). After you begin the scan, your computer automatically detects it and displays a dialog box showing you the scan progress and allowing you to view and save the scanned item.

Windows 8.1 PC Settings changes

In Windows 8.1, if you're working with devices you'll find that the PC & Devices category under PC Settings contains many more options than the Devices category in Windows 8. When you tap PC & Devices, you get settings for your Lock Screen, Display, Bluetooth, Devices, Mouse & Touchpad, Typing, Corners & Edges, Power & Sleep, AutoPlay, and PC Info.

Getting Help

*W*ith so many Windows features, you're bound to run into something that doesn't work right or isn't easy to figure out (or that this book doesn't cover). That's when you need to call on the resources that Microsoft provides to help you out.

Through the Help and Support Center, you can get help in various ways, including the following:

➡ **Access information that's stored in the Help and Support database.** You can access this information whether you're online or not. Logically enough, a database contains data; in this case, it contains information about Windows 8, organized by topics. You can search for or browse through topics using a powerful search mechanism to find articles by keywords such as *printer* or *e-mail*.

➡ **Read helpful articles.** You can take advantage of several articles that provide insight into working with the Start screen and useful Help & How-To articles on the Windows website.

Get ready to . . .

➡ Search Windows Help and Support 110

➡ Get Help Getting Started with Windows 8 112

➡ Find Information about Using the Start Screen 114

➡ Get Answers from the Windows Community 115

➡ Switch between Online and Offline Help 117

➡ Connect to Remote Assistance 118

➡ **Search Microsoft Answers.** Microsoft offers a way to search for answers in the Windows Forum to see if somebody else has had a similar problem. You can also ask a question yourself. A Microsoft employee will respond and give you advice when you post a question.

➡ **Invite someone to help you through Remote Assistance.** Get help from another person by using the Windows 8 Remote Assistance feature.

Search Windows Help and Support

1. The Help and Support window provides access to a variety of topics. Press Win+F1 to display it (see **Figure 7-1**).

2. Click in the Search field, enter a search term, and click the Search button (the button that looks like a magnifying glass).

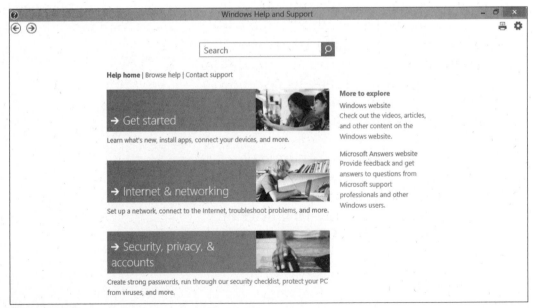

Figure 7-1

3. In the resulting screen shown in **Figure 7-2**, click an article to narrow your search or open an article, depending on the topic.

4. Click the Close button to close the Windows Help and Support window.

 If your search contains one, click a Troubleshoot item (as shown in Figure 7-2) to get a step-by-step walkthrough of possible solutions to common problems. Some troubleshooting topics will even run a check on your computer to attempt to find a solution specific to your computer. In addition you may encounter some Video links that take you to step-by-step video instruction.

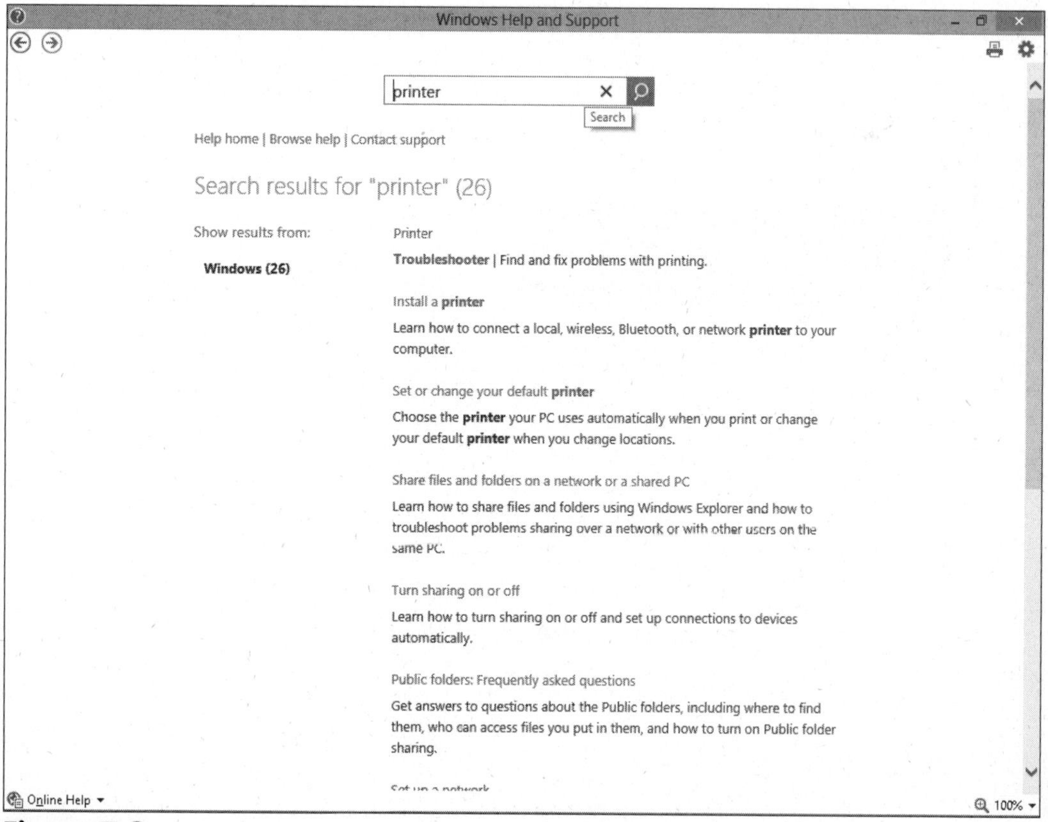

Windows Help and Support

printer

Help home | Browse help | Contact support

Search results for "printer" (26)

Show results from:

Windows (26)

Printer

Troubleshooter | Find and fix problems with printing.

Install a **printer**
Learn how to connect a local, wireless, Bluetooth, or network **printer** to your computer.

Set or change your default **printer**
Choose the **printer** your PC uses automatically when you print or change your default **printer** when you change locations.

Share files and folders on a network or a shared PC
Learn how to share files and folders using Windows Explorer and how to troubleshoot problems sharing over a network or with other users on the same PC.

Turn sharing on or off
Learn how to turn sharing on or off and set up connections to devices automatically.

Public folders: Frequently asked questions
Get answers to questions about the Public folders, including where to find them, who can access files you put in them, and how to turn on Public folder sharing.

Set up a network

Online Help

Figure 7-2

If you don't find what you need with Search, consider clicking the Browse Help tab in the Windows Help and Support window to display a list of major topics. Those topics may also give you some ideas for good search terms to continue your search.

Get Help Getting Started with Windows 8

If you need a basic tutorial on how to use Windows 8, consider using the Getting Started section of the Windows website. Here you can find videos, blogs, and articles to help you get started. Press the Windows key to display the Start screen.

1. Press Win+I to display the Settings panel of the Charm bar.

2. Click Help.

3. Click the Get Started with Windows 8 and Start link (see **Figure 7-3**).

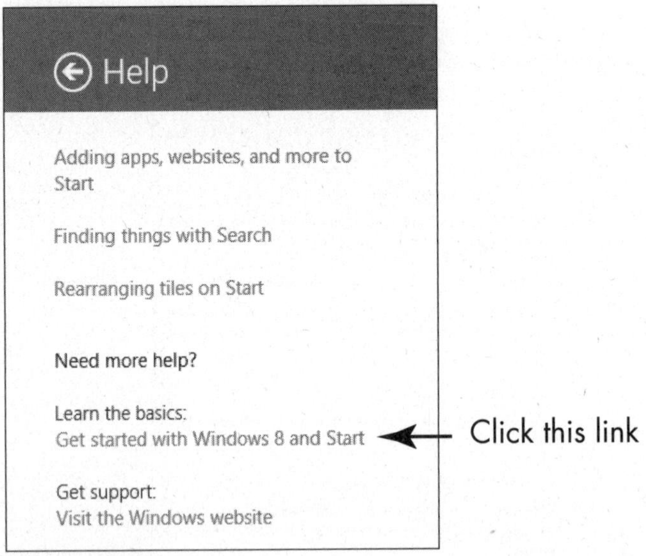

← Help

Adding apps, websites, and more to Start

Finding things with Search

Rearranging tiles on Start

Need more help?

Learn the basics:
Get started with Windows 8 and Start ◄—— Click this link

Get support:
Visit the Windows website

Figure 7-3

4. Click the Get Started link at the top of the page, as shown in **Figure 7-4**.

Click this link

Figure 7-4

5. Click the Play button (see **Figure 7-5**) to play the introductory video.

Click the Play button

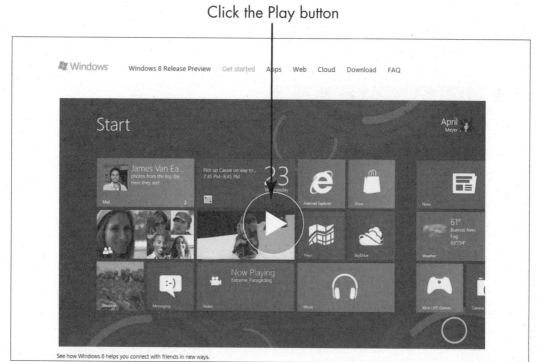

Figure 7-5

Another way to get to some of these options is to simply go to `http://windows.microsoft.com` and select from the choices presented there.

 When you first arrive at the Getting Started page shown earlier in Figure 7-4, take a moment to explore other links to read blogs or get more information on specific issues such as installing Windows 8 and Internet Explorer 10.

Find Information about Using the Start Screen

1. Because the Start screen offers an entirely new dynamic for Windows users, Microsoft built in three help topics to get you going. From the Start screen, press Win+I.

2. Click Help.

3. Click one of the three links at the top of the Help panel (see **Figure 7-6**).

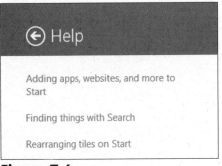

Figure 7-6

4. Scroll through the article (see **Figure 7-7**). If you want to, click any links in the article to display related information.

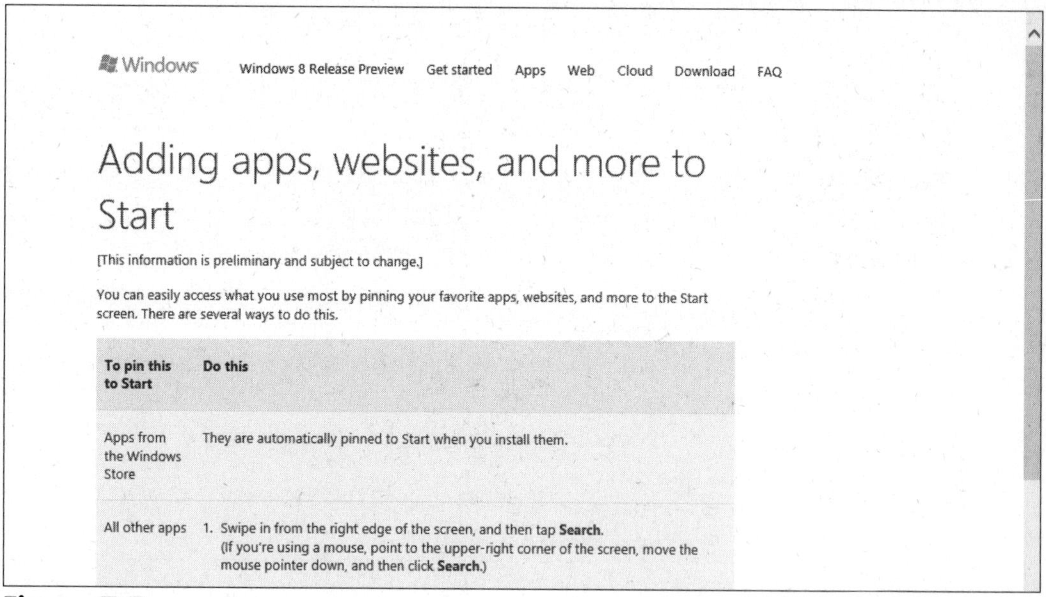

Figure 7-7

Get Answers from the Windows Community

1. If you want to see how other Windows users have solved a problem, you can visit the Windows Forum and read posted messages and the solutions suggested by Microsoft and others. You can also post your own questions. Press Win+F1 to open the Windows Help and Support window, and then click the Microsoft Answers link.

2. On the web page shown in **Figure 7-8,** click in the Search field and enter a search term. Click the Search button to search for all answers.

3. Click the title of a question that relates to your question and read the answers (see **Figure 7-9**).

4. To ask your own question, click the Ask a Question radio button above the Search field (refer to **Figure 7-8**).

5. Enter a question and then click Ask.

Enter a search term here

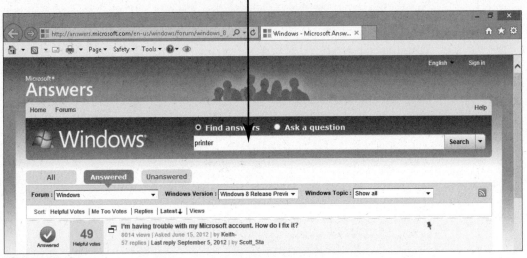

Figure 7-8

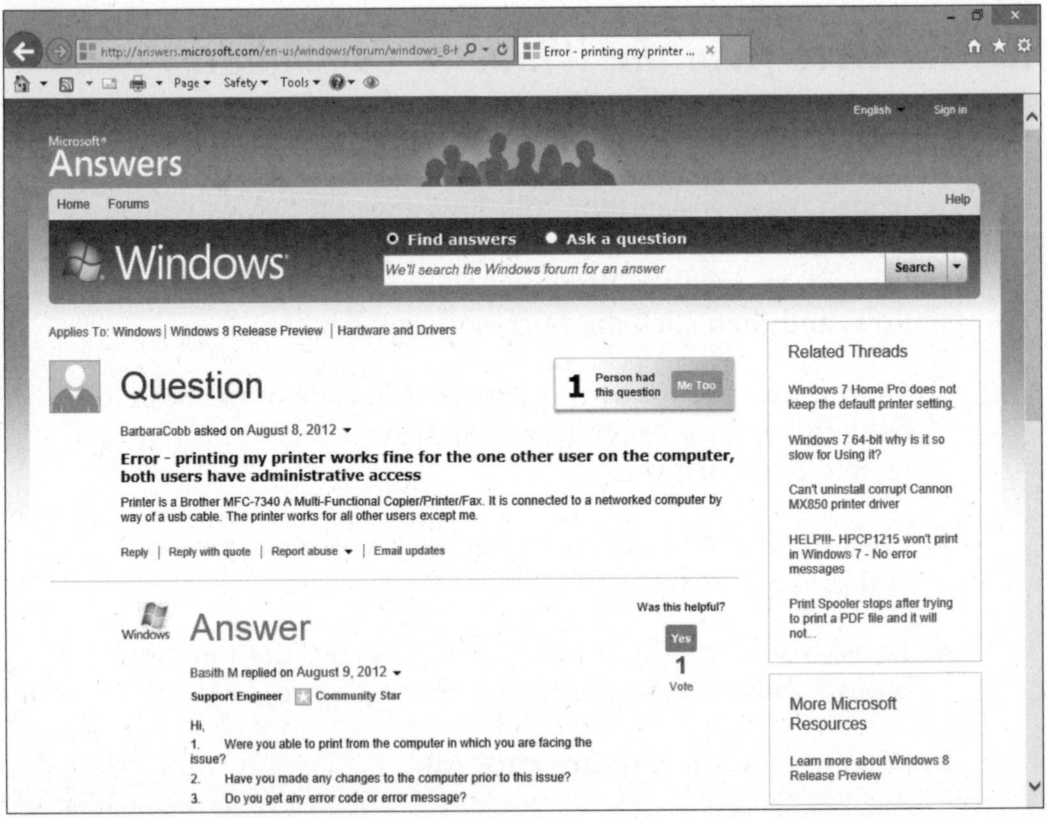

Figure 7-9

6. On the following page, click the Sign In to Post a Question button (see **Figure 7-10**) in the bottom-left corner of the screen and enter a more detailed description of your problem or question. You may have to sign up if you haven't used this site before, accepting the rules of conduct.

Sign in to post a question

Figure 7-10

7. Change the title for your question if you wish. Click the Windows Topic field and choose the appropriate topic for your question from the drop-down list.

8. If you want to get an e-mail when somebody responds to your question, be sure the Notify Me When Someone Responds to This Question check box is selected. If this isn't selected, you'll have to return to the forum and check to see if any answers have been posted.

9. Click the Submit button.

 It's a good idea to roam around the forum for a bit before you post a question to see if it's been addressed before. If you post a question that's been answered several times before, you not only waste your time and the time of others, but you may find yourself the recipient of a bit of razzing by regulars to the forum.

Switch between Online and Offline Help

1. Much of the help and support you get from Microsoft for Windows these days is driven by their online content. If you don't have an Internet connection but you need help, you do have an option. If you switch to Offline Help, you can work with the help system database built into Windows 8, though it may not be as up to date as the online help. Press Win+F1.

2. In the Windows Help and Support window, click the Online Help button (see **Figure 7-11**) in the lower-left corner.

Online Help ▼

Figure 7-11

3. Click Get Offline Help.

4. Enter a term in the Search field and click the Search button.

5. Click a topic to read more about it.

Connect to Remote Assistance

Remote Assistance can be a wonderful feature for new computer users because it allows you to permit somebody else to view or take control of your computer from their own computer no matter where they are. You can contact that person by phone or e-mail, for example, and ask for help. Then, you can send an invitation using Windows 8 Help. When that person accepts the invitation, you can give him or her permission to access your system. Be aware that by doing so you give the person access to all your files, so be sure this is somebody you trust. When that person is connected, he or she can either advise you about your problem or actually make changes to your computer to fix the problem for you. To use Remote Assistance, you and the other person first have to have Windows 8 and an Internet connection.

1. Enable Remote Assistance by typing **control panel** from the Start screen and clicking Control Panel in the results.

2. Click System and Security and then under the heading System click Allow Remote Access.

3. On the Remote tab of the System Properties dialog box that's displayed (see **Figure 7-12**), select the Allow Remote Assistance Connections to This Computer check box, and then click OK.

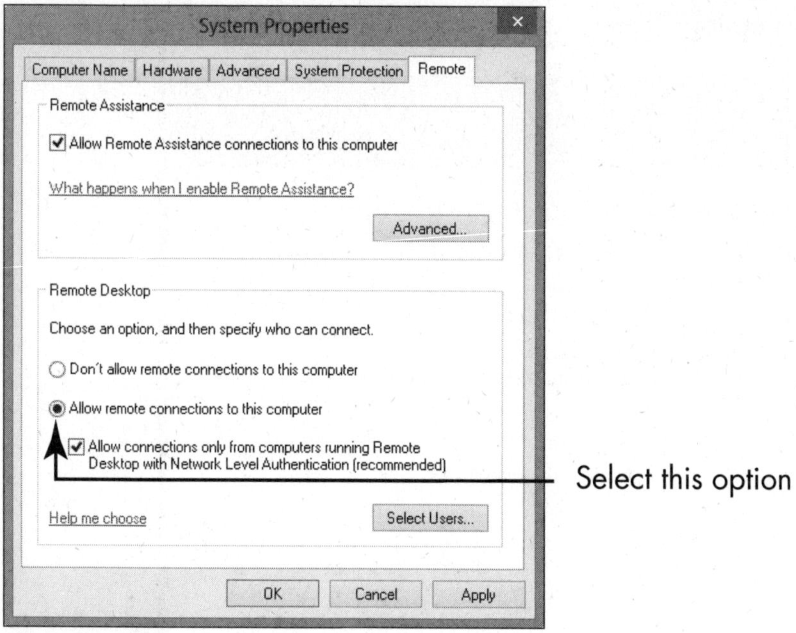

Select this option

Figure 7-12

4. Enter the search term *remote assistance* in the Control Panel Search field.

5. Click the Invite Someone to Connect to Your PC and Help You, or Offer to Help Someone Else link.

6. On the window that appears, shown in **Figure 7-13,** click the Invite Someone You Trust to Help You link. If Windows Firewall or a third-party firewall is active, you may have to disable that feature to allow remote access to your computer.

Click this option

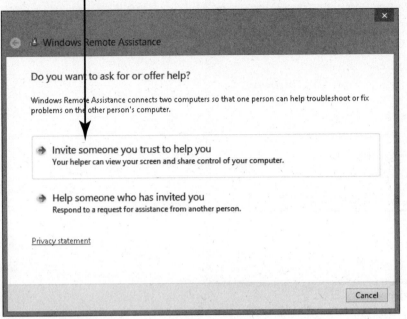

Figure 7-13

7. On the page that appears, shown in **Figure 7-14**, you can choose to use your e-mail to invite somebody to help you. You have three options:

- Click the Save This Invitation as a File option and follow the instructions to save it as a file; then you can attach the file to a message using your web-based e-mail program.

- Click the Use Email to Send an Invitation option to use a preconfigured e-mail program to send an e-mail. In the e-mail form that appears, enter an address and additional message content, if you like, and send the e-mail.

- Click Use Easy Connect to get a step-by-step wizard to help you with the remote assistance process.

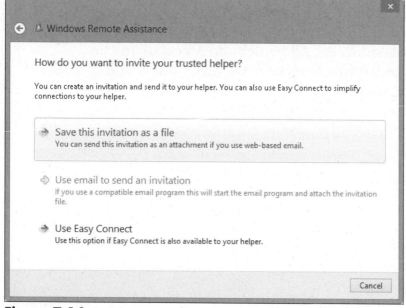

Figure 7-14

8. In the Windows Remote Assistance window, as shown in **Figure 7-15,** note the provided password and provide it to your remote helper. When that person makes an incoming connection, use the tools there to adjust settings, chat, send a file, or pause, cancel, or stop sharing.

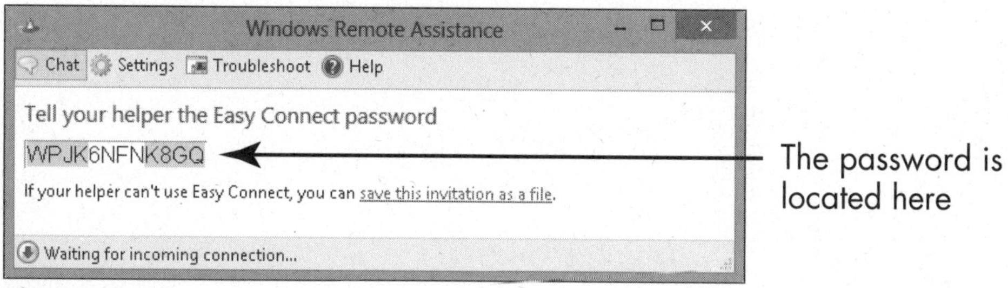

The password is located here

Figure 7-15

9. When you're finished, click the Close button to close the Windows Remote Assistance window.

 Remember that it's up to you to let the recipient know the password — it isn't included in your e-mail unless you add it in the e-mail message.

If you no longer want to use Remote Assistance it's a good idea to return to the System window of Control Panel and in the Allow Remote Access dialog box uncheck Allow Remote Assistance Connection to This Computer on the Remote tab.

Part II
Getting Things Done with Software

The 5th Wave   By Rich Tennant

"Can't I just give you riches or something?"

Working with Software Programs

*Y*ou may think of Windows 8 as a set of useful accessories, such as games, music players, and a paint program for playing around with images, but Windows 8 is first and foremost an operating system. Windows 8's main purpose is to enable you to run and manage other software programs, from programs that manage your finances to a great animated game of bingo. By using the best methods for accessing and running programs with Windows 8, you save time; setting up Windows 8 in the way that works best for you can make your life easier.

In this chapter, you explore several simple and very handy techniques for launching and moving information between applications. You go through step-by-step procedures ranging from setting program defaults to removing programs when you no longer need them.

Chapter 8

Get ready to . . .

➠ Launch a Program 126

➠ Move Information between Programs 128

➠ Set Program Defaults 130

➠ Remove a Program 131

Launch a Program

1. Launch a program by using any of the following methods:

- Click a tile on the Start screen. (For more about pinning apps to the Start screen, see Chapter 3.)

- Right-click the Start screen and click the All Apps button. This displays a list of apps arranged in categories such as Windows Accessories and Windows Ease of Access (as shown in **Figure 8-1**). Click an app to open it.

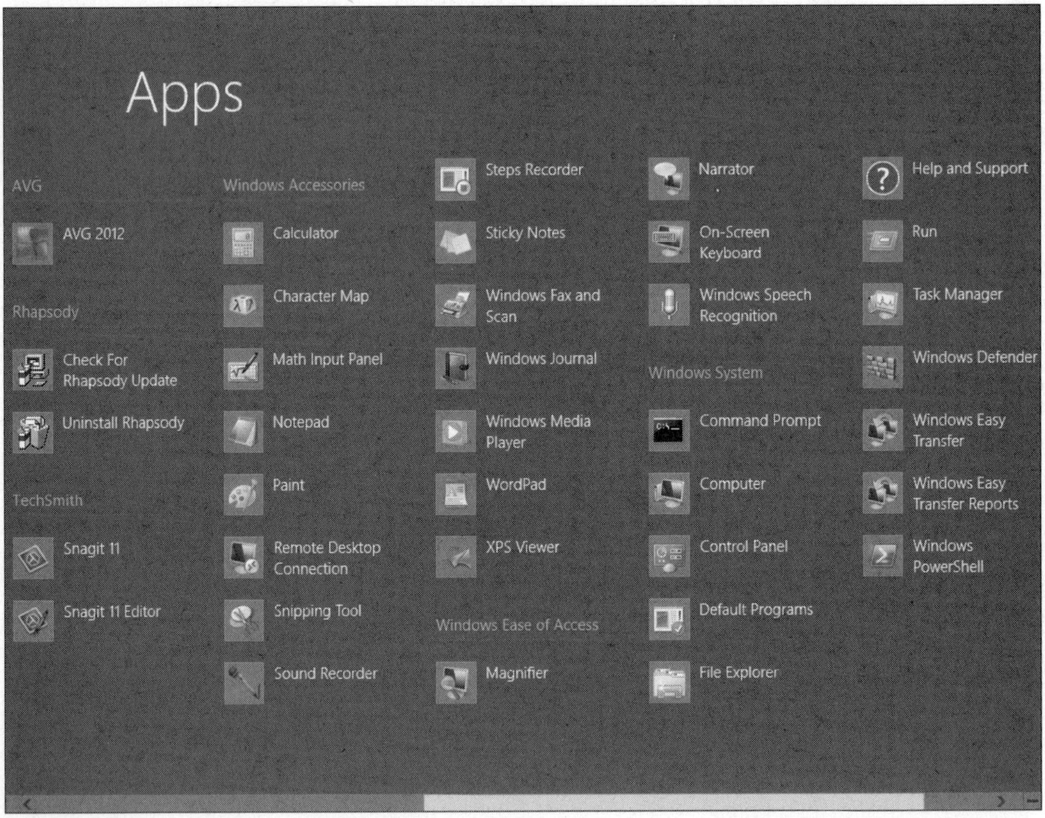

Figure 8-1

- Double-click a program shortcut icon on the desktop (see **Figure 8-2**).

- Click an item on the desktop taskbar. The taskbar should display by default; if it doesn't, press the Windows key (on your keyboard) to display it, and then click an icon on the taskbar (as shown in **Figure 8-2**). See Chapter 3 for more about working with the taskbar.

Shortcut icons on the desktop

Taskbar icons

Figure 8-2

2. When the application opens, if it's a game, play it; if it's a spreadsheet, enter numbers into it; if it's your e-mail program, start deleting junk mail . . . you get the idea.

 See Chapter 10 for more about working with apps in Windows 8.

Move Information between Programs

1. Click the Desktop tile on the Start screen.

2. Click the File Explorer icon in the taskbar to open it.

3. Browse and open documents in two programs (see the previous section for more about opening applications). Right-click the taskbar on the Windows desktop (see **Figure 8-3**) and choose Show Windows Side by Side.

4. If you don't need one of the active programs displayed, click the Minimize button in the program window so that just the program you're working with appears.

5. Select the information that you want to move (for example click and drag your mouse to highlight text or numbers, or click on a graphical object in a document), and then drag the selection to the other document window (see **Figure 8-4**).

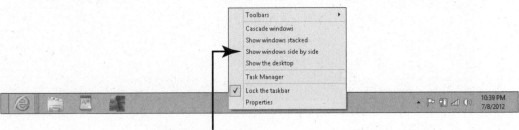

Select this option

Figure 8-3

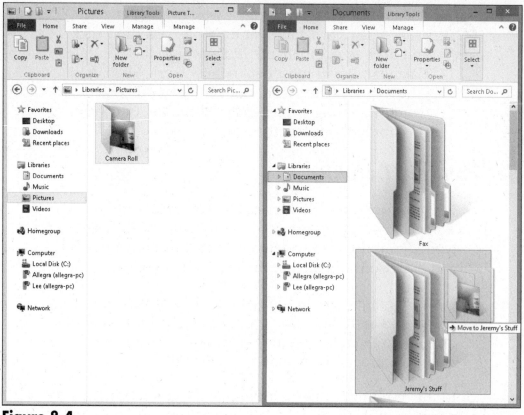

Figure 8-4

6. Release your mouse, and the information is copied to the document in the destination window.

 You can also use simple cut-and-paste or copy-and-paste keystroke shortcuts to take information from one application and move it or place a copy of it into a document in another application. To do this, first click and drag over the information in a document, and then press Ctrl+X to cut or Ctrl+C to copy the item. Click in the destination document where you want to place the item and press Ctrl+V. Alternately, you can right-click content and choose Cut, Copy, or Paste commands from the menu that appears.

Remember, dragging content won't work between every type of program. For example, you can't click and drag an open picture in Paint into the Windows Calendar. It will most dependably work when dragging text or objects from one Office or other standard word-processing, presentation, database, or spreadsheet program to another.

Set Program Defaults

1. To make working with files easier, you may want to control which programs are used to open files of different types. From the Start screen, begin to type **control panel** and click Control Panel in the results that appear.

2. Click Programs and, in the resulting Programs window shown in **Figure 8-5**, click the Set Your Default Programs link in the Default Programs section to see specifics about the programs that are set as defaults.

3. In the resulting Set Default Programs window, click a program in the list on the left (see **Figure 8-6**) and then click the Set This Program as Default option. You can also click Choose Defaults for this Program and select specific file types (such as the JPEG graphics file format or DOCX Word 2010 file format) to open in this program; click OK after you've made these selections.

Click this link

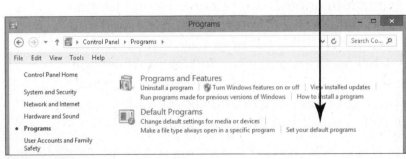

Figure 8-5

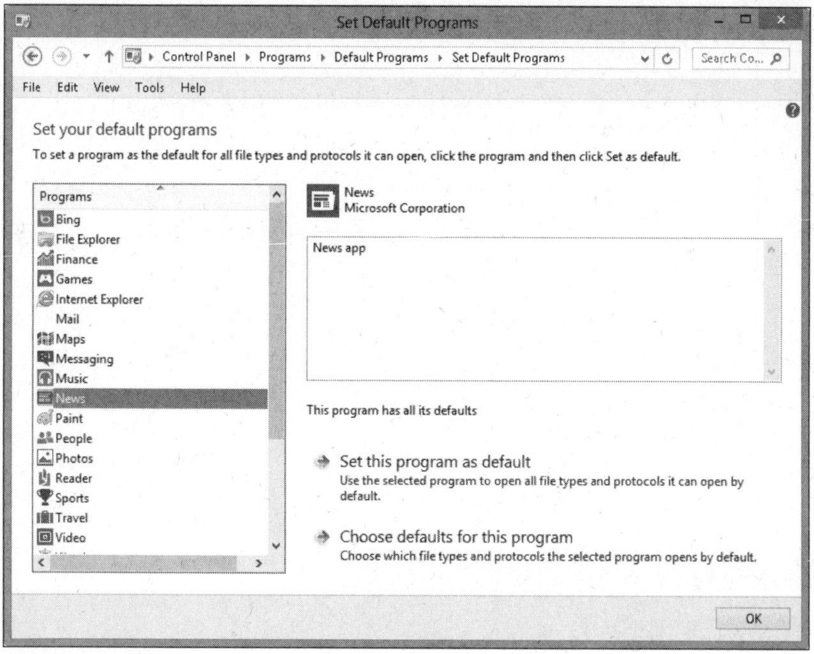

Figure 8-6

4. Click OK to save your settings.

You can also choose which devices to use by default to play media such as movies or audio files by selecting Change Default Settings for Media or Devices in the Programs window you opened in Step 2 earlier.

Remove a Program

1. If you don't need a program, removing it may help your computer's performance, which can get bogged down when your hard drive is too cluttered. From the Control Panel, click Uninstall a Program (under the Programs category).

2. In the resulting Programs and Features window, shown in **Figure 8-7,** click a program and then click the Uninstall (or sometimes this is labeled Uninstall/Change) button that appears. Although some programs will display their own uninstall screen, in most cases, a confirmation dialog box appears (see **Figure 8-8**).

Select a program to uninstall

Programs and Features

Control Panel ▸ Programs ▸ Programs and Features

Search Pr... 🔍

File   Edit   View   Tools   Help

Control Panel Home

View installed updates

Turn Windows features on or off

Uninstall or change a program

To uninstall a program, select it from the list and then click Uninstall, Change, or Repair.

Organize ▾   Uninstall

Name	Publisher	Installed On
AVG 2012	AVG Technologies	9/1/2012
FileZilla Client 3.5.3	FileZilla Project	8/16/2012
Microsoft Visual C++ 2008 Redistributable - x86 9.0.3...	Microsoft Corporation	9/1/2012
Rhapsody		8/23/2012
Snagit 11	TechSmith Corporation	8/17/2012
Visual Studio 2008 x64 Redistributables	AVG Technologies	9/1/2012

Figure 8-7

Programs and Features

⚠ Are you sure you want to uninstall Snagit 11?

☐ In the future, do not show me this dialog box   Yes   No

Figure 8-8

3. If you're sure that you want to remove the program, click Yes in the confirmation dialog box. A progress bar shows the status of the procedure; it disappears when the program has been removed.

4. Click the Close button to close the Program and Features window.

With some programs that include multiple applications, such as Microsoft Office, you get both an Uninstall and a Change option in Step 2. That's because you might want to remove only one program, not the whole shooting match. For example, you might decide that you have no earthly use for Access but can't let a day go by without using Excel and Word — so why not free up some hard drive space and send Access packing? If you want to modify a program in this way, click the Change button rather than the Uninstall button in Step 2 of this task. The dialog box that appears allows you to select the programs that you want to install or uninstall or even open the original installation screen from your software program.

Warning: If you click the Change or Uninstall button, some programs will simply be removed with no further input from you. Be really sure that you don't need a program before you remove it, that you have the original software on disc, or that you have a product key for software you downloaded from the Internet so you can reinstall it should you need it again.

Working with Files and Folders

Chapter 9

*J*oin me for a moment in the office of yester-year. Notice all the metal filing cabinets and manila file folders holding paper rather than the sleek computer workstations, ubiquitous tablets, and wireless Internet connections we use today.

Fast forward: You still organize the work you do every day in files and folders, but today the metal and cardboard have given way to electronic bits and bytes. Files are the individual documents that you save from within applications, such as Word and Excel, and you use folders and sub-folders to organize several files into groups or categories, such as by project or by year.

In this chapter, you find out how to organize and work with files and folders, including

➥ **Finding your way around files and fold-ers:** This includes tasks such as locating and opening files and folders using the tools on the new File Explorer Ribbon.

➥ **Manipulating files and folders:** These tasks cover moving, renaming, deleting, and printing a file.

➥ **Squeezing a file's contents:** This involves creating a compressed folder to reduce the size of a large file or set of files to be more manageable when back-ing up or e-mailing them.

Get ready to . . .

➥ Understand How Windows Organizes Data 136

➥ Access Recently Used Items 138

➥ Locate Files and Folders in Your Computer 139

➥ Search for Online Content 141

➥ Move a File or Folder 142

➥ Rename a File or Folder 145

➥ Create a Shortcut to a File or Folder 146

➥ Delete a File or Folder 147

➥ Create a Compressed File or Folder 148

➥ Add a File to Your Favorites List 150

➥ Back Up Files 152

➠ **Backing up files and folders:** To avoid losing valuable data, you should know how to make backup
copies of your files and folders on a recordable CD/
DVD or *flash drive* (a small stick-shaped storage
device that fits into a USB port on your computer).

Understand How Windows Organizes Data

When you work in a software program, such as a word processor, you
save your document as a file. Files can be saved to your computer hard
drive; to removable storage media such as USB flash drives (which are
about the size of a stick of gum); or to recordable DVDs (small, flat
discs you insert into a disc drive on your computer).

You can organize files by placing them in folders that you work with
in an app called File Explorer. The Windows operating system helps
you organize files and folders in the following ways:

➠ **Take advantage of predefined folders.** Windows
sets up some folders for you as libraries of content.
For example, the first time you start Windows 8 and
open File Explorer, you find folders for Documents,
Music, Pictures, and Videos already set up on your
computer. You can see them listed in File Explorer,
shown in **Figure 9-1**. (See Chapter 3 for an explanation of File Explorer.)

The Documents folder is a good place to store letters,
presentations for your community group, household
budgets, and so on. The Pictures folder is where you
store picture files, which you may transfer from a
digital camera or scanner, receive in an e-mail message from a friend or family member, or download
from the Internet. Similarly, the Videos folder is a
good place to put files from your camcorder, and the
Music folder is where you place tunes you download
or transfer from a music player.

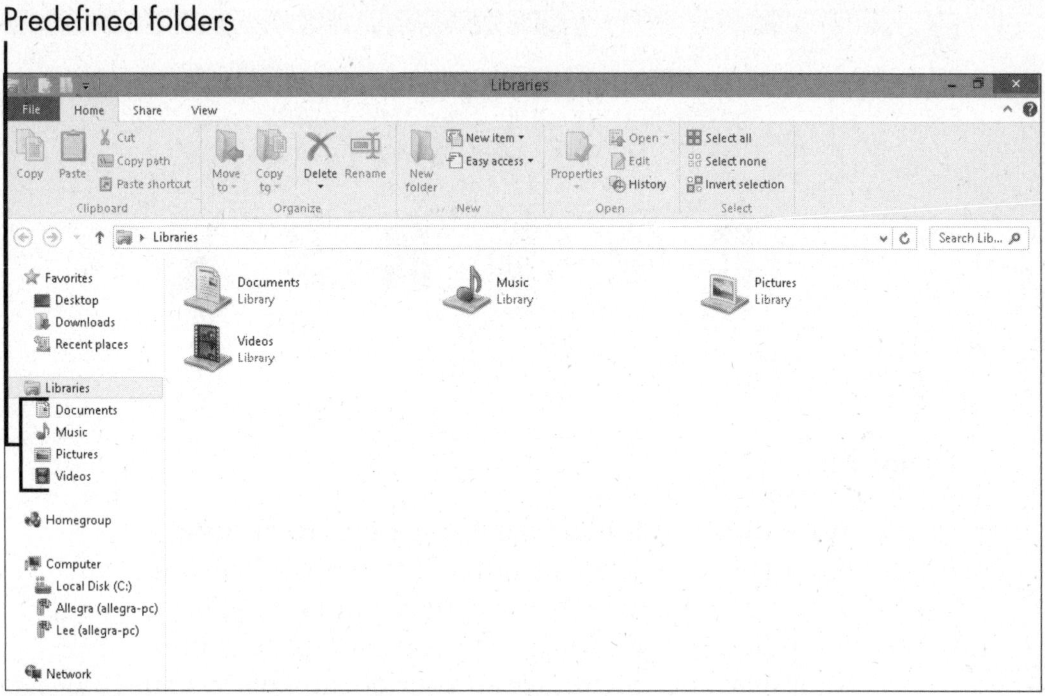

Predefined folders

Figure 9-1

➠ **Create your own folders.** You can create any number of folders and give them a name that identifies the types of files you'll store there. For example, you might create a folder called *Digital Scrapbook* if you use your computer to create scrapbooks, or a folder called *Taxes* where you save e-mailed receipts for purchases and electronic tax-filing information.

➠ **Place folders within folders to further organize files.** A folder you place within another folder is called a *subfolder*. For example, in your Documents folder, you might have a subfolder called *Holiday Card List* that contains your yearly holiday newsletter and address lists. In my Pictures folder, I organize the picture files by creating subfolders that begin with the year and then a description of the event or subject, such as *2008 Home Garden Project, 2010 Christmas, 2009 San Francisco Trip, 2010 Family Reunion, 2009 Pet Photos*, and so on. In **Figure 9-2**, you can see subfolders and files stored within the Pictures folder.

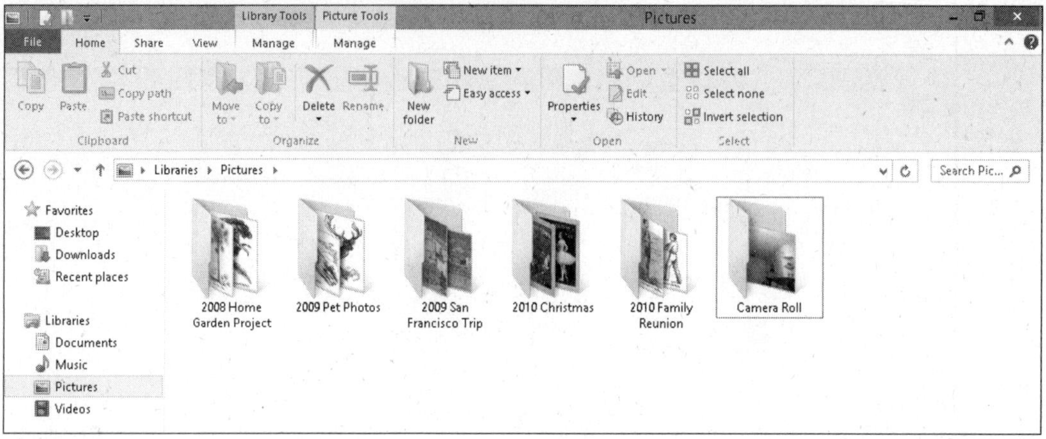

Figure 9-2

➡ **Move files and folders from one place to another.**
Being able to move files and folders helps when you
decide it's time to reorganize information on your
computer. For example, when you start using your
computer, you might save all your documents to your
Documents folder. That's okay for a while, but in time,
you might have dozens of documents saved in that one
folder. To make your files easier to locate, you can create subfolders by topic and move files into them.

Access Recently Used Items

1. If you worked on a file recently, File Explorer offers a
shortcut to finding and opening it to work on again.
From either the Start screen or desktop, press Win+R.

2. In the Run dialog box that appears (see **Figure** 9-3), type
recent and press Enter.

3. Double-click a file to open it.

 You can also hover your mouse over the top-left corner of your screen, and a list of recently used files
and apps appears. Keep your mouse on the left edge
of the screen and slide it down to the item you want,
and then click the item to open it.

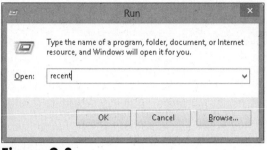

Figure 9-3

Locate Files and Folders in Your Computer

1. Can't remember what you named a folder or where on your computer or storage media you saved it? You can use Windows 8's integrated search feature to find it. First, display the Start screen (press the Windows key).

2. On the Start screen, begin typing the name of a file or folder.

3. Click the Files category in the Search panel on the right side of the screen. (See **Figure 9-4** for an example.) This limits your search results to files only, and excludes any apps or settings files that might have your search term in their name.

4. When you find the file you want, click it to open it in the application in which it was created.

Changes in Windows 8.1 searching

Type a term from the Start screen using Windows 8.1 and a single panel is displayed on the right with results, but no categories such as Apps and Music. Click an app in the results and it opens. Click other search term matches and you're taken online and shown a variety of results such as images, websites, Wikipedia articles, and more (see the figure).

Click this option

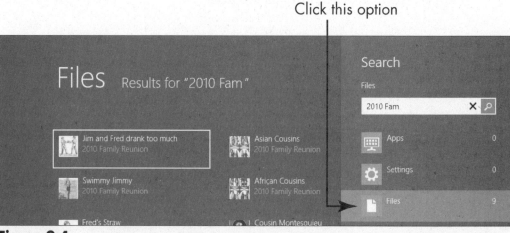

Figure 9-4

You can narrow your integrated search results to settings or apps by clicking those categories after you type the search term on the Start screen. For instance, if you want to find updates for your software, type **updates** in the Search field and click Settings. If you've forgotten whether you've installed a particular app, type the app's name in the Search field and click Apps, as shown in **Figure 9-5**.

Click this option

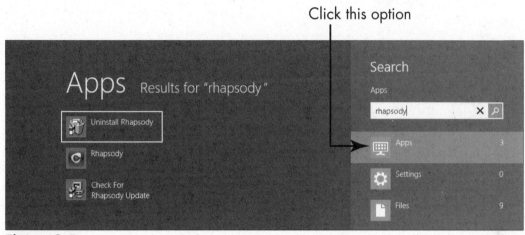

Figure 9-5

Search for Online Content

1. If you want to locate content online rather than on your computer hard drive, you can use the same integrated search feature described in the preceding task. From the Start screen, begin to type a term such as the name of a song or a location.

2. In the Search results that appear, click a category on the right, such as Music or News.

3. If the site that opens offers choices, such as several news articles (as shown in **Figure 9-6**), click the one you want.

**DACHSHUND
NEWS RESULTS**

Obese Dachshund takes on challenge of being Doxie version

OREGONIAN 20 HOURS AGO

When Portland resident Nora Vanatta agreed to foster an obese dog, she got more - about 40 pounds more, to be exact

Immaculate Conception School Fun Fair Saturday: 5 things to know about

WELLSVILLE DAILY REPORTER 1 DAY AGO

1. Dachshund racing has come back to the Immaculate Conception School Fun Fair this Saturday. Dachshunds (only) registration is at 10 a.m. Saturday in the

Pit bull owner will not be prosecuted

GILROY DISPATCH 18 HOURS AGO

The owner of the pit bull in the July attack that killed a dachshund will not be criminally prosecuted, according to Steve Lowney, the deputy district attorney handling the case. After Gilroy Police interviewed the owner, Lowney decided there was not ...

Figure 9-6

 You can see more categories in the Search pane by moving your mouse to the right edge of the screen and dragging the scrollbar down to see categories such as Travel, Sports, and Weather.

 If you click a category in the Search panel such as Maps, the results are displayed to the left of the Search panel. If you want to see another category, just click it, and the search results for that category appear. This is a great way to browse the Internet for different results related to an item of interest.

Move a File or Folder

1. Sometimes you save a file or folder in one place but in reorganizing your work decide you want to move the item to another location. To do so, click the Desktop tile on the Start screen and then click the File Explorer button in the taskbar.

2. In File Explorer, click a folder to reveal its contents, or double-click a folder or series of folders to reveal subfolders and locate the file that you want to move (see **Figure 9-7**).

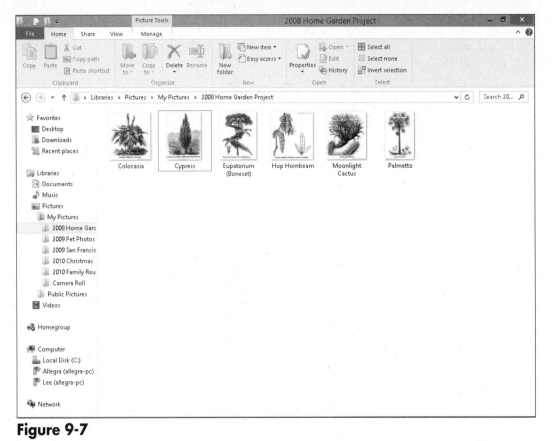

Figure 9-7

3. Take one of the following actions:

- **Click and drag** the file to another folder in the Navigation pane on the left side of the window.

- If you **right-click and drag,** you're offered options via a shortcut menu: You can move the file, copy it, or create a shortcut to it.

- **Right-click** the file and choose Send To. Then choose from the options shown in the submenu that appears (as shown in **Figure 9-8**); these options may vary slightly depending on the type of file you choose and your installed software.

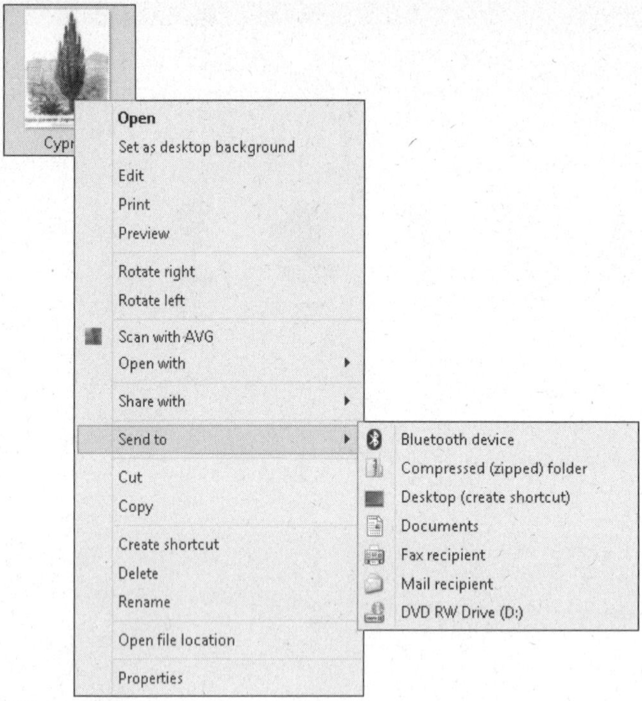

Open
Set as desktop background
Edit
Print
Preview
Rotate right
Rotate left
Scan with AVG
Open with ▶
Share with ▶
Send to ▶
Cut
Copy
Create shortcut
Delete
Rename
Open file location
Properties

Send to submenu:
- Bluetooth device
- Compressed (zipped) folder
- Desktop (create shortcut)
- Documents
- Fax recipient
- Mail recipient
- DVD RW Drive (D:)

Figure 9-8

4. Click the Close button in the upper-right corner of File
Explorer to close it.

 If you change your mind about moving an item
using the right-click-and-drag method, you can
release the mouse button and click Cancel on the
shortcut menu that appears.

 If you want to create a copy of a file or folder in
another location on your computer, right-click the
item and choose Copy. Use File Explorer to navigate
to the location where you want to place a copy, right-
click, and choose Paste or press Ctrl+V.

Rename a File or Folder

1. You may want to change the name of a file or folder to update it or make it more easily identifiable from other files or folders. Locate the file that you want to rename by using File Explorer.

2. Right-click the file and choose Rename (see **Figure 9-9**).

3. The filename is now available for editing. Type a new name, and then click anywhere outside the filename to save the new name.

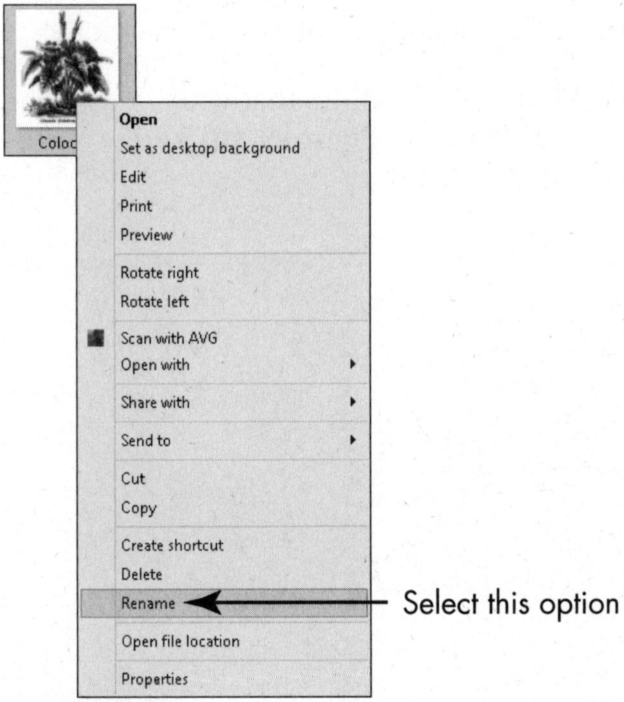

Select this option

Figure 9-9

You can't rename a file to have the same name as another file located in the same folder. To give a file the same name as another, cut it from its current location, paste it into another folder, and then follow the procedure in this task. Or open the file and save it to a new location with the same name, which creates a copy. Be careful, though: Two files with the same name can cause confusion when you search for files. If at all possible, use unique filenames.

Create a Shortcut to a File or Folder

1. You can place a shortcut to a file or folder you used recently on the desktop for quick and easy access.

2. In File Explorer, right-click the file or folder that you want and select Send To (as shown in **Figure 9-10) and then select** Desktop (Create Shortcut).

Select Desktop (Create Shortcut)

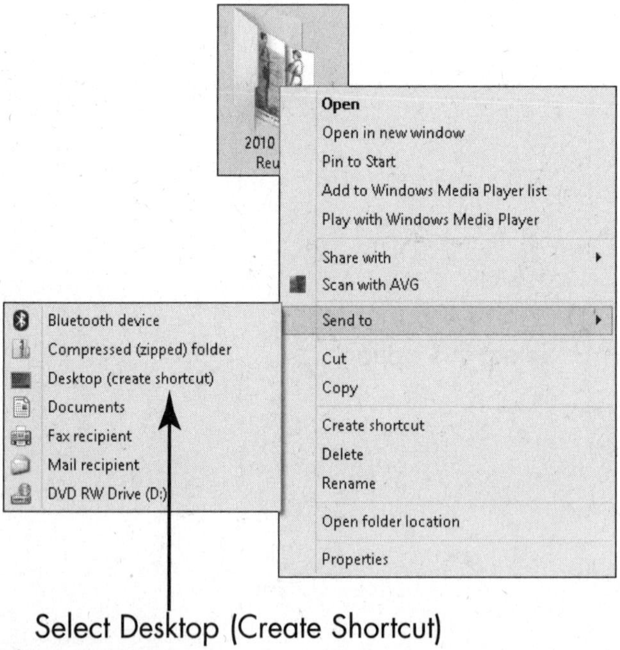

Figure 9-10

3. A shortcut appears on the desktop.

 Once you've placed a shortcut on the desktop, to open the file in its originating application or open a folder in File Explorer, simply double-click the desktop shortcut icon.

Delete a File or Folder

1. If you don't need a file or folder anymore, you can clear up clutter on your computer by deleting it. Locate the file or folder by using File Explorer. Display File Explorer, and then browse to locate the file you want to delete.

2. In File Explorer, right-click the file or folder that you want to delete and then choose Delete (see **Figure 9-11**).

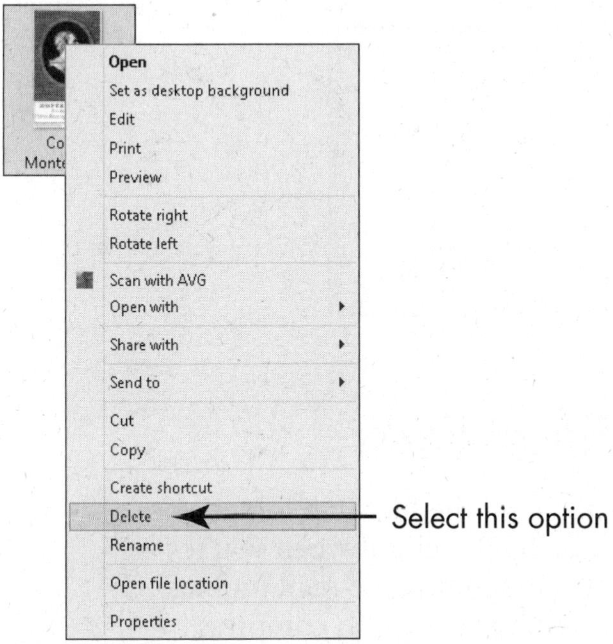

Open
Set as desktop background
Edit
Print
Preview
Rotate right
Rotate left
Scan with AVG
Open with ▶
Share with ▶
Send to ▶
Cut
Copy
Create shortcut
Delete ◀—— Select this option
Rename
Open file location
Properties

Co
Mont

Figure 9-11

3. In the Delete File dialog box (see **Figure 9-12**), click Yes to delete the file.

 When you delete a file or folder in Windows, it's not really gone. It's removed to the Recycle Bin on the desktop. Windows periodically purges older files from this folder, but you may still be able to retrieve recently deleted files and folders from it. To try to restore a deleted file or folder, double-click the Recycle Bin icon on the desktop. Right-click the file or folder and choose Restore. Windows restores the file to wherever it was when you deleted it.

 Instead of right-clicking and choosing Delete from the menu that appears in Step 2 earlier, you can click to select the file and then press the Delete key on your keyboard.

Figure 9-12

Create a Compressed File or Folder

1. To shrink the size of a file or all the files in a folder, you can compress them. This is often helpful when you're sending an item as an attachment to an e-mail message. Locate the files or folders that you want to compress by using File Explorer. (Click the File Explorer button on the taskbar, and then browse to locate the file[s] or folder[s].)

2. In File Explorer, you can do the following (as shown in **Figure 9-13**):

- **Select a series of files or folders.** Click a file or folder, press and hold Shift to select a series of items listed consecutively in the folder, and click the final item.

- **Select nonconsecutive items.** Press and hold the Ctrl key and click the items.

3. Right-click the selected items. In the resulting shortcut menu (see **Figure 9-14**), choose Send To and then choose Compressed (Zipped) Folder. A new compressed folder appears below the last selected file in the File Explorer list.

4. The folder icon is named after the last file you selected in the series, but you can rename it. Type a new name or click outside the item to accept the default name.

 You may want to subsequently rename a compressed folder with a name other than the one that Windows automatically assigns to it. See the task "Rename a File or Folder," earlier in this chapter, to find out just how to do that.

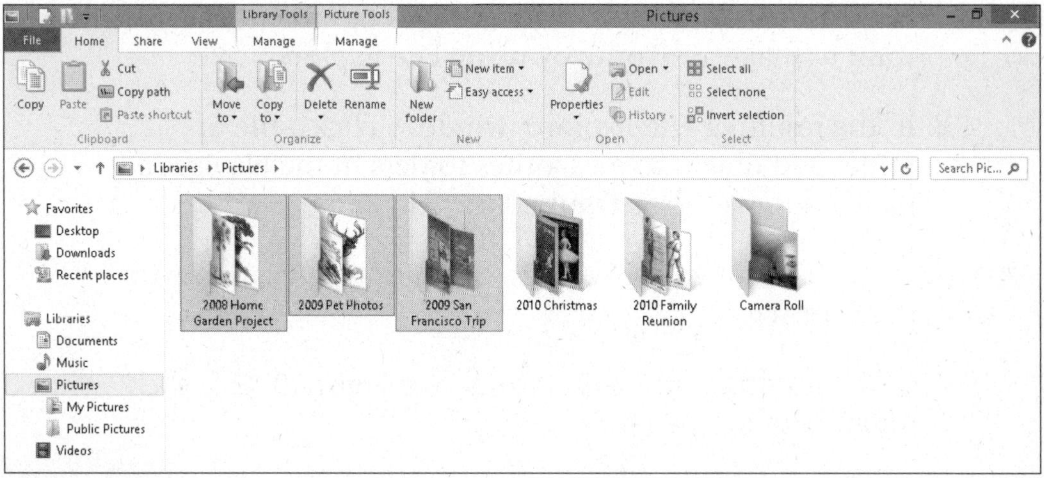

Figure 9-13

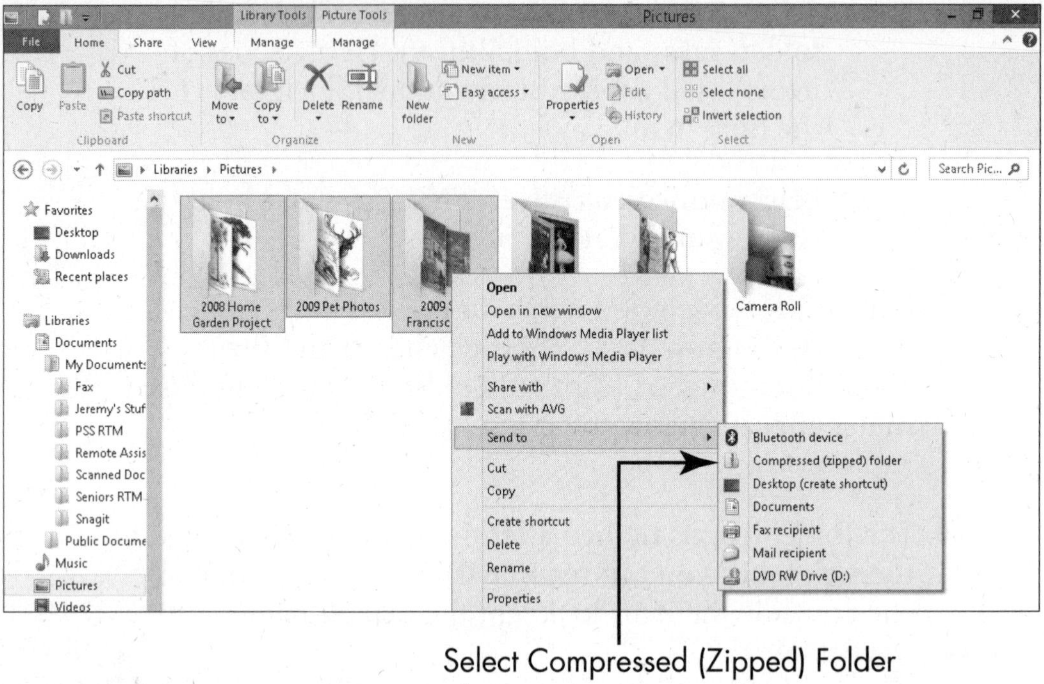

Select Compressed (Zipped) Folder

Figure 9-14

Add a File to Your Favorites List

1. The Favorites folder offers another quick way to access frequently used items. Locate the files or folders that you want to make a Favorite by using File Explorer.

2. In the resulting File Explorer window, click a file or folder and drag it to a Favorites folders in the Navigation pane on the left (see **Figure 9-15**).

3. To see a list of your Favorites, begin to type **Favorites** on the Start screen.

4. In the resulting submenu results (see **Figure 9-16**), click on an item to open it.

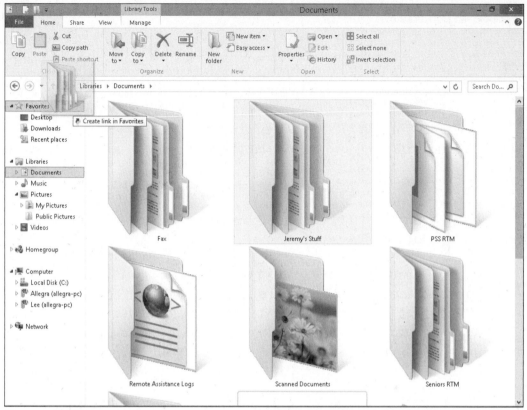

Figure 9-15

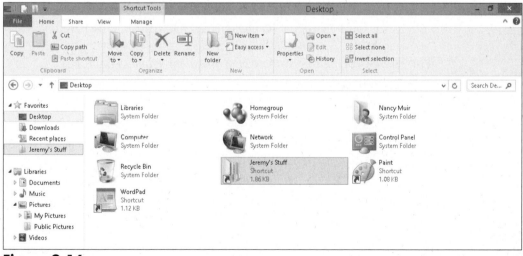

Figure 9-16

Back Up Files

1. You've put a lot of work into your files, so don't forget to back them up. If your computer is damaged or loses data, you'll have a copy safely tucked away. Place a blank writable CD-R/RW (read/writable) or DVD-R/RW in your CD-RW or DVD-RW drive (or connect a USB drive to your USB port) and then open File Explorer.

2. Select the files or folders that you want to copy to disc.

3. Click the Share tab on the Ribbon in File Explorer and click Burn to Disc.

 To save to a drive instead of burn to disc, on the Home tab, click Move To and select Choose Location from the menu. In the Move Items dialog box, click the drive associated with your USB drive and then click the folder on that drive where you want to save the files. Click the Move button.

4. Select the way to use the disc (for example USB or CD/DVD and then click Next. Files are burned to the storage device.

5. Click the Home tab and then click the Eject button, and then click the Close button to close the Document window.

 The method discussed here is a manual way to back up files, which you can do on a regular basis. However, you can also back up to a network or another drive by using the Save Back Up Copies of Your Files with File History in the Control Panel. Backing up to a CD/DVD is a little different from burning a disc in that after you back up your files, only changes that have happened to files since you last saved are saved each subsequent time a backup is run.

Working with the Weather, People, and Calendar Apps

Chapter 10

Get ready to . . .

➠ Display Weather Views 154

➠ Specify a Place in Weather 156

➠ Explore Weather around the World 157

➠ Add a Contact................. 159

➠ Edit Contact Information 161

➠ Send E-mail to Contacts 163

➠ View Contacts' Latest Postings 164

➠ Pin a Contact 166

➠ Add an Event to Your Calendar 167

➠ Invite People to an Event.... 169

Three apps that are preinstalled in Windows 8 can come in handy in planning your activities and connecting with others. Each app is represented on the Start screen by a tile that you simply click to open.

The Weather app can tell you whether you need to wear a raincoat or slather on the sunscreen. In Windows 8, you can get Bing Weather, or choose from several other weather services all from a single screen.

The People app is your contact-management resource. You can store contact information and then use information in a contact record to send an e-mail, view a profile, or post a message on that person's Facebook page or other social network.

The Calendar app lets you view your schedule by day, week, or month, and add details about events, such as the date and time, length, and whether it's a recurring event. After you've entered information about an event, you can send yourself a reminder and even invite others to the event.

Display Weather Views

1. Weather offers several sets of information in four views. Click the Weather tile on the Start screen to display Bing Weather.

2. Click the More/Less button near the bottom-right corner (see **Figure 10-1**); if this arrow faces up, less detail is displayed; if the arrow faces down, more detail is displayed.

3. Click the Options button with a minus symbol in the bottom-right corner of the screen. The choices shown in the menu in **Figure 10-2** appear, though they might vary a bit depending on which weather service you're displaying.

4. Click Historical Weather; a chart of historical weather trends is displayed (see **Figure 10-3**).

5. Scroll to the left to move from Historical Weather to Maps to Hourly Forecast and, finally, back to Bing Weather.

6. Right-click and click the Change to Celsius (or Fahrenheit) button to switch between these two temperature measurements.

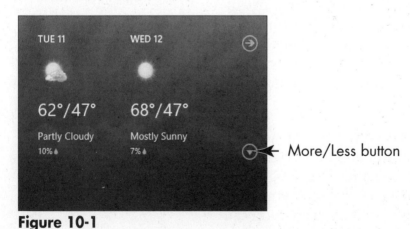

Figure 10-1

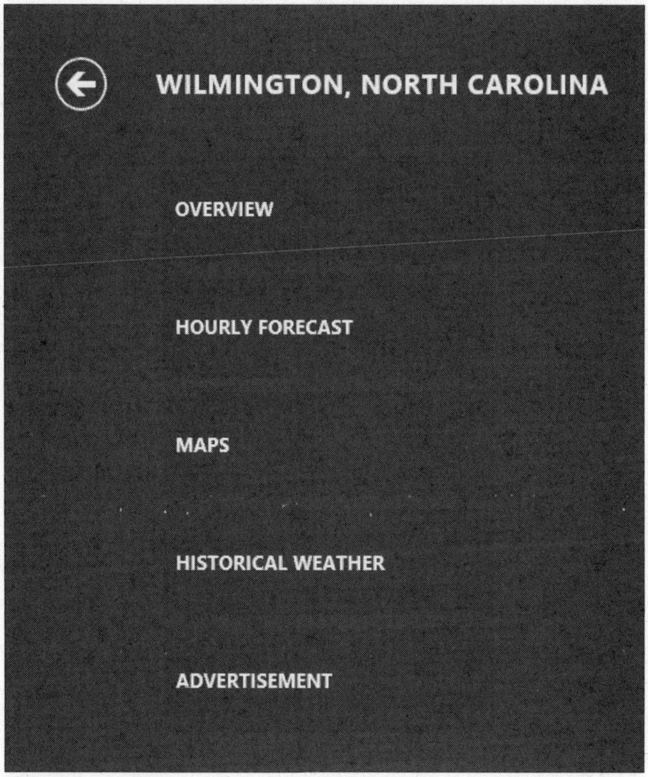

WILMINGTON, NORTH CAROLINA

OVERVIEW

HOURLY FORECAST

MAPS

HISTORICAL WEATHER

ADVERTISEMENT

Figure 10-2

7. Press the Windows key to return to the Start screen.

 If you have a touchscreen computer, you can use your finger to scroll from left to right or right to left among the four Weather views instead of going to the Weather menu and choosing a view to display.

 To view weather from a source other than Bing Weather, with the most detail displayed on the Bing Weather view, click a name above a high/low temperature such as Weather Underground or WDT (these choices change regularly) to go to that weather website.

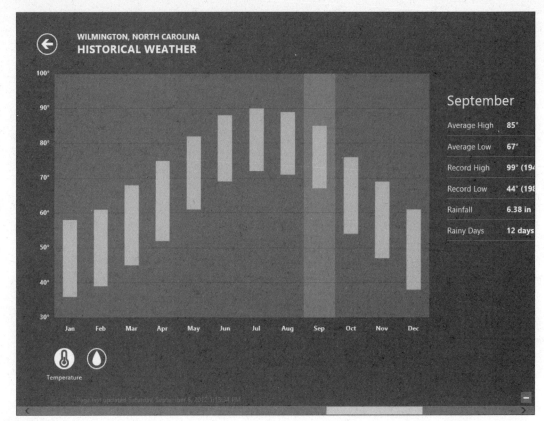

Figure 10-3

Specify a Place in Weather

1. You can specify one or more favorite places and then display detailed weather information for any of those places easily. To add a place, click the Weather tile on the Start screen.

2. Right-click anywhere onscreen to display the three tiles (see **Figure 10-4**) along the top-left of the screen.

3. Click Places.

4. Click the Add button.

Figure 10-4

5. Enter a location in the screen shown in **Figure 10-5** and then click a match for the location in the list that appears. The location is added to your Favorites.

6. Click one of the Favorite places to display information for it in the four Weather views.

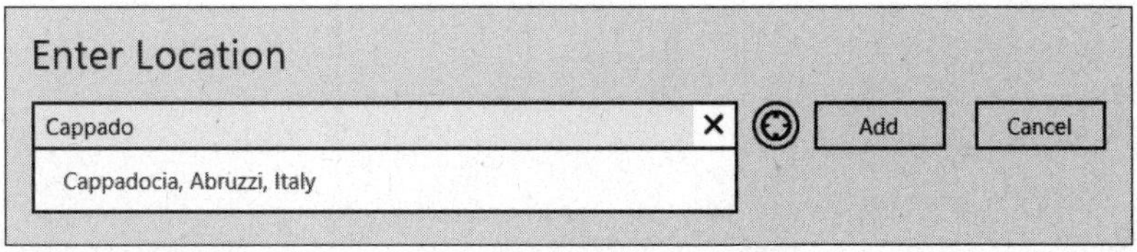

Enter Location

| Cappado | × | ◉ | Add | Cancel |

Cappadocia, Abruzzi, Italy

Figure 10-5

Explore Weather around the World

1. The Weather app isn't limited to your local weather. You can get weather for just about any city in the world. Click the Weather tile on the Start screen.

2. Right-click anywhere onscreen and then click World Weather near the top of the screen (refer to **Figure 10-4**) to display whether info in select cities.

3. Hover your mouse over a blue location dot (see **Figure 10-6**) to show alternative locations.

4. Click a location to display Bing Weather data for it.

Alternative location links

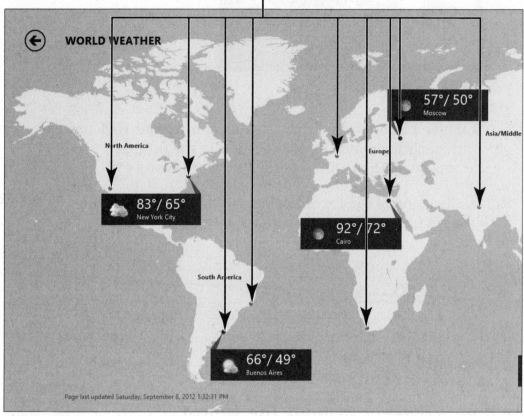

Figure 10-6

5. Click the Back arrow in the top-left corner of the screen to return to World Weather.

6. Click anywhere on the map to zoom in on a region and see more location choices (see **Figure 10-7**).

7. Click anywhere on the screen to zoom out to the world view.

8. Press the Windows key to leave the app and return to the Start screen.

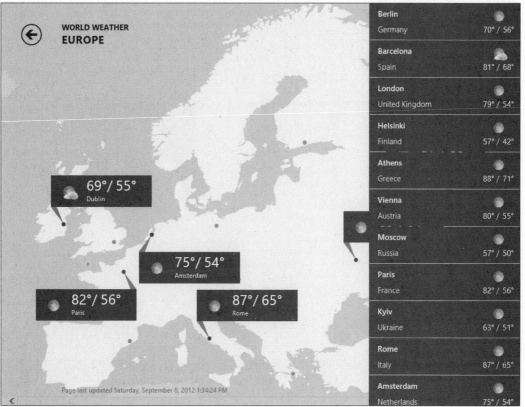

Figure 10-7

Add a Contact

1. After you've entered contacts in the People app, you can look up information about them and even send them e-mail or post messages to their social network using their contact record. To add a new contact, click the People tile on the Start screen to open the app.

2. Right-click anywhere onscreen to display the toolbar shown in **Figure 10-8.**

3. Click the New button on the toolbar.

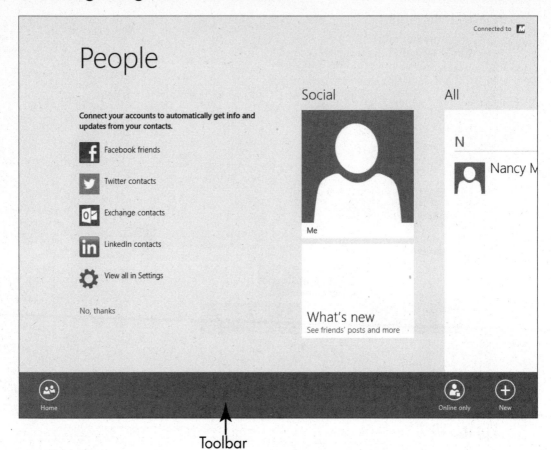

Toolbar

Figure 10-8

4. Enter contact information in the form that appears, as shown in **Figure 10-9.**

5. At the bottom of the screen, click Save.

 When you're logged into Windows 8 with a Windows Live account, contacts from that account are automatically copied into the People app. It's also possible to bring contacts from other accounts into your People app. With the People app open, press Win+I. In the Settings panel, click Accounts. Click an e-mail account and, in the dialog box that appears, make sure that the Contacts check box is selected.

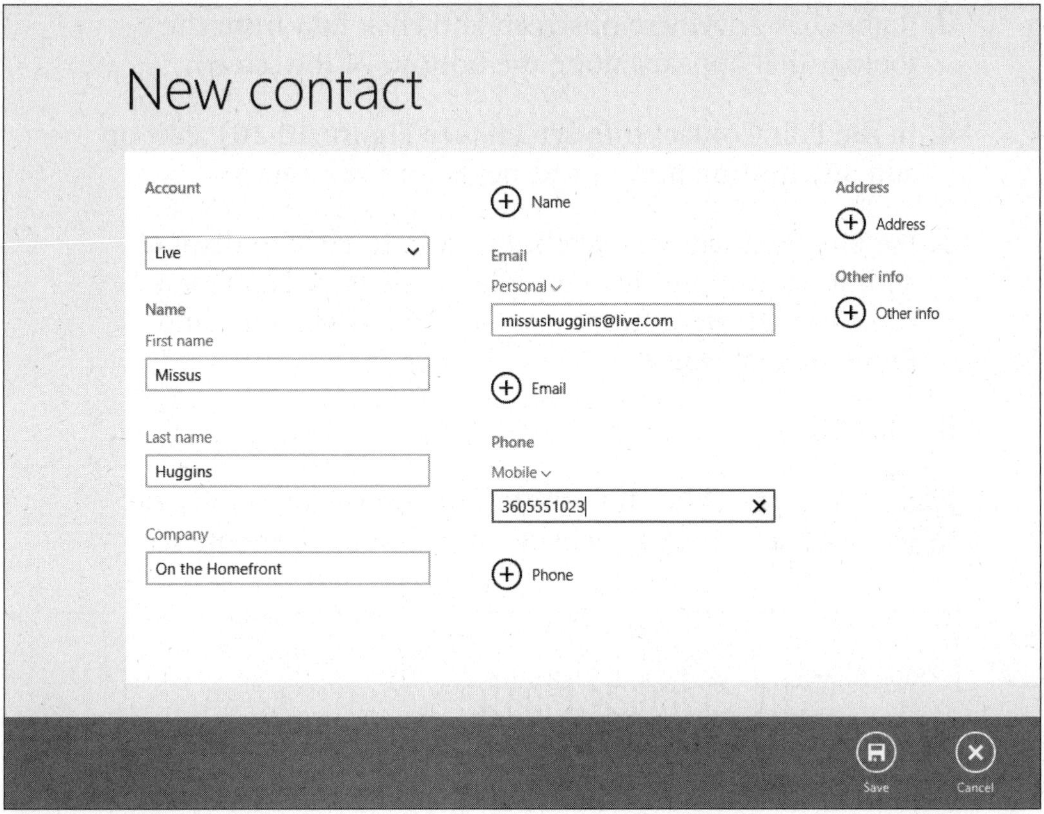

New contact

Account

Live ⌄

Name

First name

Missus

Last name

Huggins

Company

On the Homefront

⊕ Name

Email

Personal ⌄

missushuggins@live.com

⊕ Email

Phone

Mobile ⌄

3605551023   ✕

⊕ Phone

Address

⊕ Address

Other info

⊕ Other info

🖫 Save   ⊗ Cancel

Figure 10-9

 You can find contacts quickly by clicking the button with a minus symbol in the bottom-right corner of the People home screen. This displays a list of letters of the alphabet. Click on a letter to display contacts whose names begin with that letter listed alphabetically.

Edit Contact Information

1. Sometimes you get new information about a contact or find that the information you've already saved to that person's profile changes. To update the information, you can edit the contact. Click the People tile on the Start screen.

2. Click a contact.

3. Right-click anywhere onscreen and click Edit from the toolbar that appears along the bottom of the screen.

4. In the Edit Contact Info screen (see **Figure 10-10**), edit or add any information in text fields for the contact.

5. For any field with a + symbol next to it, click to display additional options; for example, if you click Name you can choose from options such as Title, Nickname, and Phonetic Last Name.

6. Click Save.

 Click the Other Info button to add or edit a job title, significant other, website, or notes for your contact.

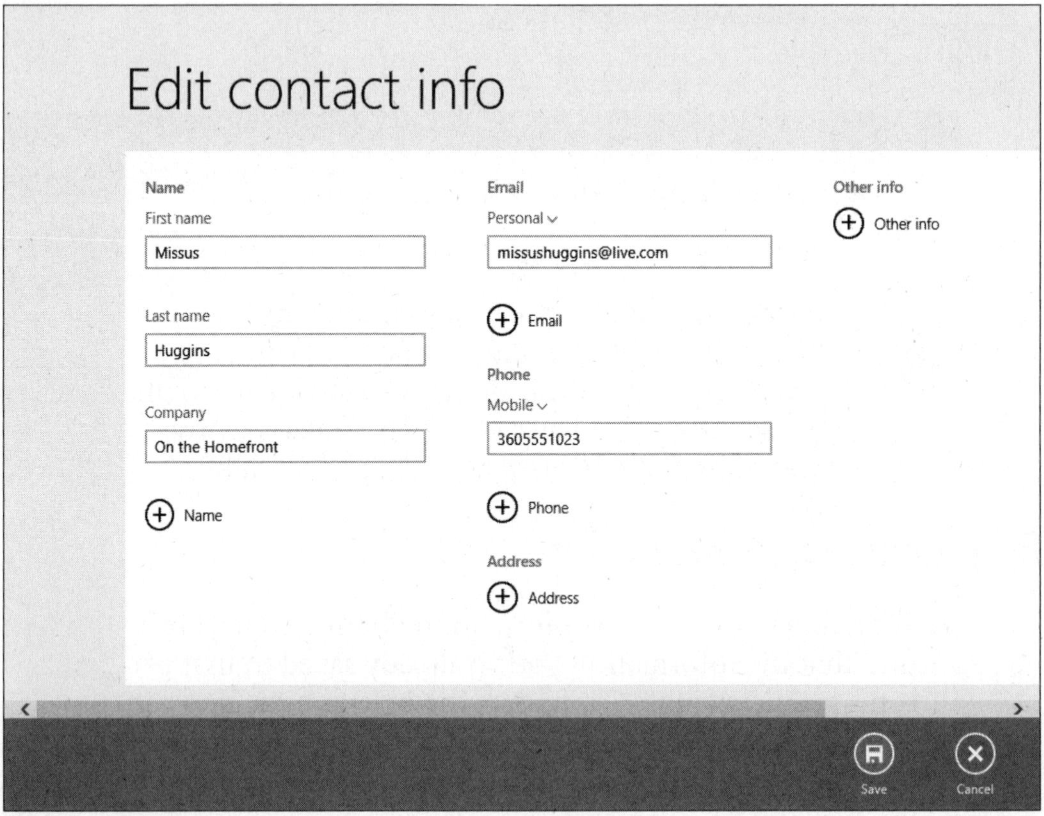

Edit contact info

Name	Email	Other info
First name	Personal ⌄	⊕ Other info
Missus	missushuggins@live.com	
Last name	⊕ Email	
Huggins	Phone	
Company	Mobile ⌄	
On the Homefront	3605551023	
⊕ Name	⊕ Phone	
	Address	
	⊕ Address	

🖫 Save   ⊗ Cancel

Figure 10-10

Send E-mail to Contacts

1. After you've added contact information, including an e-mail address, you can use the People app to quickly address an e-mail. Click the People app on the Start screen.

2. Click a contact.

3. Click on the contact's e-mail address and then click Send Email (see **Figure 10-11**).

4. Click the Hide/Show Cc & Bcc button to display those fields and then enter any addresses you want to copy on the message, as shown in **Figure 10-12**.

5. Click Add a Subject and enter a subject for the message in the Subject field.

Figure 10-11

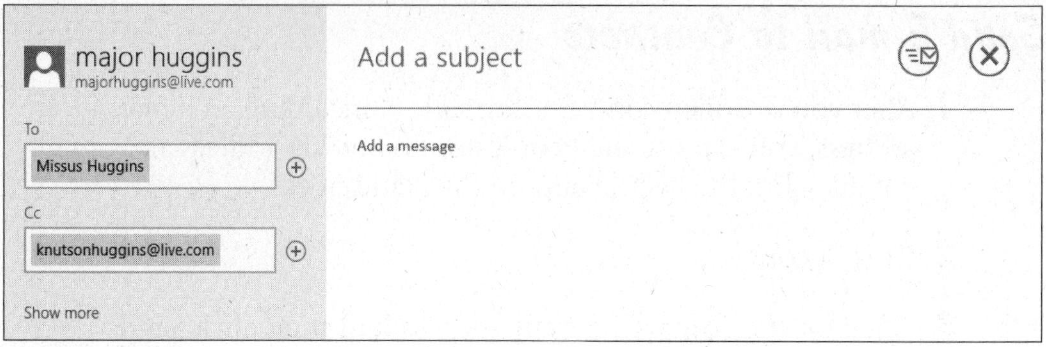

major huggins
majorhuggins@live.com

Add a subject

To

Missus Huggins   ⊕

Add a message

Cc

knutsonhuggins@live.com   ⊕

Show more

Figure 10-12

6. Click in the message area (below the Subject) and enter your message. You can right-click in the body of your message to access some useful formatting tools.

7. If you want to add attachments click Attachments, browse for a file, and then click Attach.

8. Click the Send button to the right of the Subject field.

View Contacts' Latest Postings

1. If you have contacts who are friends in your Facebook or Twitter account, you can view their latest postings easily using the People app if you have installed the Twitter or Facebook app on your computer; these apps are free from the Windows Store. Click the People tile on the Start screen.

2. Click the What's New link (see **Figure 10-13**).

3. Use the scrollbar to scroll through your contacts' latest postings, as shown in Figure 10-14.

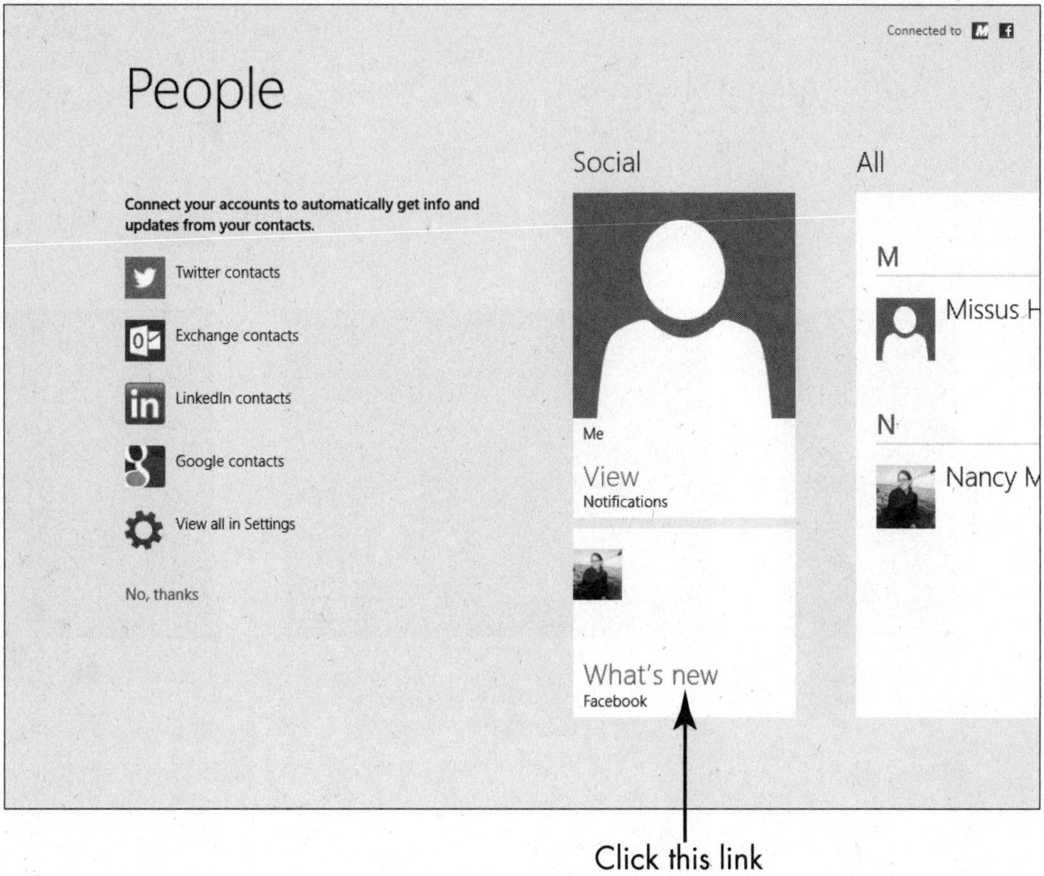

Figure 10-13

4. Click an item such as a Facebook posting to go to comments and Likes for it or Twitter to see the latest tweets.

5. Click the Back arrow to return to the list of all postings.

6. Click the Me tab in the People app to display a screen showing your latest activity; for example with Facebook this would show postings friends have made on your wall.

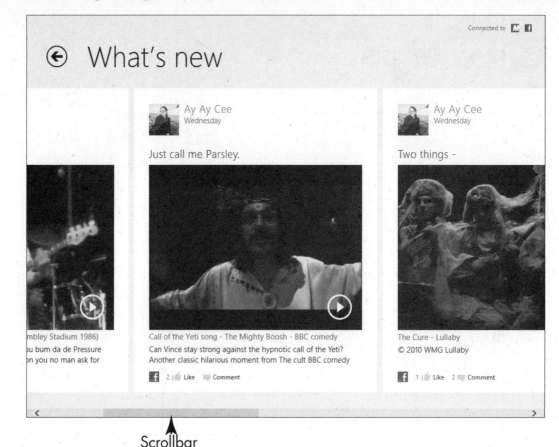

Scrollbar

Figure 10-14

Pin a Contact

1. You can pin a contact to the Start screen, which creates a tile that you can click to easily retrieve that person's information. To pin a contact, click the People tile on the Start screen.

2. Click a contact.

3. Right-click anywhere onscreen.

4. On the toolbar, click Pin to Start (see **Figure 10-15**).

Click this option

Figure 10-15

5. In the dialog box that appears, modify the name for the contact if you want to, and then click Pin to Start.

 To unpin a contact, display the Start screen and right-click the contact's tile. Click Unpin from Start in the toolbar that appears.

Add an Event to Your Calendar

1. The Calendar app is a great way to track your activities. To display and add an event to your Calendar, click the Calendar tile on the Start screen.

2. Right-click anywhere onscreen and click the view you prefer from the toolbar that appears: Day, Week, or Month (see **Figure 10-16**).

3. Click in a date or time block (depending on your view).

4. In the Details form that appears (see **Figure 10-17**), enter the details of the event in text boxes (such as Where) or choose them from drop-down lists (such as How Long).

5. If you have multiple calendar accounts associated with your computer, click the Calendar field and then select the calendar you want the event to appear in.

Figure 10-16

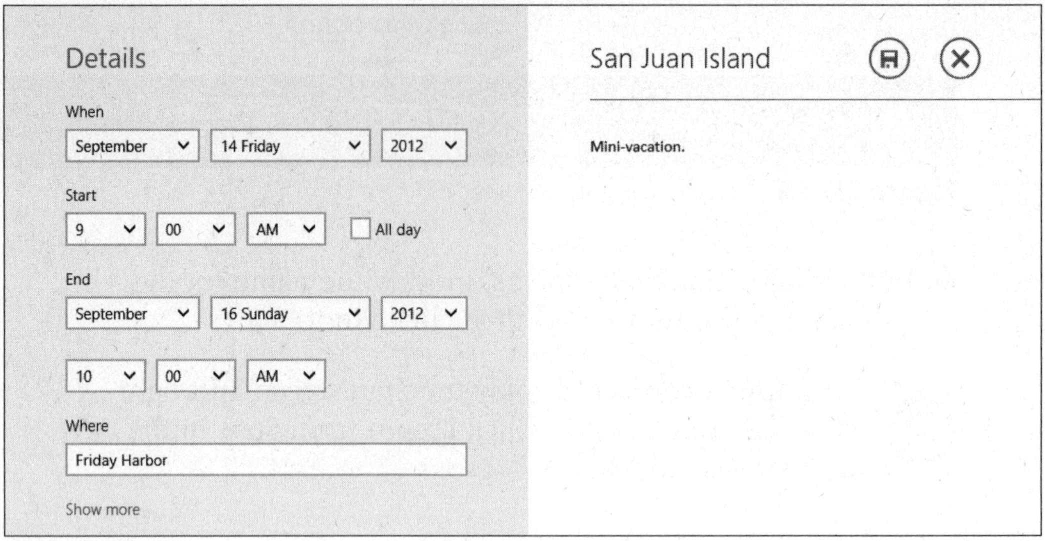

Details	San Juan Island 🖫 ⊗
When	
September ⌄ 14 Friday ⌄ 2012 ⌄	Mini-vacation.
Start	
9 ⌄ 00 ⌄ AM ⌄ ☐ All day	
End	
September ⌄ 16 Sunday ⌄ 2012 ⌄	
10 ⌄ 00 ⌄ AM ⌄	
Where	
Friday Harbor	
Show more	

Figure 10-17

6. If you want to be reminded of the event ahead of time, click the Show More link, and then click the Reminder field and select how long before the event the reminder should occur, such as 15 minutes or 1 week. To enter a title for the event click the Title field and enter it.

7. Click the Save button.

 If you want to create a recurring event such as a weekly meeting or monthly get-together with friends, use the How Often field in the Details form. This offers intervals ranging from every day to every year and creates multiple calendar entries accordingly.

 To show events from calendars associated with your computer, such as a US Holidays calendar or the calendar from an e-mail account, with the Calendar app open press Win+I. Click Options, and then click the slider associated with a calendar to show or hide it.

To edit an event after you create it, simply click it in any calendar view, modify the details, and click Save.

Invite People to an Event

1. If you're setting up an event such as your neighborhood association's meeting or a party, the Calendar app offers a handy way to get the invites out to everybody involved. To create an event and invite others to it, click in a calendar field to display a new event Details form.

2. In the Details form that appears, enter the details of the event in text boxes (such as Where) or choose them from drop-down lists (such as How Long).

3. Click the Show More link, and then click in the Who field and enter an e-mail address (as shown in **Figure 10-18**). If you want to enter multiple e-mail addresses, separate them by a comma.

4. Enter a title and message for the invitation in the area on the right and click the Send Invite button. Windows sends an e-mail with details of the event to each address you entered in the Who field.

 If you're browsing through the months or weeks in the Calendar app and want to quickly return to today's events, right-click and then click the Today button on the toolbar that appears.

Who

knutsonhuggins@live.com

Figure 10-18

Part III
Going Online

The 5th Wave   By Rich Tennant

"Since we got it, he hasn't moved from that spot for eleven straight days. Oddly enough they call this 'getting up and running' on the Internet."

Understanding Internet Basics

For many people, going online might be the major reason to buy a computer. You can use the Internet to check stock quotes, play interactive games with others, and file your taxes, for example. For seniors especially, the Internet can provide wonderful ways to keep in touch with family and friends located around the country or on the other side of the world via e-mail or instant messaging. You can share photos of your grandchildren or connect with others who share your hobbies or interests.

But before you begin all those wonderful activities, it helps to understand some basics about the Internet and how it works.

This chapter helps you understand what the Internet and World Wide Web are, as well as some basics about connecting to the Internet and navigating it. I also tell you about the Internet Explorer app, which is new in Windows 8.

Get ready to . . .

➡ Understand What the Internet Is...............................174

➡ Explore Different Types of Internet Connections..........176

➡ Set Up an Internet Connection........................ 179

➡ Practice Navigation Basics with the Start Screen IE App.............................. 181

➡ Practice Navigation Basics with the Desktop IE App 183

➡ Understand Tabs in Browsers......................... 184

➡ Understand Home Pages.... 185

➡ Set Up a Home Page in Desktop IE 186

Understand What the Internet Is

The "Internet," "links," the "web". . . . People and the media bounce around many online-related terms these days, and folks sometimes use them incorrectly. Your first step in getting familiar with the Internet is to understand what some of these terms mean.

Here's a list of common Internet-related terms:

→ The *Internet* is a large network of computers that contain information and technology tools that anybody with an Internet connection can access. (See the next section for information about Internet connections.)

→ Residing on that network of computers is a huge set of documents, which form the *World Wide Web*, usually referred to as just the *web*.

→ The web includes *websites*, which are made up of collections of *web pages* just as a book is made up of individual pages. Websites have many purposes: For example, a website can be informational, function as a retail store, or host social networking communities where people can exchange ideas and thoughts.

→ You can buy, sell, or bid for a wide variety of items in an entire online marketplace referred to as the world of *e-commerce*.

→ To get around online, you use a software program called a *browser*. Many browsers are available, and they're free. Internet Explorer (IE) is Microsoft's browser; others include Mozilla Firefox, Google Chrome, Safari, and Opera. Browsers offer tools to help you navigate from website to website and from one web page to another.

➠ Each web page has a unique address that you use to reach it, called a Universal Resource Locator (URL). You enter a URL in a browser's address bar to go to a website or a particular page within a site.

➠ When you open a website, you might see colored text or graphics that represent *hyperlinks*, also referred to as **links**. You can click links to move from place to place within a web page, within a website, or between websites. **Figure 11-1** shows some hyperlinks indicated by colored text or graphics.

🎯 A link can be a graphic (such as a company logo) or text. A text link is identifiable by colored text, which is sometimes underlined and which sometimes changes color when you hover your mouse over it. After you click a link, the link itself usually changes color to indicate that you've followed the link.

Text hyperlink   Graphical hyperlink

Figure 11-1

Explore Different Types of Internet Connections

Before you can connect to the Internet for the first time, you have to have certain hardware in place and choose your *Internet service provider* (also referred to as an *ISP* or simply a *provider*). An ISP is a company that owns dedicated computers (called *servers*) that you use to access the Internet. ISPs charge a monthly fee for this service.

You can choose a type of connection to go online. The type of connection you want determines which companies you can choose from to provide the service. For example, a DSL connection might come through your phone company, whereas a cable connection is available through your cable-TV company. Not every type of connection is necessarily available in every area, so check with phone, cable, and local Internet providers rather than national or international providers to find out your options and costs (some offer discounts to AARP members, for example).

Here are the most common types of connections, each of which offers pros and cons in terms of the quality of the signal and potential service interruptions depending on the company and your locale, so do your homework before signing on the dotted line:

➡ **Digital Subscriber Line (DSL):** This service is delivered through your phone land line, but your phone is available to you to make calls even when you're connected to the Internet. DSL is a form of broadband communication, which may use phone lines and fiber-optic cables for transmission. You have to subscribe to a broadband service (check with your phone company) and pay a monthly fee for access.

➡ **Cable:** You may instead go through your local cable company to get your Internet service via the cable that brings your TV programming rather than your phone line. This is another type of broadband service, and it's relatively fast. Check with your cable company for monthly fees.

➡ **Satellite:** Especially in rural areas, satellite Internet providers may be your only option. This requires that you install a satellite dish. DISH and Comcast are two providers of satellite connections to check into.

➡ **Wireless hotspots:** If you take a wireless-enabled laptop computer, tablet, or smartphone with you on a trip, you can piggyback on a connection somebody else has made. You will find wireless hotspots in many public places, such as airports, cafes, and hotels. If you're in range of such a hotspot, your computer usually finds the connection automatically, making Internet service available to you for free or for a fee.

➡ **Dialup:** This is the slowest connection method, but it's relatively inexpensive. With a dialup connection, you use a phone line to connect to the Internet, entering some phone numbers (*local access numbers*) that your ISP provides. Using these local access numbers, you won't incur long distance charges for your connection. However, with this type of connection, you can't use a phone line for phone calls while you're connected to the Internet, so it's no longer a popular way to connect.

Internet connections have different speeds that depend partially on your computer's capabilities and partially on the connection you get from your provider. Before you choose a provider, it's important to understand how faster connection speeds can benefit you:

➡ Faster speeds allow you to send data faster, for example to download a photo to your computer. In addition, web pages and images display faster.

➠ Dialup connection speeds run at the low end, about 56 kilobits per second, or Kbps. Most broadband connections today are around 500 to 600 Kbps. If you have a slower connection, a file might take minutes to upload. (For example, you upload a file you're attaching to an e-mail.) This same operation might take only seconds at a higher speed.

➠ Broadband services typically offer different plans that provide different access speeds. These plans can give you savings if you're economy minded and don't mind the lower speeds, or offer you much better speeds if you're willing to pay for them.

Depending on your type of connection, you'll need different hardware:

➠ A broadband connection uses an Ethernet cable and a modem, which your provider should make available, as well as a connection to your phone or cable line.

➠ Many desktop and laptop computers come with a built-in modem for dialup connections (though these are being left out more and more as people move to wireless connections) and are enabled for wireless. If you choose a broadband connection, your phone or cable company will provide you with an external modem and wireless router (usually for a price).

➠ If you have a laptop that doesn't have a built-in wireless modem, you can add this hardware by buying a wireless CardBus adapter PC card at any office supply or computer store. This card enables a laptop to pick up wireless signals.

If this all sounds like Greek to you, review your computer's user guide for information about its networking capabilities, and then visit a computer or major office supply store and ask representatives for their advice about your specific hardware.

 Many providers offer free or low-cost setup when you open a new account. If you're not technical by nature, consider taking advantage of this when you sign up.

Set Up an Internet Connection

1. The first step is to set up a connection in Windows so you can access the Internet. Begin typing the words **control panel** from the Start screen, and then click Control Panel in the Search results.

2. Click Network and Internet.

3. In the resulting window, click Network and Sharing Center.

4. In the resulting Network and Sharing Center window (see **Figure 11-2**), click the Set Up a New Connection or Network link.

Click this link

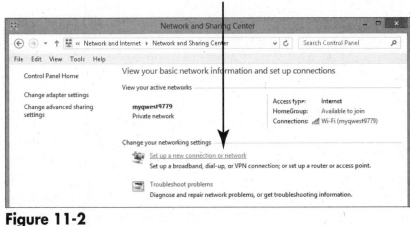

Figure 11-2

5. In the Choose a Connection Option window, click Next to accept the default option of creating a new Internet connection. If you're already connected to the Internet, a window appears; click Set Up a New Connection Anyway.

6. In the resulting dialog box, click your connection. (These steps follow the selection of Broadband.)

7. In the resulting dialog box, shown in **Figure 11-3,** enter your username and password, and change the connection name if you wish (this is optional), and then click Connect. Windows automatically detects the connection, and the Network and Sharing Center appears with your connection listed.

 In many cases, if you have a disc from your ISP, you don't need to follow the preceding steps. Just pop that DVD into your DVD-ROM drive, and in no time, a window appears that gives you the steps to follow to get set up.

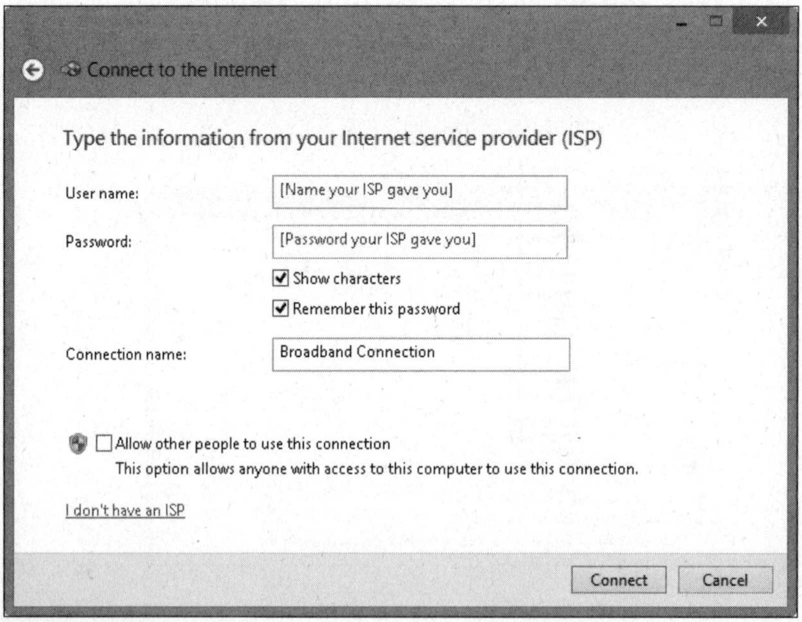

Connect to the Internet

Type the information from your Internet service provider (ISP)

User name: [Name your ISP gave you]

Password: [Password your ISP gave you]

☑ Show characters
☑ Remember this password

Connection name: Broadband Connection

☐ Allow other people to use this connection
This option allows anyone with access to this computer to use this connection.

I don't have an ISP

Connect   Cancel

Figure 11-3

Practice Navigation Basics with the Start Screen IE App

1. A browser is a program that you use to navigate, manage, and use features on the various pages of content on the web. You can practice how to get around the web using a browser such as the popular Internet Explorer 10 (IE) from Microsoft. Open IE by clicking the Internet Explorer tile on the Start screen.

   Note: This opens a different version of IE than you open from the desktop. See Chapter 12 for more info about the two versions of IE 10, and see the next task for info on using the traditional, Internet Explorer program that you might already be familiar with.

2. If the address bar isn't visible, right-click to display it along the bottom of the screen. Enter a website address in the address bar that appears (as shown in **Figure 11-4**; `http://techsmartsenior.com` is my company's website), and then press Enter.

3. On the resulting website, click a link to display another page. Try using navigation tools on the page (such as the About Us tab on the page in **Figure 11-4**) or enter another address in the address bar and press Enter to proceed to another page.

 If you don't see the address bar, right-click onscreen, but try to avoid right-clicking photos and links when you do that. Right-clicking one of those elements could display a menu or display a different page or site instead of the address bar.

 A link can be text or graphics (such as an icon or photo). A text link is identifiable by colored text, sometimes blue. After you click a link, it usually changes to another color (such as purple) to show that it's been followed.

Enter a web address here

Figure 11-4

4. Click the Back button to the left of the address bar to move back to the first page that you visited. Click the Forward button to the far right of the address bar to go forward to the second page that you visited.

If you hover your mouse pointer in the middle of the left or right edge of the screen, a backward or forward arrow is displayed. You can click the arrows to move backward or forward among other pages you've displayed.

The Refresh button (a curved arrow) to the right of the address bar is useful for navigating sites. Clicking the Refresh button redisplays the current page. This is especially useful if a page, such as on a stock market site, updates information frequently. You can also use the Refresh button if a page doesn't load correctly; it might load correctly when refreshed.

 You can quickly access frequently viewed and pinned sites by clicking in the address bar. You see the Frequent and Pinned tiles. Click a tile that represents the website you want to go to.

Practice Navigation Basics with the Desktop IE App

1. With the version of IE 10 accessed from the desktop, the address bar is always displayed across the top of the screen, as are buttons to move forward and backward among pages viewed. To open the desktop version of IE 10 from the desktop click the Internet Explorer button in the taskbar.

2. Enter an address such as www.microsoft.com in the address bar. Note you can also enter a search term here to search for online content.

3. Click the Previous button to return to the page you just left.

4. Click the Next button to go back to the second site you visited.

 In the version of IE 10 accessed from the desktop, traditional tabs are still used. See the next section, "Understand Tabs in Browsers," for more about using them.

Part III: Going Online

In the desktop version of IE 10, you can display a history of recently visited sites by clicking the arrow in the address bar.

Understand Tabs in Browsers

Several browsers use tabs (**Figure 11-5 shows tabs in the Start screen IE app**), which allow you to keep multiple web pages open at once and easily switch among them by clicking the tabs. A *tab* is a sort of window you can use to navigate to any number of web pages. You don't have to create a new tab to go to another site, but you can more quickly switch between two or more sites without a lot of clicking around or entering URLs.

Tabs

Figure 11-5

184

In desktop IE, for example, tabs across the top of the page look like tabs used to divide index cards. Click on a tab to display that page. With the Start screen's IE app, the thumbnails at the top of the page represent pages that you currently have open. (If the thumbnails don't appear, right-click the page to display them.) These thumbnails are the Start screen IE app's version of tabbed browsing. Click a thumbnail to go to the page it represents.

 With Windows 8.1 and IE 11 accessed from the Start screen, you right-click and then click the Add button (with a + in a circle) at the bottom of the screen rather than the top to add a tab. Simply enter a new URL to add a tab (see **Figure 11-6**).

 To open a new tab using the Start screen IE app, right-click the page and the tabs are displayed. Close a tab by right-clicking it and clicking the Close button.

Close button   Add button

Figure 11-6

Understand Home Pages

With Windows 8 you don't close apps as you did in previous versions of the operating system, you simply return to the Start screen and go to another app.

When you return to the Start screen after using Internet Explorer and you click the Internet Explorer tile again you simply display the last page you were viewing.

However, in the traditional desktop Internet Explorer (and other browser brands), the first page you see when you open the browser is your home page, which you can choose. In fact, you can even choose multiple home page tabs. Your home page(s) appear automatically every time you log on to the Internet, so choose one or a few sites that you go to often for this setting. See the next task, where I tell you how to set this up.

Set Up a Home Page in Desktop IE

1. Open desktop Internet Explorer. Near the upper-right corner, click the Tools icon (it looks like a gear) and choose Internet Options from the menu.

2. In the resulting Internet Options dialog box, on the General tab, enter a website address to use as your home page, as shown in **Figure 11-7,** and then click OK. Note that you can enter several home pages that will appear on different tabs every time you open IE.

   Alternatively, click one of the following preset buttons shown in **Figure 11-7:**

   • **Use Current.** Sets whatever page is currently displayed in the browser window as your home page.

   • **Use Default.** This setting sends you to the MSN website.

   • **Use New Tab.** If you're a minimalist, this setting is for you. No web page displays; you just see a blank area.

3. Click the Home Page icon (see **Figure 11-8**) on the far-right side of the IE toolbar (it looks like a little house) to go to your home page.

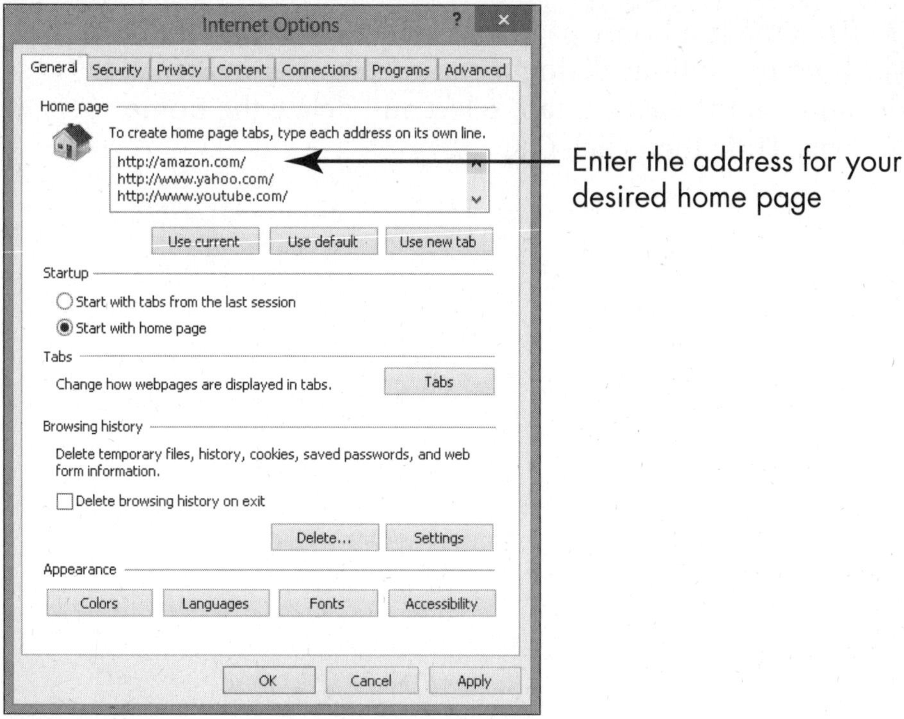

Internet Options

| General | Security | Privacy | Content | Connections | Programs | Advanced |

Home page

To create home page tabs, type each address on its own line.

    http://amazon.com/
    http://www.yahoo.com/
    http://www.youtube.com/

Enter the address for your desired home page

[Use current] [Use default] [Use new tab]

Startup

○ Start with tabs from the last session
◉ Start with home page

Tabs

Change how webpages are displayed in tabs. [Tabs]

Browsing history

Delete temporary files, history, cookies, saved passwords, and web form information.

☐ Delete browsing history on exit

[Delete...] [Settings]

Appearance

[Colors] [Languages] [Fonts] [Accessibility]

[OK] [Cancel] [Apply]

Figure 11-7

 If you're on a web page and decide that you want to add it to your home page tabs, you can easily do that. Right-click the Home button and choose Add or Change Home Page. In the Add or Change Home Page dialog box that appears, click the Add This Webpage to Your Home Page Tabs radio button, and then click Yes. Display other sites and repeat this procedure for all the home page tabs you want.

Home Page icon

Figure 11-8

To remove a home page that you've set up, go to the Internet Options dialog mentioned earlier in Step 2 and, on the General tab, select and delete the home page URL; then click OK.

Browsing the Web with Internet Explorer

A *browser* is a program that you can use to move from one web page to another, but you can also use it to perform searches for information and images. Most browsers, such as Internet Explorer (IE) and Mozilla Firefox, are available for free. Macintosh computers come with a browser called Safari preinstalled with the operating system.

Chapter 11 introduces browser basics, such as how to go directly to a site when you know the web address, how to use the Back and Forward buttons to move among sites you've visited, and how to set up the home page that opens automatically when you launch your browser.

In this chapter, you discover the ins and outs of using Internet Explorer — both the version you access from the Start screen (which I'll call Start screen IE) and the one you reach through the desktop (desktop IE).

By using either version of IE, you can

Get ready to . . .

➠ Understand Differences between the Two Versions of IE 190

➠ Search the Web 192

➠ Find Content on a Web Page 195

➠ Pin a Web Page to the Start Screen..................... 196

➠ Add a Website to Favorites 197

➠ Organize Favorites 198

➠ View Your Browsing History............................ 199

➠ Customize the Internet Explorer Toolbar.............. 201

➠ View RSS Feeds............... 202

➠ Print a Web Page 204

➠ **Navigate all around the web.** Use the IE navigation features to go back to places you've been (via the Favorites and History features), and use Google to search for new places to visit.

➠ **Customize your web-browsing experience.** You can modify what tools are available to you on Internet Explorer toolbars to make your online work easier.

➠ **Subscribe to RSS feeds.** You can request that a site alert you when it adds new content, so that you can stay up to date on news or opinions from various sources.

➠ **Print content from web pages.** When you find what you want online, such as an image or article, just use IE's Print feature to generate a hard copy.

Understand Differences between the Two Versions of IE

With Windows 8, Microsoft also introduces two new versions of Internet Explorer 10: the first you access through the Start screen and the other you access through the desktop. Here's how they differ:

➠ **Start screen IE:** This version was designed along the lines of Windows 8: a less-cluttered screen (see **Figure 12-1**); no drop-down menus and dialog boxes for making settings, just a few simple buttons and an address field along the bottom of the screen; tabs you can display showing thumbnails of recently visited sites; and Internet Options you can manage from the Settings charm. You may have to right-click the screen to display the address field and tabs.

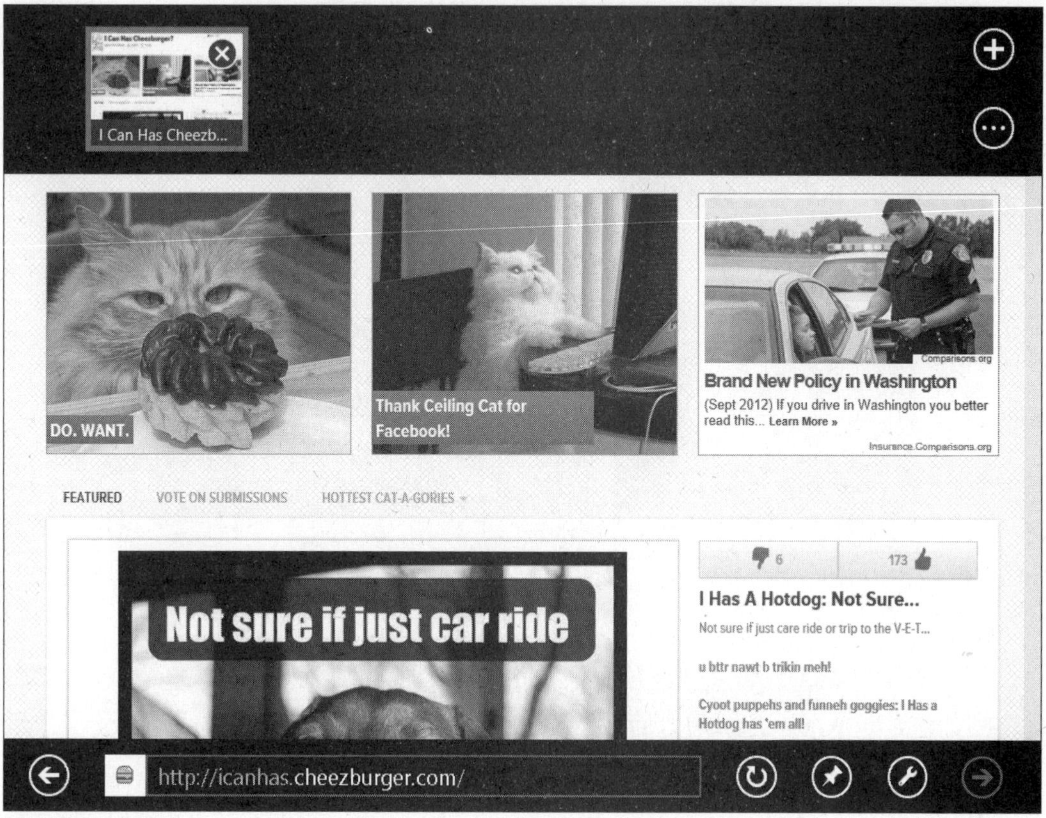

Figure 12-1

➡ **Desktop IE:** More familiar to users of previous versions of IE, desktop IE 10 offers an address field across the top of the screen, toolbars with drop-down menus such as File and Favorites, as well as tools for going to your home page and making safety and other settings (see **Figure 12-2**).

Several tasks in this chapter help you practice using both styles of Internet Explorer.

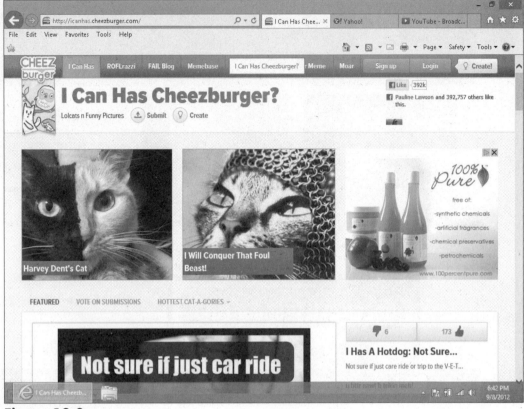

Figure 12-2

Search the Web

1. You can use words and phrases to search for information on the web using a search engine no matter which browser you use. In this example, you'll use the browser of your choice and Google, a popular search engine. Open any browser and enter `www.google.com` in the address bar.

2. Enter a search term in the search box and then click the Google Search button.

3. In the search results that appear (see **Figure 12-3**), you can click a link to go to that web page. If you don't see the link that you need, click and drag the scroll bar to view more results.

Using the Start screen IE, you might have to hover your mouse over the right edge of the screen to make the scroll bar appear, and hover your mouse over the middle of the left side of the screen to see a back arrow to move to the preceding page.

4. Click the Options button near the top-right corner (refer to **Figure 12-3**), and then click Advanced Search to change Search parameters.

5. In the resulting Advanced Search page, shown in **Figure 12-4**, modify the following parameters:

- **Find Pages With:** These options let you narrow the way words or phrases are searched; for example, you can find matches for only the exact wording you enter or enter words that you want to exclude from your results. For example, you could search *flu* and specify you don't want results that involve *swine flu*.

Click a link in the results list

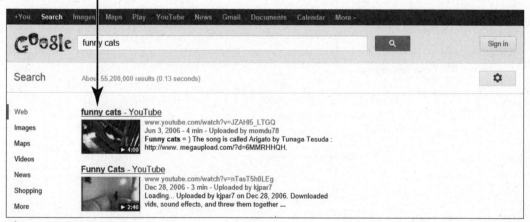

Figure 12-3

- **Then Narrow Your Results By:** Here you can select language and region. You can also limit results based on when information on the site was last updated, if you're looking for the most current information on the subject you're searching. You can specify a site address and where on the page to search. You can also adjust safety settings for your search by moving the SafeSearch slider, or adjust the reading level, file type, and *usage rights settings* (in other words, any copyrights that prohibit you from reusing content).

When you're done with the settings, click the Advanced Search button to run the search again with the new criteria.

Advanced Search	
Find pages with...	
all these words:	flu
this exact word or phrase:	
any of these words:	
none of these words:	swine
numbers ranging from:	to
Then narrow your results by...	
language:	any language
	Find pages in the language you select.
region:	any region
	Find pages published in a particular region.
last update:	anytime
	Find pages updated within the time you specify.
site or domain:	.edu,.org ✕
	Search one site (like wikipedia.org) or limit your results to a domain like .edu, .org or .gov
terms appearing:	anywhere in the page

Figure 12-4

Knowing how search engines work can save you time. For example, if you search by entering *golden retriever*, you typically get sites that contain both words or either word. If you put a plus sign between these two keywords (*golden+retriever*), you get only sites that contain both words.

Find Content on a Web Page Using Start Screen IE

1. Click the Internet Explorer tile on the Start screen, enter a URL in the address field, and press Enter. Right-click a blank area onscreen, click the Settings button (it has a small wrench symbol on it), and choose Find on Page.

2. In the resulting Find toolbar that appears on the bottom of the screen, as shown in **Figure 12-5,** enter the word that you want to search for. As you type, all instances of the word on the page are highlighted.

Enter a search term here

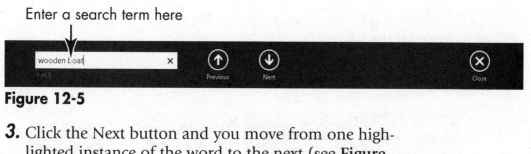

Figure 12-5

3. Click the Next button and you move from one highlighted instance of the word to the next (see **Figure 12-6**). If you want to move to a previous instance, click the Previous button.

Previous button   Next button   Close button

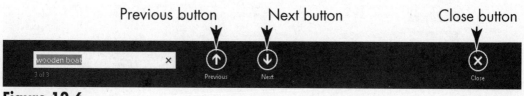

Figure 12-6

4. When you're done searching on a page, click the Close button at the right end of the Find on Page toolbar.

 Many websites have a Search This Site feature that allows you to search not only the displayed web page but all web pages on a website, or to search by department or category of item in an online store. Look for a Search text box and make sure that it searches the site — and not the entire Internet.

Pin a Web Page to the Start Screen

1. You can pin a web page and even a search results page to your Start screen as a tile so you can quickly open it again just by clicking the tile. Click the Internet Explorer tile on the Start screen and display a page or search results.

2. Right-click and click the Pin button in the address field toolbar.

3. In the dialog box that appears (see **Figure 12-7**), enter a name for the tile.

4. Click Pin to Start.

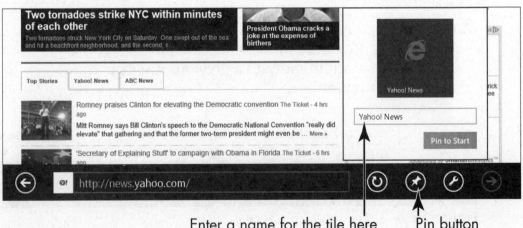

Enter a name for the tile here   Pin button

Figure 12-7

To unpin an item from the Start screen right-click it and then click the Unpin from Start button on the toolbar that appears.

Add a Website to Favorites

1. If there's a site you intend to revisit, you may want to save it to IE's Favorites folder so you can easily go there again. To use this feature, open IE from the desktop, enter the URL of a website that you want to add to your Favorites list, and then press Enter.

2. Click the Favorites button (a star near the top-right corner of the browser screen) to display the Favorites pane, and then click the Add to Favorites button.

3. In the resulting Add a Favorite dialog box, shown in **Figure 12-8**, modify the name of the Favorite listing to something easily recognizable. If you wish, choose another folder or create a folder to store the Favorite in.

4. Click the Add button to add the site and click the Close button to close the Favorites Center. When you want to return to the site, click the Favorites button and then click the name of the site from the list that's displayed (see **Figure 12-9**).

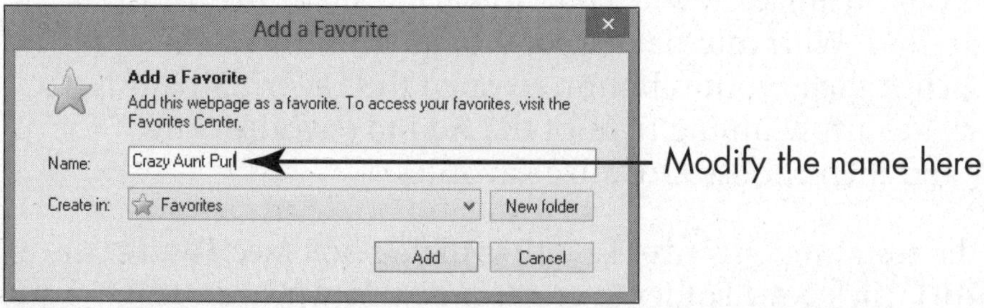

Add a Favorite	×
⭐ **Add a Favorite**	
Add this webpage as a favorite. To access your favorites, visit the Favorites Center.	
Name: `Crazy Aunt Purl` ◄───────────	Modify the name here
Create in: ⭐ Favorites ▾ New folder	
Add Cancel	

Figure 12-8

Favorites button

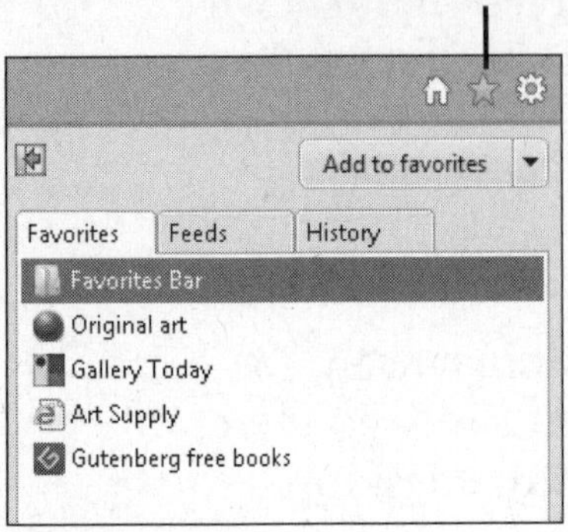

Add to favorites ▾

| Favorites | Feeds | History |

Favorites Bar
Original art
Gallery Today
Art Supply
Gutenberg free books

Figure 12-9

 Regularly cleaning out your Favorites list is a good idea — after all, do you really need the sites that you used to plan last year's vacation? With the Favorites Center displayed, right-click any item and then choose Delete or Rename to modify the Favorites listing.

 You can keep the Favorites Center as a side pane in Internet Explorer by displaying it and then clicking the Pin the Favorites Center button (it has a left-facing green arrow on it and is located in the top-left corner of the pane).

Organize Favorites

1. You can organize favorites into folders to make them easier to find. With Internet Explorer open from the desktop, click the Favorites button to open the Favorites pane. Click the arrow on the right of the Add to Favorites button and then choose Organize Favorites.

2. In the resulting Organize Favorites dialog box (see **Figure 12-10**), click New Folder to create a new folder to store items in and give it a name, or click an item in the Favorites list and then click Move, Rename, or Delete to organize or clean up your favorites list.

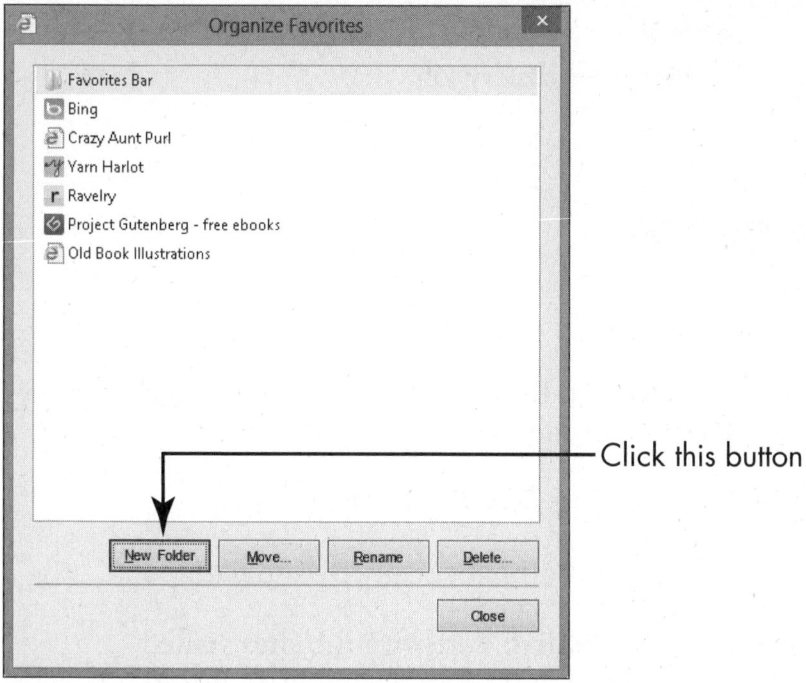

Organize Favorites

Favorites Bar
Bing
Crazy Aunt Purl
Yarn Harlot
Ravelry
Project Gutenberg - free ebooks
Old Book Illustrations

Click this button

New Folder   Move...   Rename   Delete...

Close

Figure 12-10

3. When you finish organizing your Favorites, click Close.

 If you create new folders in these steps, you manually transfer files into those folders. To do this, just display the Favorites Center and click and drag a file listed there onto a folder.

View Your Browsing History using Desktop IE

1. If you went to a site recently and want to return there again but can't remember the name, you might check your browsing history to find it. In the desktop Internet Explorer application, click the Favorites button and then click the History tab to display the History pane (see **Figure 12-11**).

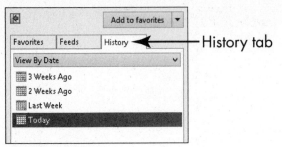 History tab

Figure 12-11

2. Click the down-arrow on the View By button (see **Figure 12-12**) and select a sort method:

- **View By Date:** Sort favorites by date visited.

- **View By Site:** Sort alphabetically by site name.

- **View By Most Visited:** Sort with the sites visited most at the top of and those visited least at the bottom of the list.

- **View By Order Visited Today:** Sort by the order in which you visited sites today.

3. In the History pane, you can click to drill down to sites or pages on a particular site visited on a particular day and then click an item to go to it. The History pane closes.

 You can also choose the arrow on the right of the Address bar to display sites you've visited.

 Choose Search History on the menu on the History tab to display a search box you can use to search for sites you've visited.

 In the Start screen IE, you can right-click and then click a thumbnail of a recently visited site at the top of the screen to go there.

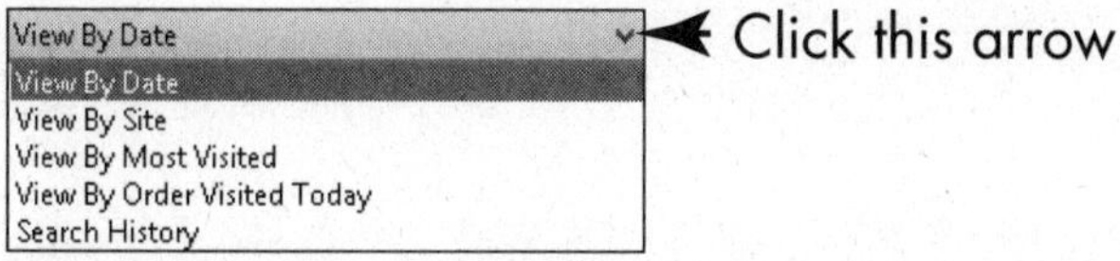

◄ Click this arrow

Figure 12-12

Customize the Internet Explorer Toolbar

1. You can customize the toolbars that offer common commands in IE 10 so that the commands you use most often are included. Open IE from the desktop.

2. Click the Tools button, choose Toolbars, and then choose Customize. The Customize Toolbar dialog box (shown in **Figure 12-13**) appears.

3. Click a tool on the left and then click the Add button to add it to the toolbar.

4. To remove a tool from the toolbar, click a tool on the right and then click the Remove button.

5. When you're finished, click Close to save your new toolbar settings. The new tools appear; click the double-arrow button on the right of the toolbar (see **Figure 12-14**) to display any tools that IE can't fit onscreen.

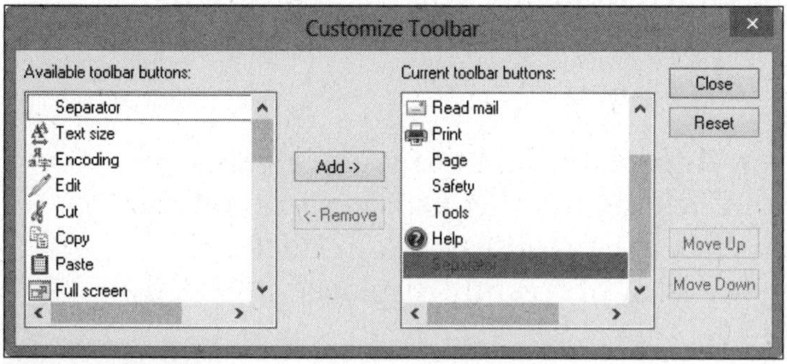

Figure 12-13

Click here to see more tools

Figure 12-14

 You can use the Move Up and Move Down buttons in the Customize Toolbar dialog box to rearrange the order in which tools appear on the toolbar. To reset the toolbar to defaults, click the Reset button in that same dialog box.

 If you want to add some space between tools on the toolbar so they're easier to see, click the Separator item in the Available Toolbar Buttons list and add it before or after a tool button.

View RSS Feeds

1. You can subscribe to RSS feeds in desktop IE by clicking the Favorites button, displaying the Feeds tab, and clicking the See Suggested Sites button. Click a listed site, click the arrow on the Views Feeds on the Page button in the toolbar (it has three white lines on it), and click the site name. On the following screen, click Subscribe to This Feed.

2. You can now view information sent to you via RSS feeds using IE desktop. Click the Internet Explorer icon on the taskbar and then click the Favorites button. Click the Feeds tab to display a list of recently displayed RSS feeds (see **Figure 12-15**).

3. Click a feed to open it, and then click a feed story to display it (see **Figure 12-16**).

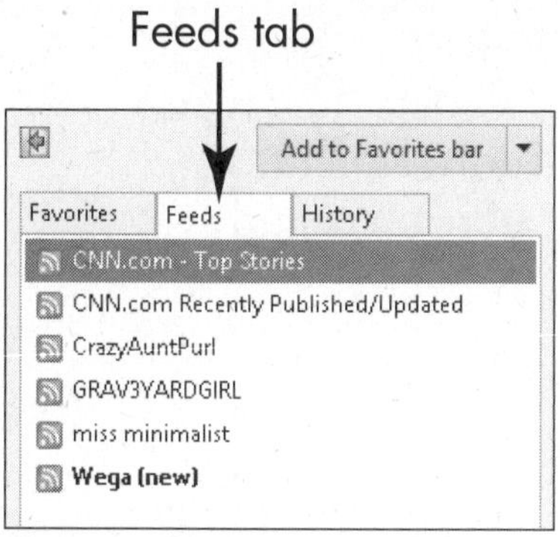

Feeds tab

Figure 12-15

4. You can also press Alt+J to view any active feeds listed on the currently displayed page.

 The View Feeds on This Page button is grayed out when there are no RSS feeds on the current page, and it turns orange when feeds are present.

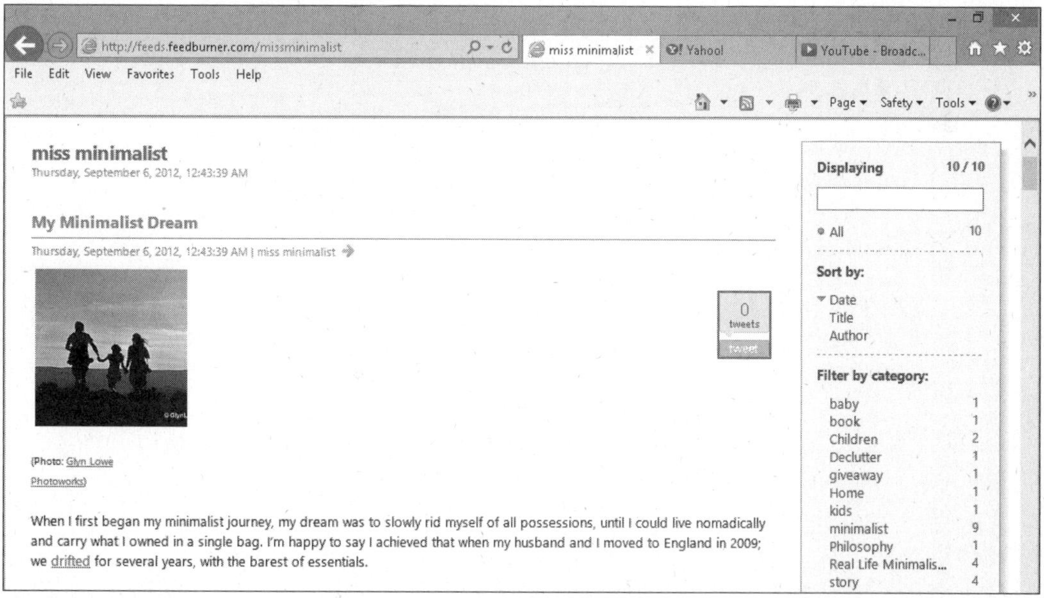

Figure 12-16

Though Internet Explorer has an RSS feed reader built in, you can explore other feed readers. Just type **RSS feeds** into Internet Explorer's Address field to find more information and listings of readers and RSS feed sites.

Print a Web Page

1. If a web page includes a link or button to print or display a print version of a page, click that and follow the instructions.

2. If the page doesn't include a link for printing, click the Print button on the desktop IE toolbar.

3. In the resulting Print dialog box, decide how much of the document you want to print, and then select one of the options in the Page Range area, as shown in **Figure 12-17**.

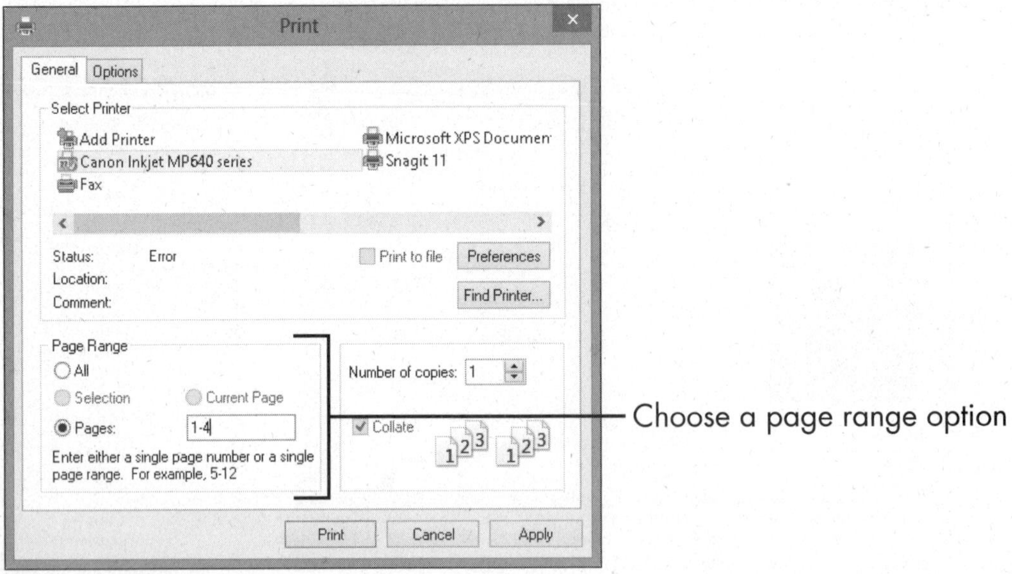

Figure 12-17

— Choose a page range option

Note that choosing Current Page or entering page numbers in the Pages text box of the Print dialog box doesn't mean much when printing a web page — the whole document might print because web pages aren't divided into pages as word-processing documents are.

4. Click the up arrow in the Number of Copies text box to print multiple copies. If you want to collate multiple copies, select the Collate check box.

5. After you adjust all settings you need, click Print.

Use Start Screen IE 11 Settings

When you are working in an app such as Internet Explorer, the Settings you access from the Windows Charm bar are specific to that app. In Internet Explorer 11, these settings vary somewhat from IE 10. To work with Settings in IE 11:

1. With the Start screen IE open, press Win+I to open the Charm bar Settings.

2. Click Options in the list of settings that appears.

3. In the panel that appears (see **Figure 12-18**), make selections for the following settings:

- **Appearance:** Use the On/Off slider to always show the address bar and tabs, and the Zoom feature to enlarge or reduce the size of pages in your browser.

- **Home Pages:** Click the Customize button here to choose your IE home pages.

- **History:** Click the Select button here to control what browsing data you want to retain or delete from your laptop.

- **Passwords:** Turn on this feature to be able to go to the next page on a website; information will be sent to Microsoft if you turn this feature on so that they can improve your browsing experience.

- **Phone Numbers:** Turn this setting on to be able to call phone numbers you find on a website.

- **Fonts and Encoding:** With this on, IE adjusts for text on a web page that doesn't seem to be in your preferred language.

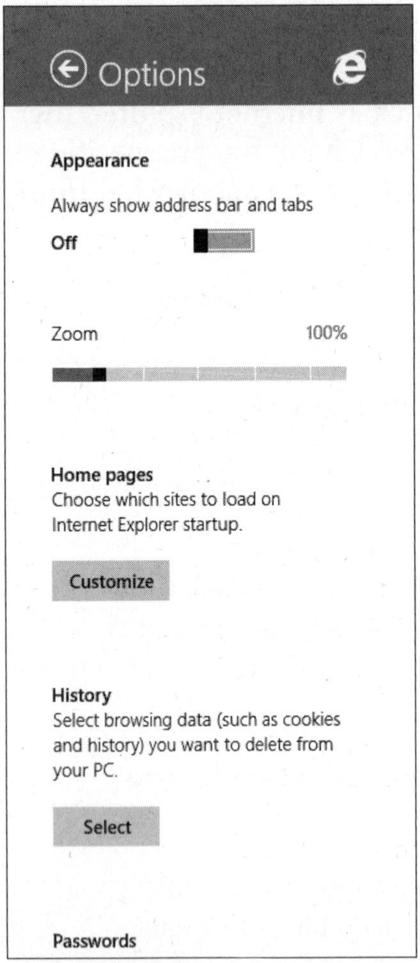

Figure 12-18

Staying Safe While Online

Getting active online carries with it certain risks, like most things in life. But just as you know how to drive or walk around town safely when you know the rules of the road, you can stay relatively safe online.

In this chapter, you discover some of the risks and safety nets that you can take advantage of to avoid risk, including

➡ **Understand what risks exist.** Some risks are human, in the form of online predators wanting to steal your money or abuse you emotionally; other risks come from technology, such as computer viruses. For the former, you can use the same common sense you use when interacting offline to stay safe. For the latter, there are tools and browser settings to protect you.

➡ **Be aware of what information you share.** Abuses such as ID theft occur most often when you or somebody you know shares information about you that's nobody's business. Find out how to spot who is exposing information (including you) and what information to keep private, and you'll become much safer online.

Get ready to . . .

➡ Understand Technology Risks on the Internet 208

➡ Use Suggested Sites 211

➡ Download Files Safely 212

➡ Turn on InPrivate Browsing 214

➡ Use SmartScreen Filter 215

➡ Change Privacy Settings 216

➡ Understand Information Exposure 218

➡ Keep Your Information Private 222

➡ Spot Phishing Scams and Other E-mail Fraud 224

➡ Create Strong Passwords ... 226

➡ **Avoid scams and undesirable content.** You can use the Windows 8 Content Advisor (Family Safety in Windows 8.1) to limit the online locations that your computer can visit so you don't encounter sites you consider undesirable. You can also find out how to spot various e-mail scams and fraud so you don't become a victim.

➡ **Create safe passwords**. Passwords don't have to be hard to remember, just hard to guess. I provide some guidance in this chapter about creating passwords that are hard to crack.

Understand Technology Risks on the Internet

When you buy a car, it has certain safety features built in. Sometimes after you drive it off the lot, you might find that the manufacturer slipped up and either recalls your car or requests that you go to the dealer's service department for replacement of a faulty part. In addition, you need to drive defensively to keep your car from being damaged in daily use.

Your computer is similar to your car in terms of the need for safety. It comes with an operating system (such as Microsoft Windows) built in, and that operating system has security features. Sometimes that operating system has flaws — or new threats emerge after it's first released — and you need to install an update to keep it secure. And as you use your computer, you're exposing it to dangerous conditions and situations that you have to guard against.

Threats to your computer security can come from a file you copy from a disc you insert into your computer, but most of the time, the danger is from a program that you download from the Internet. These downloads can happen when you click a link, open an attachment in an e-mail, or download a piece of software without realizing that *malware* (malicious software) is attached to it.

You need to be aware of these three main types of dangerous programs:

➠ A *virus* is a little program that some nasty person thought up to spread around the Internet and infect computers. A virus can do a variety of things but, typically, it attacks your data by deleting files, scrambling data, or making changes to your system settings that cause your computer to grind to a halt.

➠ *Spyware* consists of programs responsible for tracking what you do with your computer. Some spyware simply helps companies you do business with track your activities so that they can figure out how to sell things to you; other spyware is used for more insidious purposes, such as stealing your passwords.

➠ *Adware* is the computer equivalent of telemarketing phone calls at dinner time. After adware is downloaded onto your computer, you'll see annoying pop-up windows trying to sell things to you all day long. Beyond the annoyance, adware can quickly clog up your computer. The computer's performance slows down, and it's hard to get anything done at all.

To protect your information and your computer from these various types of malware, you can do several things:

➠ **You can buy and install an antivirus, antispyware, or antiadware program.** It's critical that you install an antivirus program, such as those from McAfee, Symantec, or Trend Micro, or the freely downloadable AVG Free (see **Figure 13-1**).

People come up with new viruses every day, so it's important that you use software that's up to date with the latest virus definitions and that protects your computer from the latest threats. Many antivirus programs are purchased by yearly subscription, which gives you access to updated virus definitions that the company constantly gathers throughout the year. Be sure to update the definitions of viruses on your computer regularly using this software, and then run a scan of your computer on a regular basis. For convenience, you can use settings in the software to activate automatic updates and scans. Consult your program's Help tool for instructions on how to use these features.

➡ **Install a program that combines tools for detecting adware and spyware.** Windows 8 has a built-in program, Windows Defender, which includes an anti-spyware feature. (I cover Windows Defender tools in Chapter 21.) If you don't have Windows 8, you can purchase programs such as Spyware Doctor (from PC Tools) or download free tools such as Spybot or Spyware Terminator.

Figure 13-1

➡ **Use Windows tools to keep Windows up to date with security features, and fixes to security problems.** You can also turn on a firewall, which is a feature that stops other people or programs from accessing your computer over an Internet connection without your permission. (I cover Windows Defender and firewalls in Chapter 21.)

➡ **Use your browser's privacy and security features,** such as the Suggested Sites and InPrivate Browsing features in IE 10.

Use Suggested Sites

1. To allow Internet Explorer to suggest sites you might like that are related to the currently displayed site, open desktop Internet Explorer and click the Options button. Choose Suggested Sites, and a check mark appears next to that option, as shown in **Figure 13-2.** When a prompt appears, asking if you want to discover websites you might like based on sites you've visited, click Yes.

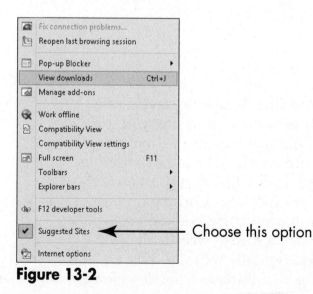

Choose this option

Figure 13-2

2. Click the Suggested Sites button on the Favorites toolbar. (If the toolbar isn't displayed, right-click the toolbar area and choose Favorites Bar.) A list of suggested sites appears (see **Figure 13-3**).

3. Click a site name to open its website.

 Suggested Sites uses your browsing history to come up with suggestions, so when you first activate it, it may take a little while before the feature comes up with useful suggestions.

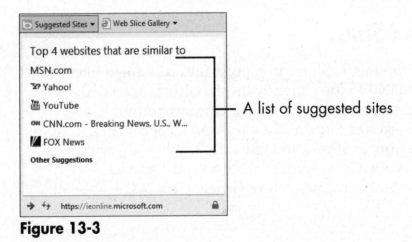

Figure 13-3

Download Files Safely

1. The two tricks to downloading files while staying safe from malware is to only download from sites you trust and to never download file attachments to e-mails that you aren't completely sure are safe. The most dangerous files to download are executable files that sport an .exe extension at the end of the filename. Clicking on these will run a program of some kind, and could therefore pose an active threat. Open a trusted website that contains downloadable files. Typically websites offer a Download button or link that initiates a file download.

If you don't know of a file to download but want to practice these steps, try www.adobe.com. From that site, you can download the free Adobe Reader or Adobe Flash add-on, which are handy and popular utility programs.

2. Click the appropriate link to proceed. Windows might display a dialog box asking your permission to proceed with the download; click Yes.

3. In the toolbar that appears along the bottom of the screen, shown in **Figure 13-4,** choose either option:

- **Click Run to download the file to a temporary folder.** You can run a software installation program, for example. However, beware: If you run a program you obtained from the Internet, you could be introducing dangerous viruses to your system. You might want to set up an antivirus program to scan files before downloading them.

- **Click Save to save the file to your hard drive.** In the Save As dialog box, select the folder on your computer or removable storage media (a USB flash drive, for example) where you want to save the file.

 Make sure you choose a folder that's easy for you to remember and return to later when you need the file. If you're downloading software, you need to locate the downloaded file (in whichever folder you saved it) and double-click it to install or run it.

 If you're worried that a particular file might be unsafe to download (for example, if it's from an unknown source, or if you discover that it's an executable file type, which could contain a virus), click Cancel in the File Download dialog box.

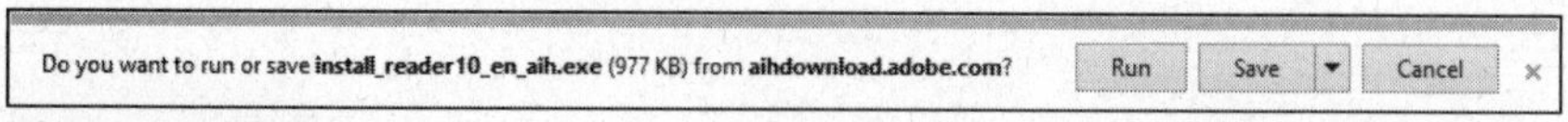

Do you want to run or save **install_reader10_en_aih.exe** (977 KB) from **aihdownload.adobe.com**?   Run   Save ▼   Cancel ✕

Figure 13-4

If a particular file will take a long time to download (some can take 20 minutes or more), you may have to babysit it. If your computer goes into standby mode, it could pause the download. If your computer automatically downloads Windows updates, it may cause your computer to restart automatically as well, cancelling or halting your download. Check in periodically to keep things moving along.

Turn on InPrivate Browsing

1. InPrivate Browsing is a feature that stops IE from saving information about your browsing session, such as cookies and your browsing history. InPrivate Browsing allows you to block or allow sites that automatically collect information about your browsing habits. InPrivate Browsing is turned off by default. To turn it on you can open Start screen IE and follow these steps:

2. Right-click a blank spot on the desktop and then click the Tab Tools button (the button with three dots on it) in the tab area at the top of the screen (see Figure 13-5).

3. Choose New InPrivate Tab. A message appears, telling you that InPrivate Browsing is on.

Tab Tools button

Figure 13-5

4. You can now surf the web privately by clicking in the
Address bar and doing one of the following: Type a web
address, click a Frequent tile, or click a Pinned tile.

5. To turn InPrivate Browsing off, right-click to display tabs,
and then click the Close button to close the InPrivate tab,
as shown in Figure 13-6.

 If you don't want to use InPrivate Browsing but
would like to periodically clear your browsing history
manually, with IE open, press Win+I and click Internet
Options. In the Delete Browsing History section,
click the Delete button. (In Windows 8.1, click
Options and then in the History section click Select.
Then click to choose what you want to delete. Click
the Delete button to delete selected items.)

Close button

Figure 13-6

Use SmartScreen Filter

When you activate SmartScreen Filter, you allow Microsoft to check its
database for information on the websites you visit. Microsoft alerts
you if any of those websites are known to generate phishing scams or
download malware to visitors' computers. SmartScreen Filter is on by
default, but if it gets turned off, to turn it on again, open desktop IE
10 and follow these steps:

1. Click the Options button, hover your mouse over Safety,
and then choose Turn On SmartScreen Filter. In the confirmation dialog box that appears, click OK.

2. To use SmartScreen Filter, go to a website you want to check. Click the Tools button, hover your mouse over Safety, and choose Check This Website. Click OK to authorize the check.

3. The SmartScreen Filter window appears (see **Figure 13-7**), indicating whether it found any threats. Click the OK button to close the message.

 Once it's turned on, SmartScreen Filter automatically checks websites and will generate a message if you visit one that has reported problems. However, that information is updated only periodically, so if you have concerns about a particular site, use the procedure given here to check the latest information about the website.

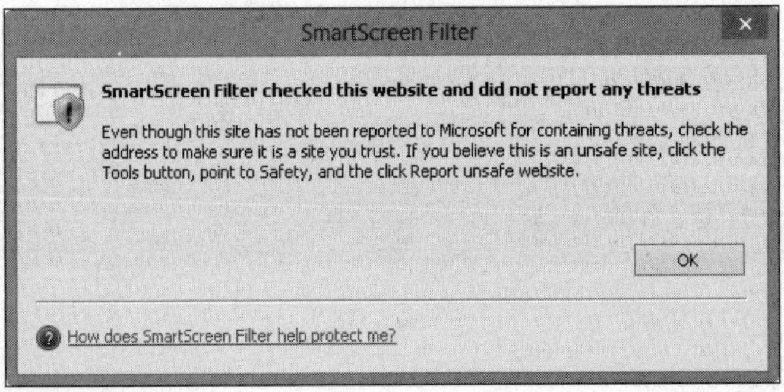

SmartScreen Filter

SmartScreen Filter checked this website and did not report any threats

Even though this site has not been reported to Microsoft for containing threats, check the address to make sure it is a site you trust. If you believe this is an unsafe site, click the Tools button, point to Safety, and the click Report unsafe website.

OK

How does SmartScreen Filter help protect me?

Figure 13-7

Change Privacy Settings

1. You can modify how IE 10 deals with privacy settings to keep information about your browsing habits or identity safer. From the Start screen, begin typing **control panel** and click the Control Panel app in the results.

2. Click Network and Internet, and then click Internet Options.

3. In the Internet Properties dialog box, click the Privacy tab, as shown in **Figure 13-8.**

4. Drag the slider up or down to make different levels of security settings.

5. Read the choices and select a setting that suits you.

6. Click the Sites button to specify sites to always or never allow the use of cookies. In the resulting Per Site Privacy Actions dialog box (shown in **Figure 13-9**), enter a site in the Address of Website box and click either Block or Allow.

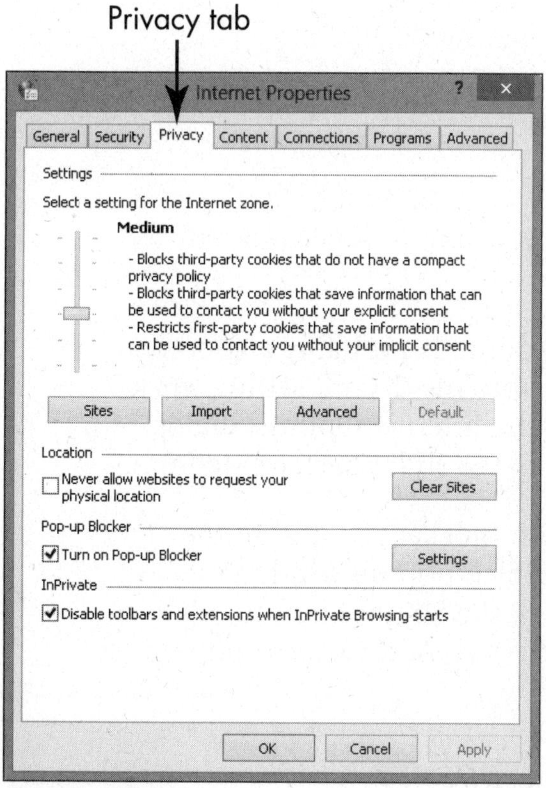

Privacy tab

Figure 13-8

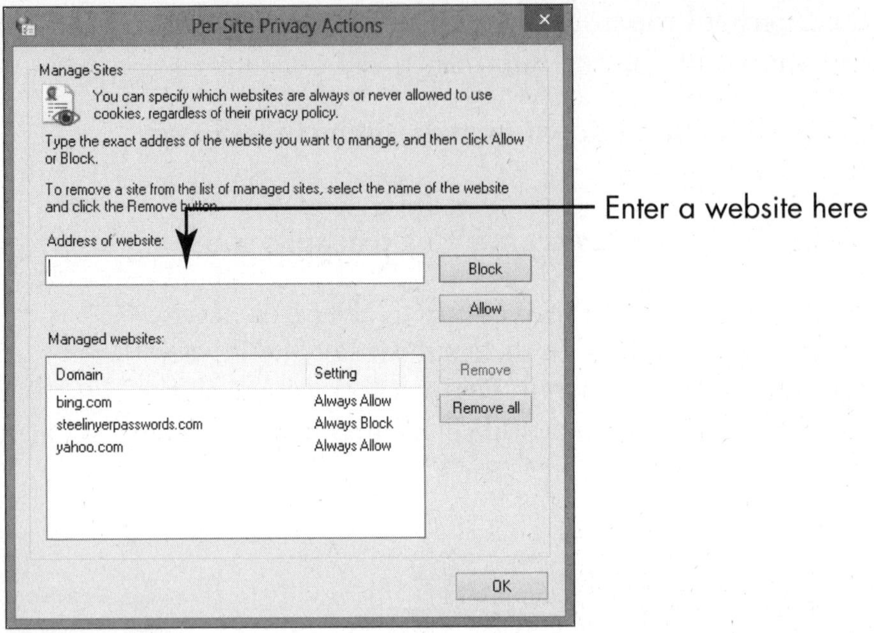

Per Site Privacy Actions

Manage Sites

You can specify which websites are always or never allowed to use cookies, regardless of their privacy policy.

Type the exact address of the website you want to manage, and then click Allow or Block.

To remove a site from the list of managed sites, select the name of the website and click the Remove button. ──────── Enter a website here

Address of website:

| | Block |
| Allow |

Managed websites:

Domain	Setting
bing.com	Always Allow
steelinyerpasswords.com	Always Block
yahoo.com	Always Allow

Remove

Remove all

OK

Figure 13-9

7. Click OK, and then click OK again, to save your new settings.

 The default setting, Medium, is probably a good bet for most people. To restore the default setting, click the Default button on the Internet Options dialog box's Privacy tab or drag the slider back to Medium.

 You can also use pop-up blocker settings on the Privacy tab to specify which pop-up windows to allow or block. Just click the Settings button, enter a website name, and then click Add to allow pop-ups from that site.

Understand Information Exposure

Many people think that if they aren't active online, their information isn't exposed. But you aren't the only one sharing your information. Consider how others might handle information about you.

➡ **Employers:** Many employers share information about employees. Consider carefully how much information you're comfortable with sharing through, for instance, an employee bio posted on your company website. How much information should be visible to other employees on your intranet? When you attend a conference, is the attendee list shown in online conference documents? And even if you're retired, there may still be information about you on your former employer's website. Review the site to determine if it reveals more than you'd like it to — and ask your employer to take down or alter the information if needed.

➡ **Government agencies:** Some agencies post personal information, such as documents concerning your home purchase and property tax (see **Figure 13-10**), on publicly available websites. Government agencies may also post birth, marriage, and death certificates, and these documents may contain your Social Security number, loan number, copies of your signature, and so on. You should check government records carefully to see if private information is posted and, if it is, demand that it be removed.

➡ **Family members and friends:** They may write about you in their blogs, post photos of you, or mention you on special-interest sites such as those focused on genealogy.

➡ **Clubs and organizations:** Organizations with whom you volunteer, the church you attend, and professional associations you belong to may reveal facts such as your address, age, income bracket, and how much money you've donated.

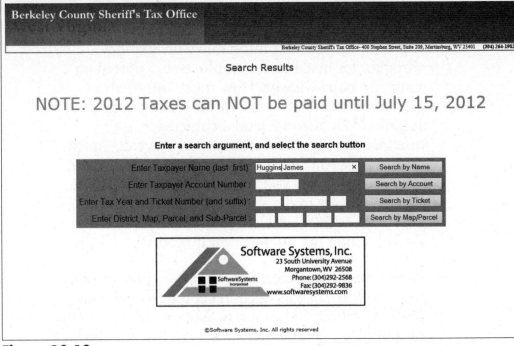

Figure 13-10

➡ **Newspapers:** If you've been featured in a newspaper article, you may be surprised to find the story, along with a picture of you or information about your work, activities, or family, by doing a simple online search. If you're interviewed, ask for the chance to review the information that the newspaper will include, and be sure that you're comfortable with exposing that information.

➡ **Online directories:** Services such as www.white pages.com, shown in **Figure 13-11,** or www. anywho.com list your home phone number and address, unless you specifically request that these be removed. You may be charged a small fee associated with removing your information — a so-called privacy tax — but you may find the cost worthwhile.

Online directories often include the names of members of your family, your e-mail address, the value of your home, your neighbors' names and the values of their homes, an online mapping tool to provide a view of your home, driving directions to your home, and your age. The record may also include previous addresses, schools you've attended, and links for people to run background checks on you. A smart con person can use all that information to convince you that he's a friend of a friend or even a relative in distress who needs money.

 Because services get new information from many sources, you'll need to check back periodically to see if your information has again been put online — if it has, contact the company or go through its removal process again.

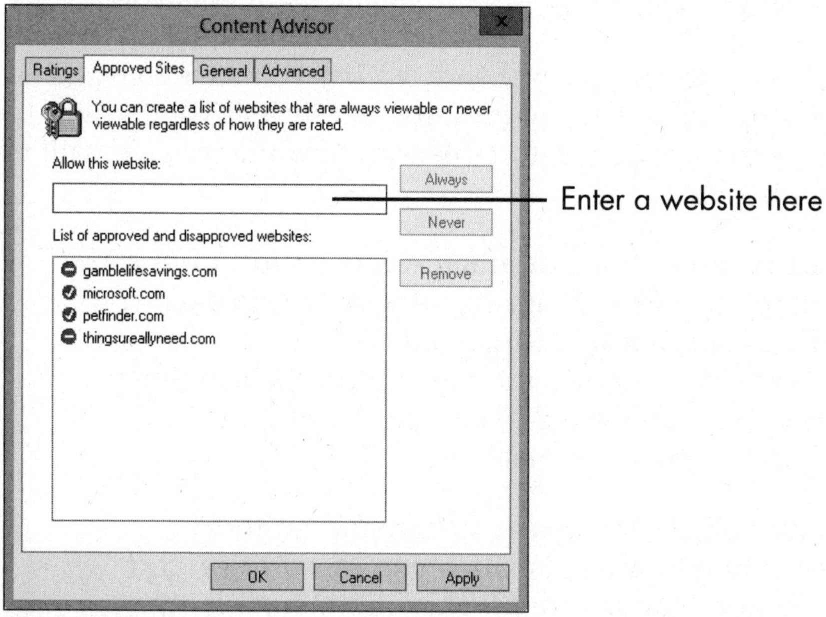

Enter a website here

Figure 13-11

Try entering your home phone number in any browser's address line; chances are you'll get an online directory listing with your address and phone number (although this doesn't work for cellphone numbers).

Keep Your Information Private

Sharing personal information with friends and family enriches your relationships and helps you build new ones. The key is to avoid sharing information online with the wrong people and shady companies because, just as in the real world, exposing your personal information is one of your biggest risks.

Criminals come in all flavors, but the more savvy ones collect information in a very systematic way. Each piece of information is like a series of brushstrokes that, over time, form a very clear picture of your life. And after criminals collect and organize the information, they never throw it away because they may be able to use it many times over.

Fortunately, information exposure is a risk you have a great deal of control over. Before sharing information, such as your date of birth, make sure that you're comfortable with how the recipient will use the information.

➡ **Address and phone number:** Abuse of this information results in you receiving increased telemarketing calls and junk mail. Although less common, this information may also increase a scammer's ability to steal your identity and make your home a more interesting target for break-ins.

➡ **Names of husband/wife, father, and mother (including mother's maiden name), siblings, children, and grandchildren:** This information is very interesting to criminals, who can use it to gain your confidence and then scam you, or use it to guess your passwords or secret-question answers, which often include family members' names. This information may also expose your family members to ID theft, fraud, and personal harm.

➡ **Information about your car:** Limit access to license plate numbers; VINs (vehicle identification numbers); registration information; make, model, and title number of your car; your insurance carrier's name and coverage limits; loan information; and driver's license number. The key criminal abuse of this information includes car theft (or theft of parts of the car) and insurance fraud. The type of car you drive may also indicate your financial status, and that adds one more piece of information to the pool of data criminals collect about you.

➡ **Information about work history:** In the hands of criminals, your work history can be very useful for "authenticating" the fraudster and convincing people and organizations to provide him or her with more about your financial records or identity.

➡ **Information about your credit status:** This information can be abused in so many ways that any time you're asked to provide this online, your answer should be "No." Don't fall for the temptation to check your credit scores for free through sites that aren't guaranteed as being reputable. Another frequent abuse of credit information is found in free mortgage calculators that ask you to put in all kinds of personal information in order for them to determine what credit you may qualify for.

Many people set automatic responders in their e-mail, letting people know when they'll be away from their offices. This is really helpful for colleagues, but exercise caution and limit who you provide the information to. Leaving a message that says, "Gone 11/2–11/12. I'm taking the family to Hawaii for ten days," may make your house a prime target for burglary. And you'll probably never make the connection between the information you exposed and the offline crime.

You may need to show your work history, particularly on resumes you post on Internet job or business-networking sites. Be selective about where you post this information, create a separate e-mail account to list on the resume, and tell what kinds of work you've done rather than give specifics about which companies and what dates. Interested, legitimate employers can then contact you privately, and you won't have given away your life history to the world. After you've landed the job, take down your resume. Think of it as risk management — when you need a job, the risk of information exposure is less than the need to get the job.

Spot Phishing Scams and Other E-mail Fraud

As in the offline world, the Internet has a criminal element. These cyber-criminals use Internet tools to commit the same crimes they've always committed, from robbing you to misusing your good name and financial information. Know how to spot the types of scams that occur online and you'll go a long way toward steering clear of Internet crime.

Before you click a link that comes in a forwarded e-mail message or forward a message to others, ask yourself:

➡ **Is the information legitimate?** Sites such as `www.truthorfiction.com`, `www.snopes.com` (see **Figure 13-12**), or `http://urbanlegends.about.com` can help you discover if an e-mail is a scam.

➡ **Does a message ask you to click links in e-mail or instant messages?** If you're unsure whether a message is genuinely from a company or bank that you use, call them, using the number from a past statement or the phone book. *Remember:* Don't call a phone number listed in the e-mail; it could be a fake. To visit a company's or bank's website, type the address in yourself if you know it or use your own bookmark rather than clicking a link. If the website is new to you, search for the company online and use that link to visit its site. Don't click the link in an e-mail, or you may land on a site that looks right — but is in reality a good fake.

➡ **Does the e-mail have a photo or video to download?** If so, exercise caution. If you know the person who sent the photo or video, it's probably fine to download, but if the photo or video has been forwarded several times and you don't know the person who sent it originally, be careful. It may deliver a virus or other type of malware to your computer.

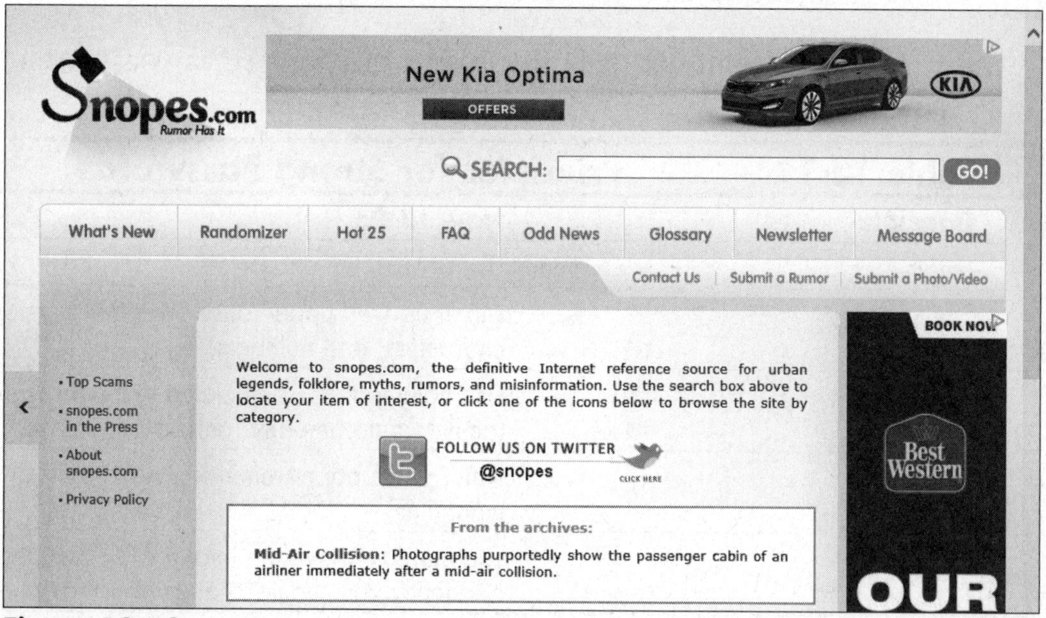

Figure 13-12

In addition to asking yourself these questions, also remember the following:

➠ **If you decide to forward (or send) e-mail to a group, always put their e-mail addresses on the Bcc: (or Blind Carbon Copy) line.** This keeps everyone's e-mail safe from fraud and scams.

➠ **Think *before* you click.** Doing so will save you and others from scams, fraud, hoaxes, and malware.

Create Strong Passwords

A strong password can be one of your best friends in protecting your information in online accounts and sites. Never give your password to others, and change passwords on particularly sensitive accounts, such as bank and investment accounts, regularly.

Table 13-1 outlines five principles for creating strong passwords.

Table 13-1	Principles for Strong Passwords
Principle	**How to Do It**
Length	Use at least ten characters.
Strength	Mix it up with upper- and lowercase letters, characters, and numbers.
Obscurity	Use nothing that's associated with you, your family, your company, and so on.
Protection	Don't place paper reminders near your computer.
Change	The more sensitive the information, the more frequently you should change your password.

Look at **Table 13-2** for examples of password patterns that are safe but also easy to remember.

Table 13-2	Examples of Strong Passwords
Logic	**Password**
Use a familiar phrase typed with a variation of capitalization and numbers instead of words (text message shorthand).	L8r_L8rNot2day = Later, later, not today 2BorNot2B_ThatIsThe? = To be or not to be, that is the question.
Incorporate shortcut codes or acronyms.	CSThnknAU2day = Can't Stop Thinking About You today 2Hot2Hndle = Too hot to handle
Create a password from an easy-to-remember phrase that describes what you're doing, with key letters replaced by numbers or symbols.	1mlook1ngatyahoo = I'm looking at Yahoo (I replaced the Is with 1s.) MyWork@HomeNeverEnds
Spell a word backward with at least one letter representing a character or number.	$lidoffaD = Daffodils (The $ replaces the s.) y1frettuB = Butterfly (The 1 replaces the l.) QWERTY7654321 = This is the 6 letters from left to right in the top row of your keyboard, plus the numbers from right to left across the top going backward.
Use patterns from your keyboard. (See **Figure 13-13.**) Make your keyboard a palette and make any shape you want.	1QAZSDRFBHU8 is really just making a W on your keyboard. (Refer to **Figure 13-13.**)

Figure 13-13

Keeping In Touch with Mail

Chapter 14

Get ready to . . .

➡ Set Up an Internet-Based E-mail Account 230

➡ Set Up Accounts in Mail 232

➡ Get to Know Mail 234

➡ Open Mail and Receive Messages 236

➡ Create and Send E-mail 238

➡ Send an Attachment 240

➡ Read a Message 241

➡ Reply to a Message 242

➡ Forward E-mail 243

➡ Make Account Settings in Mail 244

An e-mail program is a tool you can use to send messages to others. These messages are delivered to the recipient's e-mail inbox, usually within seconds. You can attach files to e-mail messages and even put images within the message body. You can get an e-mail account through your Internet provider or through sites such as Yahoo! and Microsoft Live Hotmail. These accounts are typically free.

When you have one or more e-mail accounts, you can set them up in the Mail app in Windows 8, and then use that app to send and receive e-mail for all your Outlook.com and Gmail accounts in one place. Mail uses the information you store in the People app for addressing your e-mails, and it can sync contacts from your individual accounts to People if you choose.

With Windows 8.1, you can set up Yahoo! and AOL accounts in addition to Outlook and Google. If you prefer, you can instead use your provider's e-mail interface in your Internet browser. Some of these programs provide more tools for working with e-mail, such as more sophisticated tools to format message text or add

a signature (for example your company name and phone number) to every message you send.

To make your e-mailing life easy, this chapter takes a look at these tasks:

➠ **Choose an e-mail provider.** Find out how to locate e-mail providers and what types of features they offer.

➠ **Set up your e-mail accounts in the Mail app.** Make settings to access your Windows Live Hotmail or Gmail account from within the Mail app so you can check all your messages in one place. This is useful if you use both work and home e-mail accounts, for example. If you do access work e-mail from home you can use the Microsoft Exchange type of account to do so (check with your work network administrator about how to do this).

➠ **Receive, send, and forward messages.** Deal with the ins and outs of receiving and sending e-mail.

➠ **Make settings for each account.** Set up how often content is downloaded, and whether to sync your e-mail, contacts, and calendar information from each account.

Set Up an Internet-Based E-mail Account

Your Internet service provider (ISP) — whether that's your cable or phone company or a small local provider — probably offers you a free e-mail account along with your service. You can also get free accounts from many online sources, such as Yahoo!, AOL, Gmail, and Windows Live Mail. Note that the Mail app in Windows 8 is currently set up to work with Windows Live Hotmail and Gmail accounts — as well as Microsoft Exchange accounts, which are typically business accounts such as your company might provide.

Here are some tips for getting your own e-mail account:

➠ **Using e-mail accounts provided by an ISP:** Check with your ISP to see whether an e-mail account comes with your connection service. If it does, your ISP should provide instructions on how to choose an *e-mail alias* (that's the name on your account, such as SusieXYZ@aol.com) and password, and instructions on how to sign into the account.

➠ **Searching for an e-mail provider:** If your ISP doesn't offer e-mail, or you prefer to use another service because of features it offers, use your browser's search engine to look for what's available. Don't use the search term *free e-mail* because results for any search with the word *free* included are much more likely to return sites that will download bad programs like viruses and spyware onto your computer. Besides, just about all e-mail accounts today are free! Alternatively, you can go directly to services such as Yahoo, AOL, or Gmail by entering their addresses in your browser's address field (for example, www. gmail.com).

➠ **Finding out about features:** E-mail accounts come with certain features that you should be aware of. For example, each account includes a certain amount of storage for your saved messages. (Look for one that provides 10 gigabytes or more.) The account should also include an easy-to-use address book feature to save your contacts' information. Some services provide better formatting tools for text, as well as calendar and to-do list features.

Whatever service you use, make sure it has good junk-mail filtering to protect you from unwanted e-mails. You should be able to modify junk-mail filter settings so that the service places messages from certain senders or with certain content in a junk-mail folder, where you can review the messages with caution or delete them.

➠ **Signing up for an e-mail account:** When you find an e-mail account you want to use, sign up (usually there will be a Sign Up or Get An Account button or link to click) by providing your name and other contact information and selecting a username and password. The username is your e-mail address, in the form of UserName@*service*.com, where the *service* is, for example, Yahoo!, Windows Live Hotmail, or AOL. Some usernames might be taken, so have a few options in mind.

➠ **Making sure your username is a safe one:** If possible, don't use your full name, your location, age, or other identifiers. Such personal identifiers might help scam artists or predators find out more about you than you want them to know.

Set Up Accounts in Mail

1. You can set up the Windows 8 Mail app to manage Outlook and other accounts so you can receive all your e-mail messages in one place. Click the Mail tile on the Start screen.

2. Press Win+I and click the Accounts link shown in **Figure 14-1.**

3. Click the Add an Account link shown in **Figure 14-2.**

4. Click a provider option as shown in **Figure 14-3.**

5. In the resulting window (see **Figure 14-4**), enter the account address and your password and click Connect.

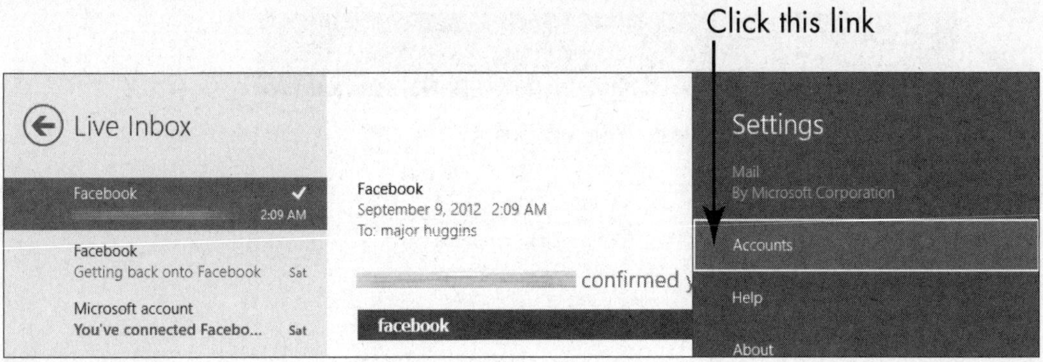

Click this link

Figure 14-1

Click this link

Figure 14-2

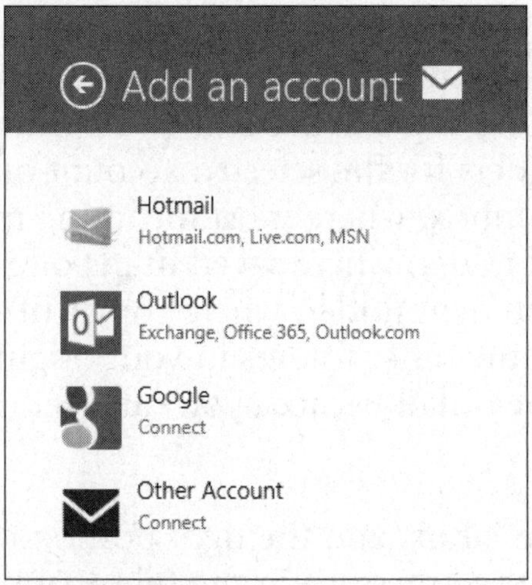

Figure 14-3

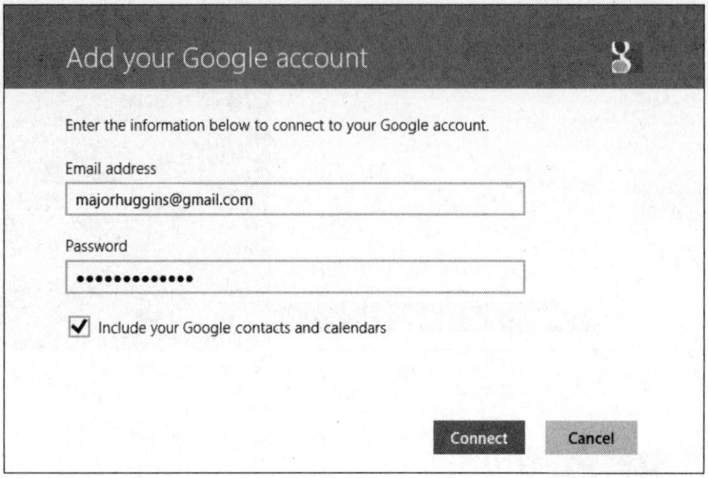

Add your Google account

Enter the information below to connect to your Google account.

Email address

majorhuggins@gmail.com

Password

••••••••••••

☑ Include your Google contacts and calendars

Connect   Cancel

Figure 14-4

6. Mail takes a moment to set up the account. Click the account in the list of accounts on the left side of the Mail screen to open its inbox and view messages.

Get to Know Mail

Mail (see **Figure 14-5**) may look a bit different from other e-mail programs that use menus and tools to take actions such as deleting an e-mail, creating a new e-mail, and so on. Mail has a sparser, cleaner interface in line with the whole Windows 8 approach. You have a list of e-mail accounts and a list of folders for the selected account on the left. Some typical folders are your Inbox, where most incoming mail appears; your Outbox; your Drafts folder, where saved drafts of e-mails are saved ready to be sent; and your Sent folder, where copies of sent e-mails are stored. You can set up any other folders in your original e-mail program such as Hotmail or Gmail because you can't set these up in Mail.

The section on the left displays the Inbox, and the right portion of the screen shows the contents of a selected message in the Inbox or other folder (see **Figure 14-6**).

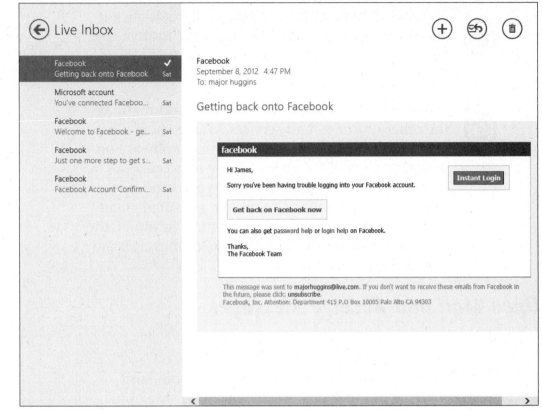

Figure 14-5

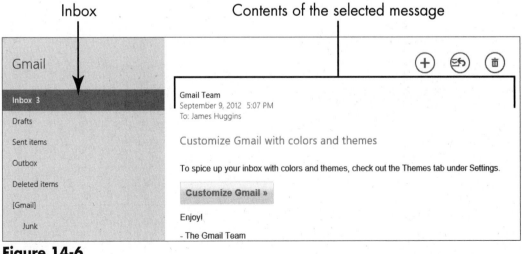

Figure 14-6

To move a message from your Inbox, right-click it and then click the Move button on the toolbar that appears. Click a folder, and the message is moved there.

 When you access Windows Live Mail and many of the other online e-mail services, you're using a program that's hosted online, rather than software on your computer. That makes it easy to access your mail from any computer because your messages and folders are kept online. If you use an e-mail client such as Outlook to access your e-mail accounts, the client software and your downloaded messages are stored on your computer.

Open Mail and Receive Messages

1. Click the Mail tile on the Start screen.

2. Click the account you want to read mail from, and the contents of the Inbox are displayed, as shown in **Figure 14-7**.

Inbox contents

Figure 14-7

3. Click a message, and its contents appear in the right side of the screen. Use the scroll bar to move through the message contents.

4. If the message has an attachment, you'll see a paper clip symbol (see **Figure 14-8**) next to it in the Inbox. Click the attachment once, and it displays a thumbnail, and then click the thumbnail and choose one of the following from the menu that appears:

- **Open:** The file opens in the app that Windows 8 associates it with.

- **Open With:** Use this option when you want to choose which program in which the attachment opens.

- **Save:** Windows 8 opens the associated library (such as Pictures for an image), where you can enter a name and click Save to save the file in that library.

Icon indicating an attachment

New button

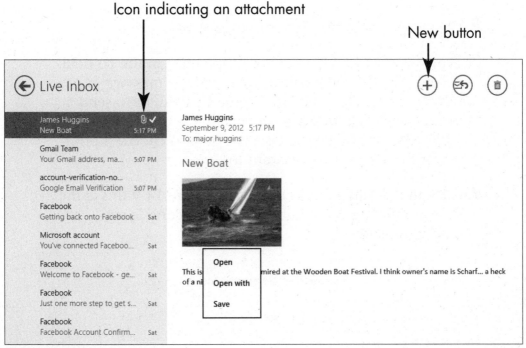

Figure 14-8

If your mail doesn't come through, it's probably because your e-mail provider's servers are experiencing technical problems. Just wait a little while. If you still can't get mail, make sure your connection to the Internet is active. Mail may show your Inbox, but if you've lost your connection, it can't receive new messages.

 Note that if an e-mail has a little exclamation point next to it in your Inbox, somebody has flagged it as urgent. It's usually best to check out those e-mails first!

Create and Send E-mail

1. Creating e-mail is as simple as filling out a few fields in a form. Open Mail and click the account from which you want to send the e-mail.

2. Click the New button (refer to **Figure 14-8**).

3. Type the e-mail address of the recipient(s) in the To field. If you want to send a courtesy copy of the message to other people enter addresses in the Cc field, or to send a blind copy, click the More Details link and enter an address(es) in the Bcc fields. You can also choose a priority for the message if you want to.

4. Click in the Add a Subject field (in **Figure 14-9** this is the field at the top on the right) and type a concise yet descriptive subject.

The Add a Subject field

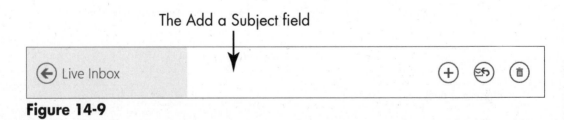

Figure 14-9

5. Click in the message pane beneath the subject and type your message (see **Figure 14-10**).

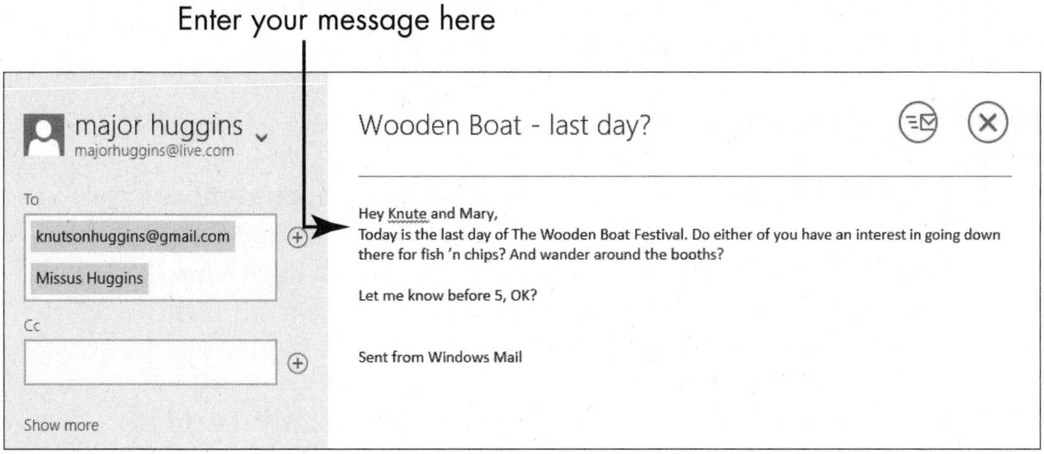

Enter your message here

major huggins ⌄
majorhuggins@live.com

Wooden Boat - last day?

To

knutsonhuggins@gmail.com ⊕

Missus Huggins

Cc

⊕

Show more

Hey Knute and Mary,
Today is the last day of The Wooden Boat Festival. Do either of you have an interest in going down there for fish 'n chips? And wander around the booths?

Let me know before 5, OK?

Sent from Windows Mail

Figure 14-10

Don't press Enter at the end of a line when typing a message. Mail and most e-mail programs have an automatic text-wrap feature that does this for you. Do be concise. If you have lots to say, consider sending a letter by snail mail or overnight delivery. Most people tire of reading text onscreen after a short while.

Keep e-mail etiquette in mind as you type. For example, don't type in ALL CAPITAL LETTERS. This is called shouting, which is considered rude. Do be polite even if you're really, really angry. Your message could be forwarded to just about anybody, just about anywhere, and you don't want to get a reputation as a hothead.

6. When you finish typing your message, click the Send button. The message is on its way!

Remember that when you're creating an e-mail, you can address it to a stored address in the People app. Click the + button to the right of an address field, and the People app appears. You can then select a contact(s) from there. Mail also allows you to just begin to type a stored contact in an address field (To, Bcc, or Cc), and it provides a list of likely options as you type. Just click the correct name when it appears in the list to enter it.

Send an Attachment

1. It's very convenient to be able to attach a document or image file to an e-mail that the recipient can open and view on his end. To do this, open Mail and click your e-mail account. Click New to create a new e-mail message, address it, and enter a subject.

2. Right-click and choose Attachments (see **Figure 14-11**) on the toolbar that appears at the bottom of the screen.

Click this option

Figure 14-11

3. The Documents library appears. Locate the file or files that you want and select it (or them) and then click it.

4. Click the Attach button. A thumbnail of the attached file appears in the message body (see **Figure 14-12**) indicating that it's uploaded. If you have other attachments from other folders on your computer, you can click the Attachments link again and repeat the previous steps as many times as you like to add more attachments.

5. Click the Send button to send the message and attachment.

Thumbnail of the attached file

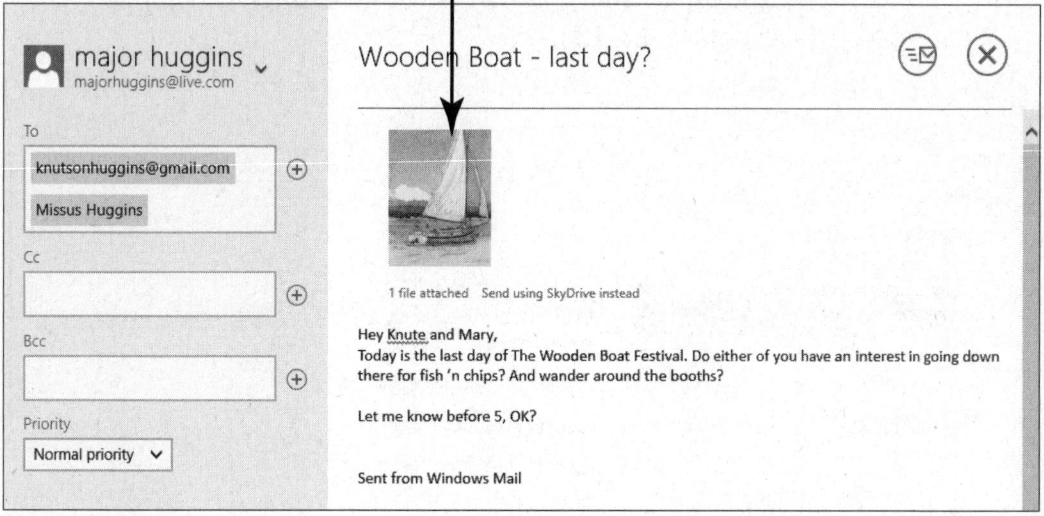

major huggins ⌄
majorhuggins@live.com

Wooden Boat - last day?

To

knutsonhuggins@gmail.com ⊕

Missus Huggins

Cc

⊕

Bcc

⊕

Priority

Normal priority ⌄

1 file attached   Send using SkyDrive instead

Hey Knute and Mary,
Today is the last day of The Wooden Boat Festival. Do either of you have an interest in going down there for fish 'n chips? And wander around the booths?

Let me know before 5, OK?

Sent from Windows Mail

Figure 14-12

 You can attach as many files as you like to a single e-mail by repeating steps in this task. Your limitation is size. Various e-mail programs have different limitations on the size of attachments, and some prevent you from attaching certain types of files for security reasons. If you attach several documents and your e-mail fails to send, consider clicking the Send Using SkyDrive Instead link in the message window to use Microsoft's file-sharing service instead. See Chapter 15 for more about using SkyDrive.

If you change your mind about sending a message while you're creating it, just click the Close button (it's in the top-right corner with an X in it) and choose Save Draft or Delete.

Read a Message

1. When you receive an e-mail, your next step is to read it. Click an e-mail message in your Inbox. Unread messages are in bold and messages you've read are unbolded.

2. Click in the message body and use the scroll bar in the message window to scroll down through the message and read it (see **Figure 14-13**).

Scroll bar

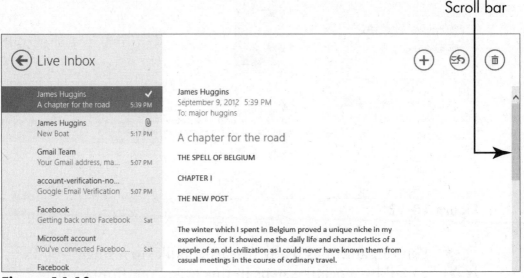

Figure 14-13

3. If you want to delete the message, simply click the Trash button in the top-right corner.

 If you'd like to save an attachment to a storage disc or your hard drive, right-click the thumbnail of it in the message, choose the location to save the file to, and then click Save.

Reply to a Message

1. If you receive an e-mail and want to send a message back, use the Reply feature. Open the message you want to reply to, click the Respond button, and then select one of the following reply options, as shown in **Figure 14-14:**

- **Reply:** Send the reply to only the author.

- **Reply All:** Send a reply to the author as well as to everyone who received the original message.

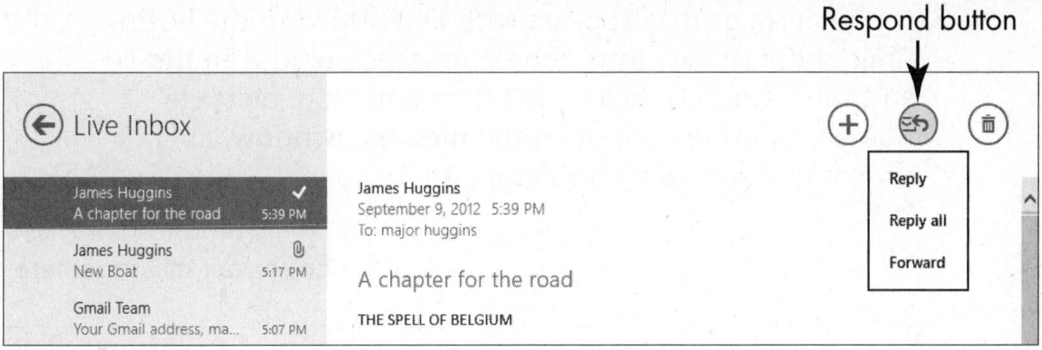

Respond button

Live Inbox

| James Huggins | ✓ | James Huggins |
| A chapter for the road | 5:39 PM | September 9, 2012 5:39 PM |

To: major huggins

| James Huggins | 📎 |
| New Boat | 5:17 PM |

A chapter for the road

| Gmail Team | |
| Your Gmail address, ma... | 5:07 PM |

THE SPELL OF BELGIUM

Reply

Reply all

Forward

Figure 14-14

2. In the resulting e-mail form (see **Figure 14-15**), enter any additional recipient(s) in the To and/or Cc text boxes; to send a blind copy you can click Show More to display the Bcc field. Type your message in the message window.

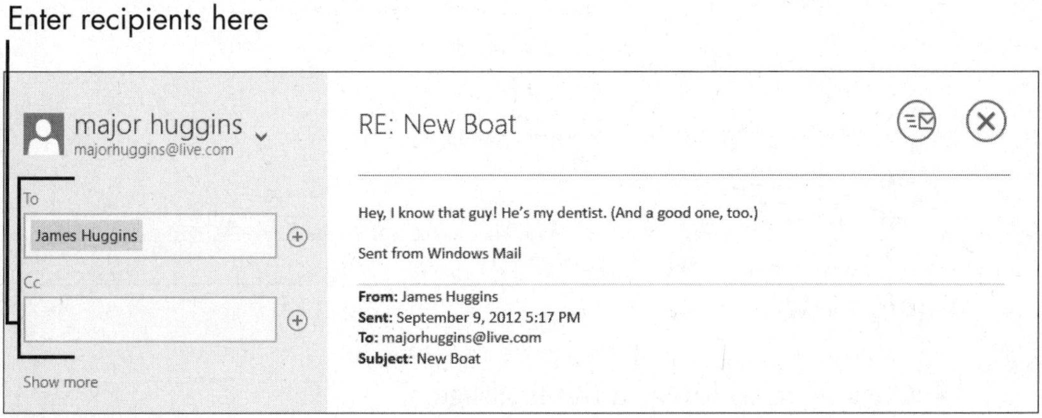

Enter recipients here

major huggins
majorhuggins@live.com

RE: New Boat

To

James Huggins

Cc

Show more

Hey, I know that guy! He's my dentist. (And a good one, too.)

Sent from Windows Mail

From: James Huggins
Sent: September 9, 2012 5:17 PM
To: majorhuggins@live.com
Subject: New Boat

Figure 14-15

3. Click the Send button to send the reply.

Forward E-mail

1. To share an e-mail you receive with others, use the Forward feature. Open the e-mail message that you want to forward in Mail.

2. Click the Respond button, and then click Forward.

3. In the message that appears with FW: added to the beginning of the subject line, enter a new recipient(s) in the To and/or Cc and Bcc fields, and then enter any message that you want to include in the message window, as shown in the example in **Figure 14-16**.

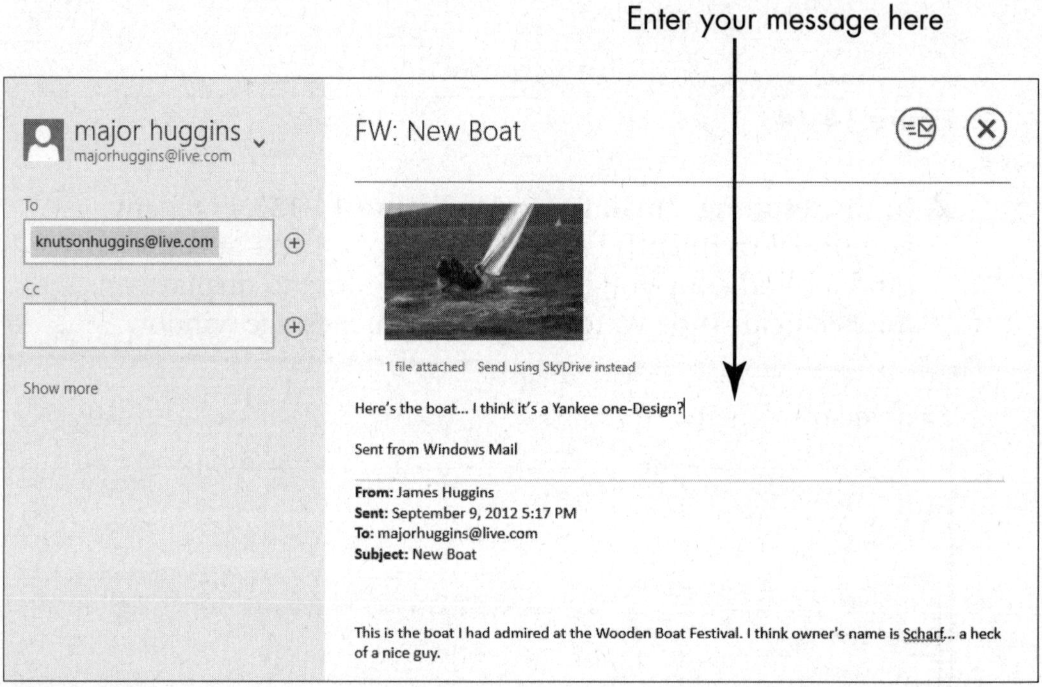

Enter your message here

major huggins
majorhuggins@live.com

To
knutsonhuggins@live.com

Cc

Show more

FW: New Boat

1 file attached   Send using SkyDrive instead

Here's the boat... I think it's a Yankee one-Design?

Sent from Windows Mail

From: James Huggins
Sent: September 9, 2012 5:17 PM
To: majorhuggins@live.com
Subject: New Boat

This is the boat I had admired at the Wooden Boat Festival. I think owner's name is Scharf... a heck of a nice guy.

Figure 14-16

4. Click Send to forward the message.

Make Account Settings in Mail

1. Each account that you set up in Mail has its own settings. Click the Mail tile on the Start screen.

2. From within Mail, press Win+I, and then click Accounts in the Settings panel (see **Figure 14-17**).

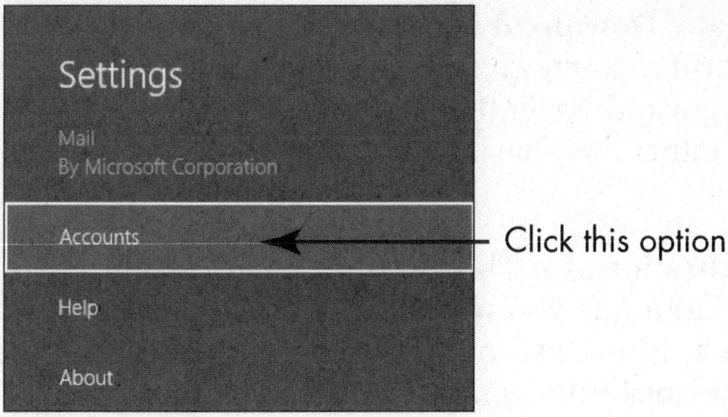

Settings

Mail
By Microsoft Corporation

Accounts ← —— Click this option

Help

About

Figure 14-17

3. Click the account for which you want to change settings. In the panel displayed in **Figure 14-18,** you can make the following changes:

- **Download New Content.** You can click this field and, from the drop-down list that appears, choose to download content when a message arrives or every 15, 30, or 60 minutes. If you prefer, you can choose to download items manually by clicking the Manual option here.

- **Download Content From.** This is a handy setting if you're away from Mail for a while and have been checking messages in your browser. If so, you may not want to download a month's worth of messages you've already read, so choose another setting from this drop-down list, such as The Last 3 Days.

- **Content to Sync.** Syncing involves having certain actions and content delivery or deletions coordinated among different accounts. You can choose to download various items, depending on your e-mail provider, such as e-mail, contacts, or calendar appointments using this command.

- **Automatically Download External Images.** Turn this setting off if you're concerned about the content of images and prefer that you manually download them rather than having them automatically downloaded.

- **Show Notifications for This Account.** If you want Windows 8 to notify you when e-mail arrives, turn this on. To activate this, you must also check Mail in the list of apps from which you can get notifications in the Notifications area of PC Settings.

- **Remove Account.** If you decide you don't want Mail to access an account anymore, click the Remove Account button. For the account you use to log in to Windows 8, you'll have to do this procedure though the PC Settings window (press Win+I and then click Change PC Settings).

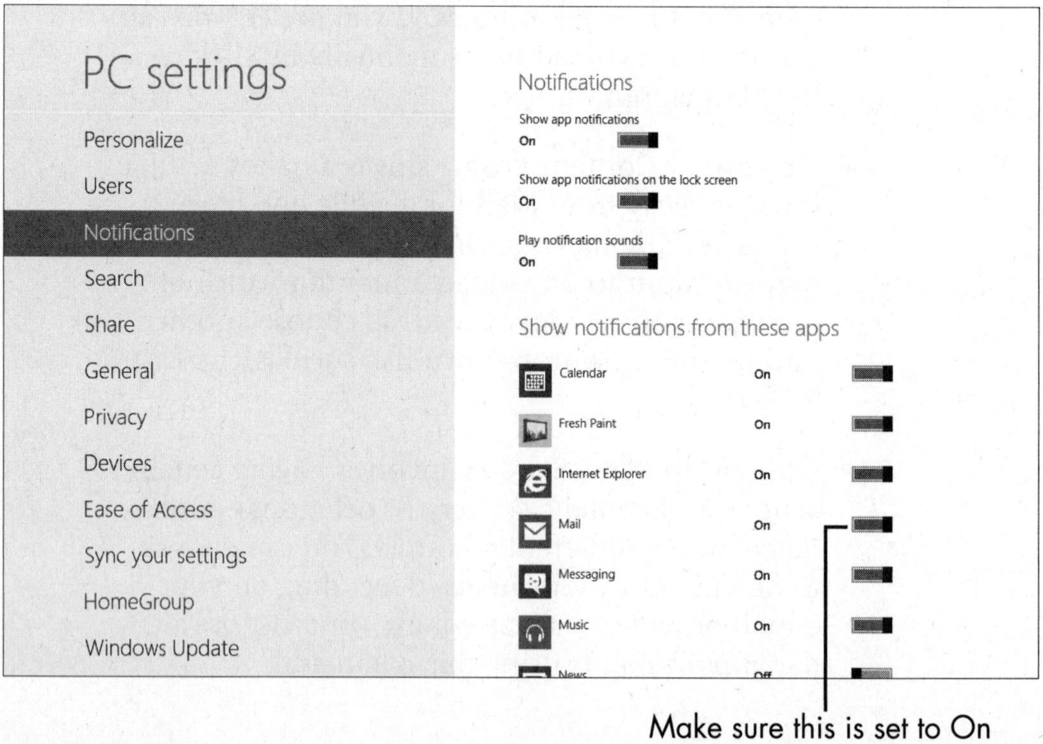

Make sure this is set to On

Figure 14-18

PC Settings in Windows 8.1

PC Settings in Windows 8.1 are rather different than in Windows 8. For example, to change Display settings, you first click PC & Devices and on the next panel of options, you then click Display. The figure shows an example of how several PC Settings are now available to you in secondary menus in Windows 8.1.

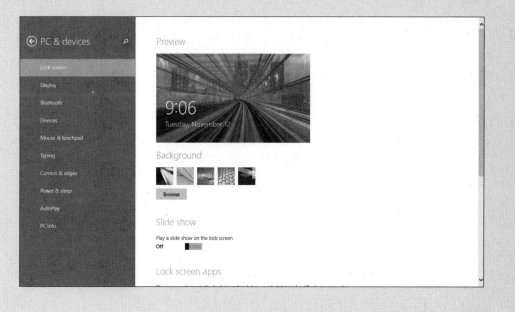

Working in the Cloud

Chapter 15

You may have heard the term *cloud* bandied about. The term comes from the world of computer networks, where certain functionality isn't installed on computers but resides on the network itself, in the so-called cloud.

Today, the definition of the term has broadened to include functionality that resides on the Internet. If you can get work done without using an installed piece of software — or if you store and share content online — you're working in the cloud.

In this chapter, you discover the types of applications you might use in the cloud, saving you the cost and effort of buying and installing software. In addition, I explore two Windows 8 features that help you access your own data in the cloud: Sync and SkyDrive. Sync allows you to share the settings you've made in Windows 8 on one computer with other Windows 8 computers. SkyDrive is a file-sharing service that has been around a while, but with Windows 8, sharing files from your computer with others or with yourself on another computer is tightly integrated.

Get ready to . . .

➡ Use Applications Online 250

➡ Add Files to SkyDrive 252

➡ Share Files Using SkyDrive 253

➡ Create a New SkyDrive Folder 255

➡ Share a SkyDrive Folder with Others 256

➡ Turn On the Sync Feature... 257

➡ Choose which Settings You Want to Sync............. 258

Use Applications Online

Certain apps, such as Maps and People, are built into Windows 8. You may purchase or download and install other apps, such as Fresh Paint or Angry Birds, or applications such as Microsoft Word or Excel. Although these apps and applications may connect to the Internet to get information — such as the latest traffic info, or software help files — the software itself is installed on your computer.

Today, you have the option of using software in the cloud, meaning that you never install the software on your computer but simply make use of it online. Here are some examples you can explore:

➠ **Google Docs:** This suite of online software (available at www.docs.google.com; see **Figure 15-1**) includes word processor, spreadsheet, presentation, drawing, and form design software products you can use by logging into a Gmail account. These applications are compatible with popular office software such as Microsoft Word and PowerPoint.

➠ **E-mail clients:** When you log into Gmail or Windows Live Hotmail, you're using the software in the cloud. In addition, some e-mail clients that access various e-mail accounts, such as Outlook, connect with file-sharing sites. Rather than attaching files to e-mail messages, you're given the option of uploading and sharing them on the file- sharing site. You can do that with Windows Live Hotmail and SkyDrive.

➠ **Photo-sharing sites:** Sites such as Flickr (www.flickr.com), shown in **Figure 15-2,** allow you to upload and download photos to them without ever installing an app on your computer. A variation on this is a site such as Viewbook (www.viewbook.com), where you can create an online portfolio of art samples or business presentations, for example, to share with others.

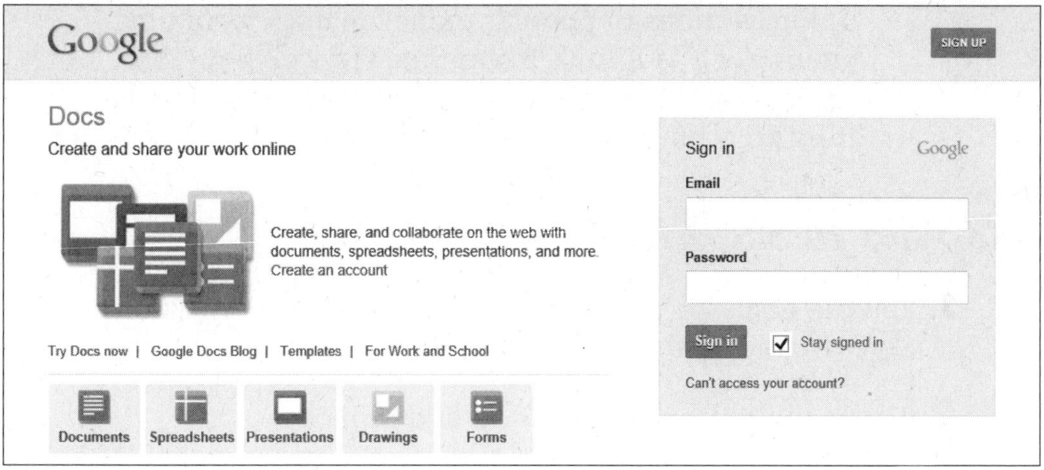

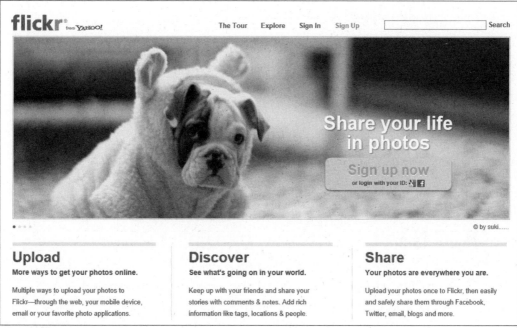

Figure 15-1

Figure 15-2

⟶ **Financial applications:** You might use a site such as
Online Investment Portfolio (www.online
investmentportfolio.com) to maintain an
online portfolio of investments and generate charts
to help you keep track of trends. You can also use

online versions of popular money-management programs, such as Intuit's free online service Mint (www.
mint.com), through which you can access your data
from any computer or mobile device.

Add Files to SkyDrive

1. You can easily add files to SkyDrive at any time. Click the
SkyDrive tile on the Start screen.

2. Click a folder (see **Figure 15-3**), and it opens.

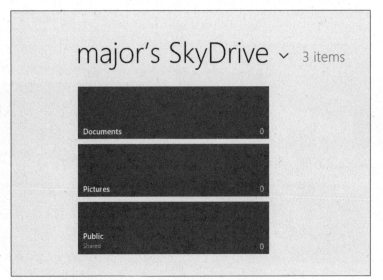

major's SkyDrive ⌄ 3 items

Documents   0

Pictures   0

Public
Shared   0

Figure 15-3

3. Right-click in a blank area of the screen and then click
the Upload button in the toolbar that appears.

4. Drag the scroll bar at the bottom on the screen (see
Figure 15-4) to locate a file. (If you don't see the file you
need, click the Go Up button; more folders are
displayed.)

5. Click a file.

6. Click Add to SkyDrive.

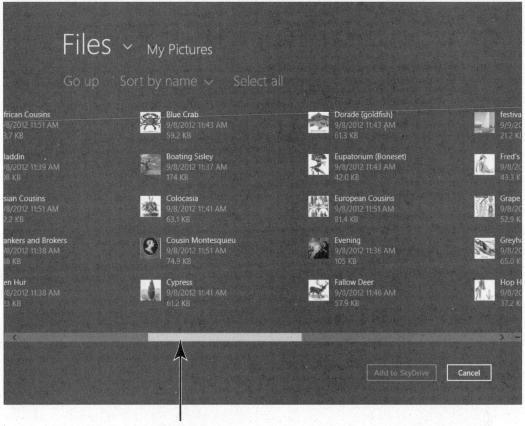

Scroll bar

Figure 15-4

 You may want to delete a file from SkyDrive, as the free storage is limited to 7 gigabytes (GB). First, find the file in SkyDrive that you want to delete, and right-click it. Click Manage, and then click Delete. In the pop-up menu that appears, click Delete.

Share Files Using SkyDrive

1. SkyDrive is a Microsoft file-sharing service that you can use to upload and share files with others. With Windows 8, you can share larger files such as videos and photos via SkyDrive as you're working with the Mail app. Sharing files online can be easier than sending them as attachments because e-mail programs typically limit how much data you can send at one time. You can share items from within apps such as Camera (assuming you have a camera built in to your computer, which most computers today have). Click the Camera tile on the Start screen.

2. Click a video to play it (if you haven't recorded any video with the camera, go to Chapter 17 and record a short video).

3. Press Win+C to display the Charms bar.

4. Click Share. Different apps you can use to share appear, such as the Mail or SkyDrive app (see **Figure 15-5**).

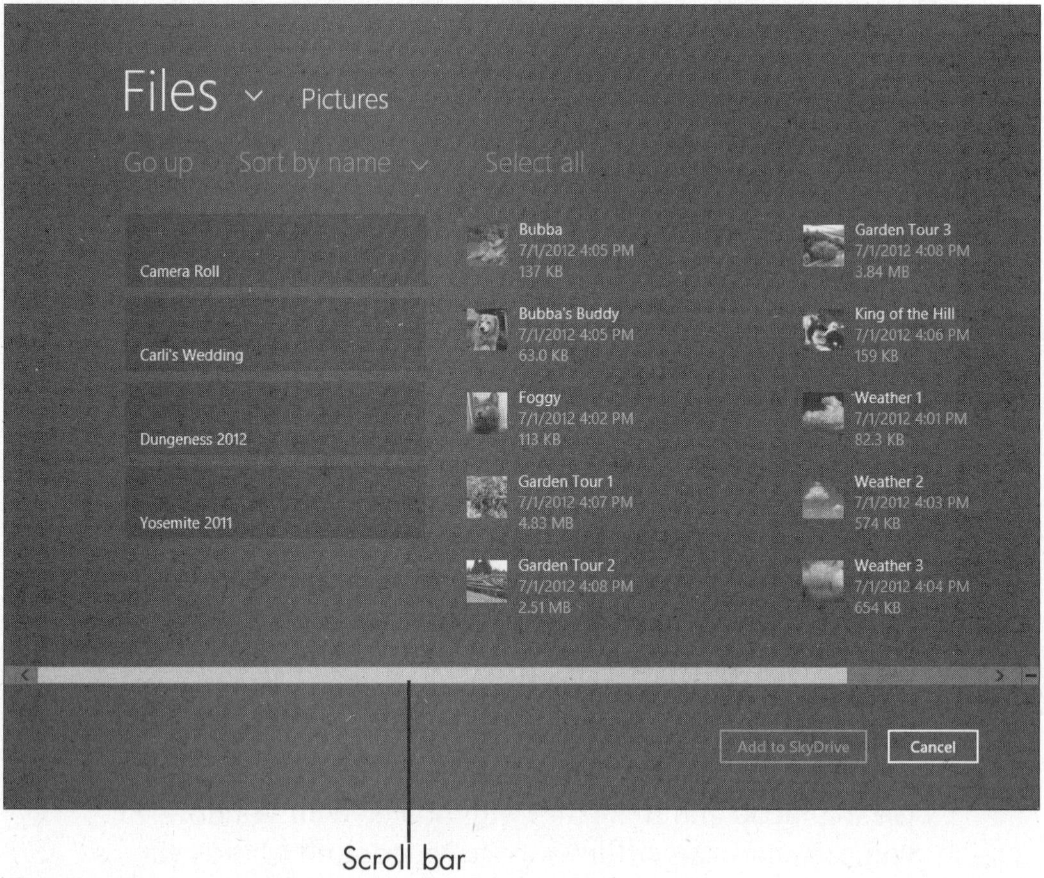

Scroll bar

Figure 15-5

5. Click Mail.

6. Click Send Using SkyDrive Instead, and then enter the e-mail address that's associated with your SkyDrive account (all Windows Live Hotmail accounts come with a SkyDrive account).

7. Click Send.

8. Now open your e-mail account and click View New Folder on SkyDrive.

 After you've shared something using SkyDrive, you can view the contents of SkyDrive by clicking the SkyDrive tile on the Start screen.

Create a New SkyDrive Folder

1. You can keep your shared files in order by placing them in folders on SkyDrive. After you've placed content in folders, you can then share those folders with others. This ability to share individual folders gives you a measure of security, as you don't have to share access to your entire SkyDrive content with anybody. Click the Internet Explorer tile on the Start screen.

2. Right-click to display the Address field (see **Figure 15-6**), type https://skydrive.live.com, and press Enter.

Address field

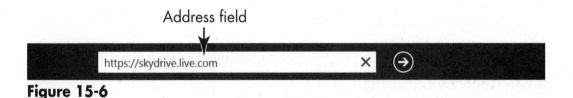

Figure 15-6

3. Click New Folder and enter a name for the new folder.

When you click the SkyDrive tile on the Start screen, you see folders of content stored online. When you go to the SkyDrive site by entering `www.skydrive.com` into any browser's address field, you have more options for displaying your content by criteria such as name, date modified, and with whom your folders are shared.

Share a SkyDrive Folder with Others

1. SkyDrive's purpose is to allow you to share files with others. Sharing can involve allowing others to view content, or granting permission to edit it. Open SkyDrive in a browser and then click Files to display the Files list (see **Figure 15-7**).

Files list

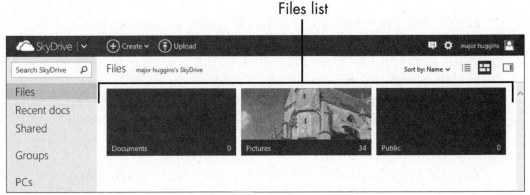

Figure 15-7

2. Right-click a folder.

3. Choose Share, and then enter an e-mail address (see **Figure 15-8**). A warning may appear about sharing and your privacy. Click Continue to proceed.

4. You can enter a note, though this is optional.

5. If you don't want to allow the person you're sharing with to edit files, deselect the Recipients Can Edit check box.

6. Click Send.

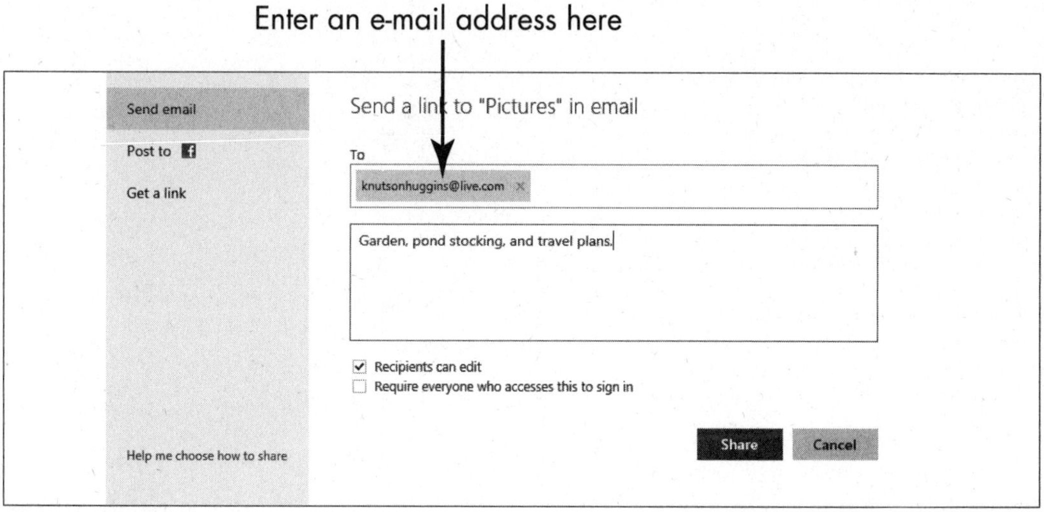

Enter an e-mail address here

Send a link to "Pictures" in email

Send email	
Post to 🖪	
Get a link	To
	knutsonhuggins@live.com ✕
	Garden, pond stocking, and travel plans.
	☑ Recipients can edit
	☐ Require everyone who accesses this to sign in
Help me choose how to share	Share Cancel

Figure 15-8

> When you share a word-processing file with another person on SkyDrive and grant permission to edit it, she can edit it in a Word Web App (a cloud version of Microsoft Word) or open the document in Microsoft Word on her computer.

Turn On the Sync Feature

1. You can use the Sync feature to share your PC settings among Windows 8 devices so you don't have to redo the settings on each device. To sync, you have to turn on the sync feature. With the Sync feature turned on, sign into your Windows Live account on another device, and all your settings will be synced from the cloud. To begin, press Win+I.

2. Click Change PC Settings, and then click Sync Your Settings.

3. Click the Sync Settings On This PC On/Off button (see **Figure 15-9**).

Make sure this is set to On

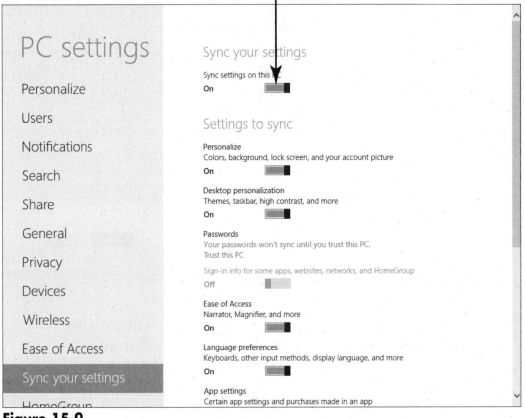

Figure 15-9

 Syncing works only with Windows 8 settings and settings for apps that you buy from the Windows Store.

Choose which Settings You Want to Sync

1. When you turn on syncing, you can choose what you
want to share. For example, you can share language preferences, passwords, or Ease of Access settings — it's up to
you. To set up what you want to sync, begin by pressing
Win+I.

2. Click Change PC Settings.

3. Click Sync Your Settings.

4. In the Settings to Sync section, click the On/Off buttons for the various settings you want to share (refer to **Figure 15-9**). With Sync turned on selected settings are synced automatically among Windows 8 devices.

 If you're charged for data or Internet connection time — for example on a Windows 8 tablet with 3G — go to Sync Settings in the PC Settings and click the On/Off button under Sync Settings over Metered Internet Connections. You might want to keep the next item, Sync Settings over Metered Connections Even When I'm Roaming, off, as syncing settings while roaming can cost you a lot.

Syncing with Windows 8.1

In Windows 8.1, you make different sync settings than in the previous tasks. Here are the steps you take for the previous two tasks for Windows 8.1:

1. Press Win+I and then click Change PC Settings.

2. Click SkyDrive and in the following screen click Sync Settings.

3. Click the On setting for Sync Settings on this PC (see the figure).

4. Scroll down and you can turn sync on or off for various items such as Web Browser and Ease of Access.

(continued)

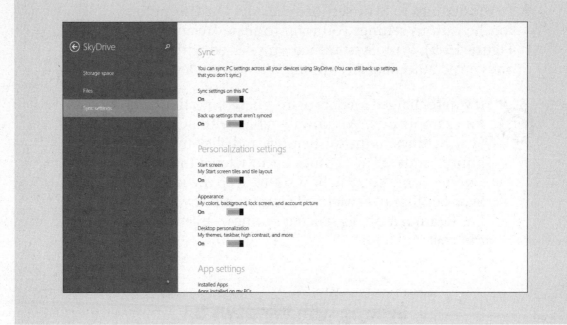

Connecting with People Online

The Internet offers many options for connecting with people and sharing information. You'll find discussion boards, blogs, and chat on a wide variety of sites, from news sites to recipe sites, sites focused around grief and health issues, and sites that host political- or consumer-oriented discussions.

There are some great senior chat rooms for making friends, and many sites allow you to create new chat rooms on topics at any time.

Instant messaging (IM), on the other hand, isn't a website but a service. Using software such as the Windows 8 Messaging app, IM allows you to chat in real time with your contacts. You can access instant-messaging programs via your computer or your cellphone.

As with any site where users share information, such as social networks and blogs, you can stay safer if you know how to sidestep some abuses, including *data mining* (gathering your personal information for commercial or criminal intent), *social engineering* ploys that try to gain your trust and access to your money, ID theft scams, and so forth. If you're careful to protect your privacy, you can enjoy socializing without worry.

Get ready to . . .

➡ Use Discussion Boards and Blogs 262

➡ Participate in Chat 264

➡ Send and Receive Instant Messages (IMs)................. 266

➡ Work with the Messaging App................................... 267

➡ Use Webcams 270

➡ Get an Overview of Collaborative and Social Networking Sites 271

➡ Sign Up for a Social Networking Service........... 273

➡ Understand How Online Dating Works.................. 275

➡ Select a Dating Service...... 277

➡ Share Content with Others... 278

Finally, Windows 8 offers some neat sharing features that allow you to share content such as music or videos with others via services such as e-mail or Facebook by using the Share charm.

In this chapter, I look at some ways of sharing information content and tell you how to do so safely.

Use Discussion Boards and Blogs

A *discussion board* is a place where you can post written messages, pictures, and videos on a topic. Others can reply to you, and you can reply to their postings. In a variation on discussion boards, you'll find *blogs* (web logs) everywhere you turn, and you can also post your comments about blog entries.

Discussion boards and blogs are *asynchronous*, which means that you post a message (just as you might on a bulletin board at the grocery store) and wait for a response. Somebody might read it that hour — or ten days or several weeks after you make the posting. In other words, the response isn't instantaneous, and the message isn't usually directed to a specific individual.

You can find a discussion board or blog about darn-near every topic under the sun, and these are tremendously helpful when you're looking for answers. They're also a great way to share your expertise — whether you chime in on how to remove an ink stain, provide historical trivia about button styles on military uniforms, or announce the latest breakthroughs in your given field. Postings are likely to stay up on the site for years for people to reference.

1. To try using a discussion board, enter this URL in your browser's address field: `http://answers.microsoft.com/en-`. (Some discussion boards require that you become a member, with a username, and sign in before you can post, though this site doesn't.)

2. On the top-right side of the screen, the default language is English but you can click another language of your choice and then click a topic area, such as Home and Entertainment.

3. In the topic list that appears, click another topic, such as IE, to see more options. Continue to click until you get to a specific discussion board, such as the one shown in **Figure 16-1**.

4. When you click a posting that has replies, you'll see that the replies are organized in the middle of the page in easy-to-follow threads, which arrange postings and replies in an outlinelike structure. You can review the various participants' comments as they add their ideas to the conversation.

5. To reply to a posting yourself, first click the posting and then click the Reply link, fill in your comments (see **Figure** 16-2), and click Submit.

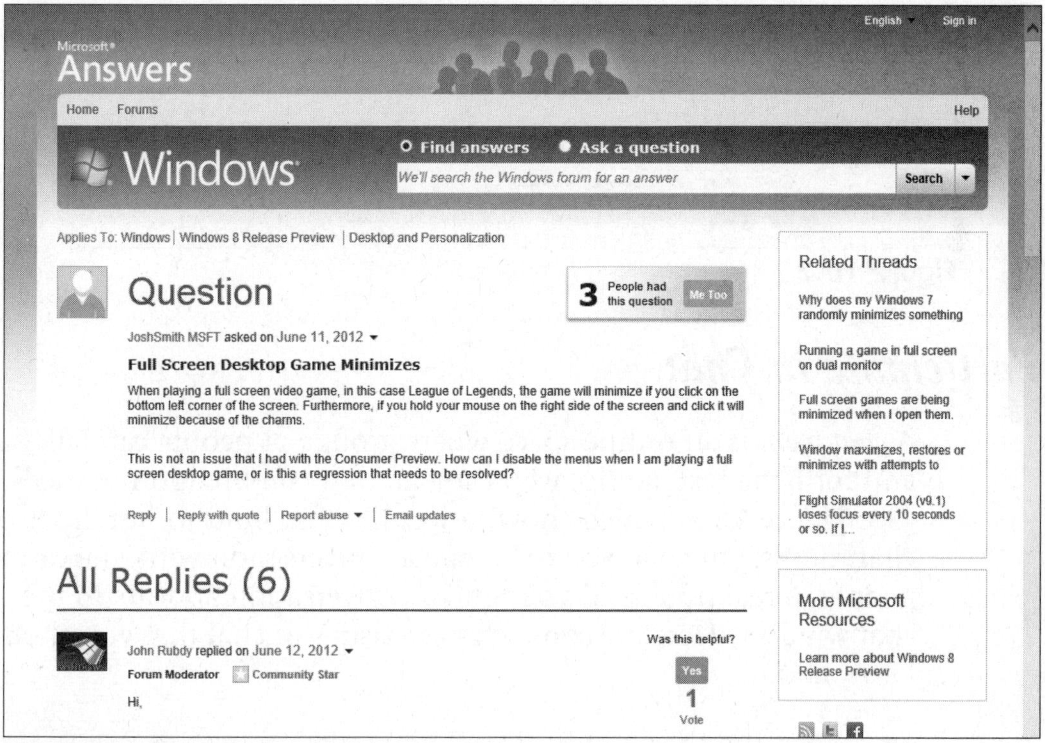

Figure 16-1

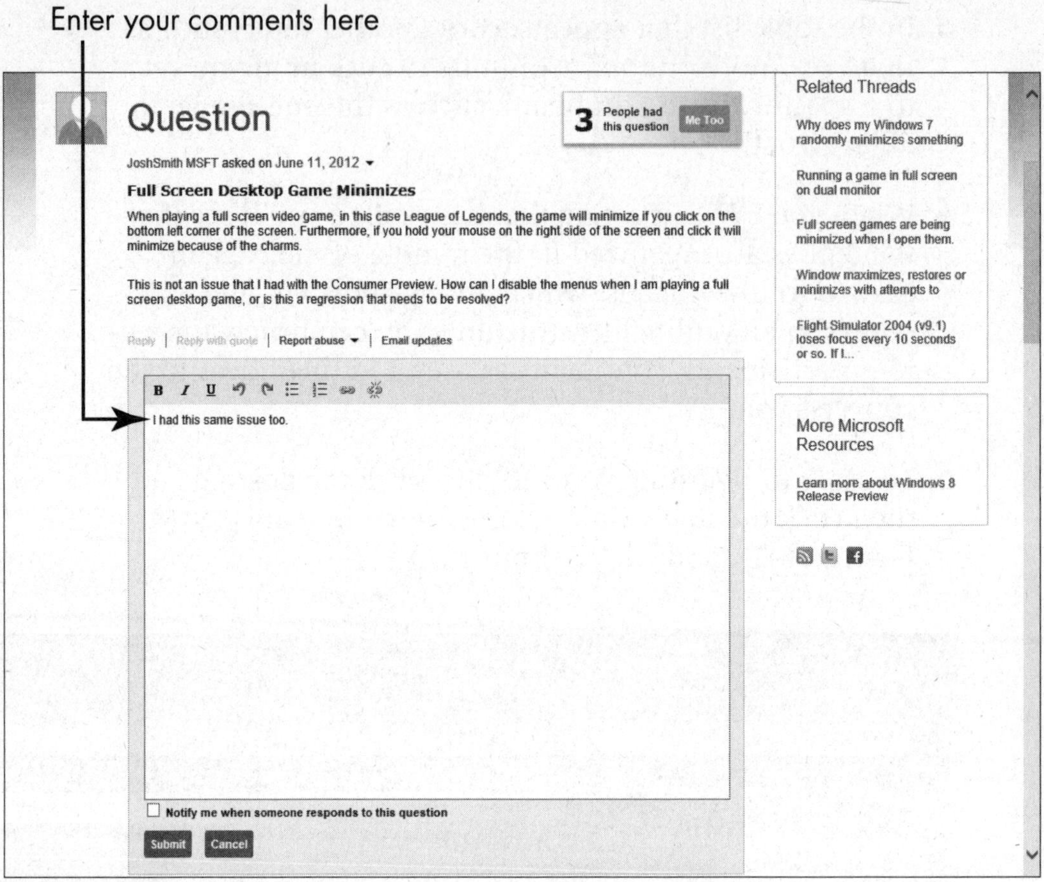

Enter your comments here

Figure 16-2

Participate in Chat

A *chat room* is an online space where groups of people can talk back and forth via text, audio, web camera, or a combination of media. (See **Figure 16-3**, which shows a website that links to hundreds of chat rooms.) In chat, you're having a conversation with one or more people in real time, and your entire conversation appears in the chat window. Here are some characteristics of chat that you should know about:

➡ When the chat is over, unless you save a copy, the conversation is typically gone.

➡ Interactions are in real time (synchronous), which means you can interact with others in the moment.

Figure 16-3

➡ Several people can interact at once, although this can take getting used to as you try to follow what others are saying and jump in with your own comments.

➡ When you find a chat you want to participate in, sign up to get a screen name, and then you simply enter the chat room, type your message, and submit it. Your message shows up in the stream of comments, and others may — or may not — reply to it.

 When you're talking to someone in a chat room with multiple people, you might be able to, if you'd like, invite him to enter a private chat room, which keeps the rest of the folks who wandered into the chat room out of your conversation. Also, others can invite you into private chat rooms. Be careful who you interact with in this way, and be sure you understand the motivations for making your conversation private. This may be entirely reasonable, or it may be that you're dealing with someone with suspect motivations.

 Before you get started, check out the website's Terms of Use and privacy, monitoring, and abuse-reporting procedures to understand the safety protections that are in place. Some sites are well monitored for signs of abusive content or interactions; others have no monitoring at all. If you don't like the terms, find a different site.

Send and Receive Instant Messages (IMs)

Instant messaging (often called just *IMing*) used to be referred to as real-time e-mail. It used to be strictly synchronous, meaning that two (or more) parties could communicate in real time, without any delay. It still can be synchronous, but now you can also leave a message that the recipient can pick up later.

Instant messaging is a great way to stay in touch with younger generations who rarely use e-mail. IM is ideal for quick, little messages where you just want an answer without forming a formal e-mail, as well as for touching base and saying hi. Text messaging on cellphones is largely the same phenomena: This isn't a tool you'd typically use for a long, meaningful conversation, but it's great for quick exchanges.

Depending on the IM service you use, you can do the following:

➡ Write notes to friends, grandchildren, or whoever.

➡ Talk as if you were on the phone.

➡ Send photos, videos, and other files.

➡ Use little graphical images, called *emoticons* (such as smilies or winks) and *avatars*, to add fun to your IM messages.

➡ See participants via web cameras.

➠ Get and send e-mail.

➠ Search the web, find others' physical location using Global Positioning System (GPS) technology, listen to music, watch videos, play games, bid on auctions, find dates, and more.

➠ Track the history of conversations and even save transcripts of them to review later.

Instant messaging programs vary somewhat, and you have several to choose from, including the Messaging app that's included in Windows 8. Other messaging apps include Yahoo! Messenger (available at `http://messenger.yahoo.com`), and AOL Instant Messenger, also known as AIM (available at `www.aim.com`). Gmail also has a built-in IM feature.

Work with the Messaging App

To get started with a new messaging program, you need to follow the general steps in the upcoming list. But as with any software, if you aren't sure how to use its features, consult its Help documentation for specific instructions.

1. To get started using a messaging program, try working with the Windows 8 Messaging app (note that this app is gone in Windows 8.1). If you've signed into Windows with a Windows Live account, you're automatically signed in to use Messaging. Click the Messaging tile on the Start screen.

2. Right-click the screen, click the Invite button (see **Figure 16-4**), and then choose Add a Friend.

—Click this button

Figure 16-4

3. In the following screen, enter the name or e-mail address of somebody in your contacts and click Next.

4. Click the Invite button (see **Figure 16-5**). After the person accepts your invitation, he or she will appear in the list of Messaging contacts when you next start an IM session.

5. Move your mouse to the upper-left corner and then click the Messaging app in the list of recently used apps to display the Messaging home screen again. Click the New Message button.

6. Click a Messaging contact from the People app that appears and then click the Select button.

7. On the Messaging screen, type a message in the field at the bottom of the screen (see **Figure 16-6**) and press Enter. The message appears as the first message in the conversation. Read your friend's response when it appears, and type additional comments to carry on your conversation.

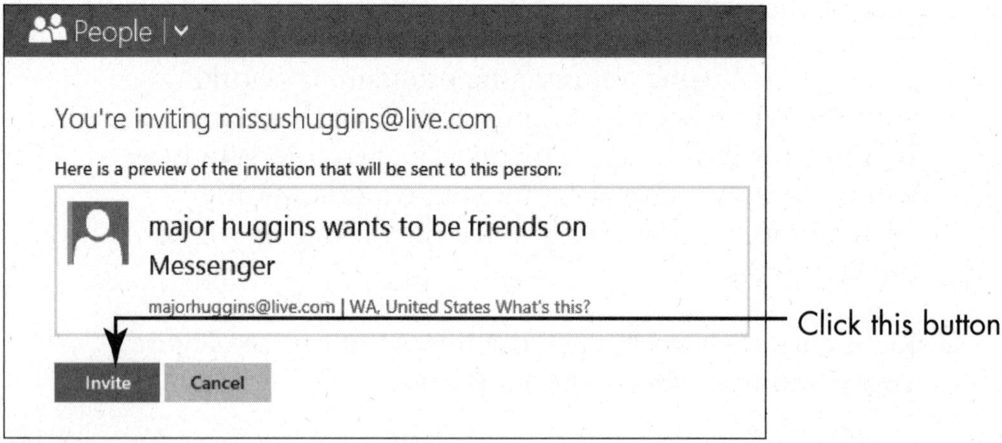

Figure 16-5

Are you having a good day? ☺ ————— Enter your message here

Figure 16-6

 You can send IMs (instant messages) from a computer to a mobile phone (and vice versa) and from one mobile phone to another. If you include your mobile phone number as part of your IM profile, anyone who can see your profile can view it. This is useful information for both friends and criminals, so it's important to consider whether you want your number exposed — especially if you have many people on your contact list who you don't personally know.

 If you want to communicate with folks you know through services such as Facebook or LinkedIn, after clicking Add a Friend in the preceding steps, click a service's icon and follow the instructions for that individual service to connect and locate your friends.

 IM is one place where people use shortcut text. Some of this will be familiar to you, such as FYI (for your information) and ASAP (as soon as possible). Other short text may be less familiar, such as LOL (laughing out loud). Visit www.swalk.com for a table of common shortcut text terms. Knowing these will make communicating with younger folks more fun.

 Consider what you're saying and sharing in IM and how you'd feel if the information were made public. IM allows you to store your conversation history, which is super-useful if you need to go back and check something that was said, but it has its downside. Anything you include in an IM can be forwarded to others. If you're at work, keep in mind that many employers monitor IM (and e-mail) conversations.

If you run across illegal content — such as child pornography — downloading or continuing to view this for any reason is illegal. Report the incident to law enforcement immediately.

Use Webcams

Webcams are relatively inexpensive, and many laptops now come with webcams embedded in their lids. (See **Figure 16-7.**) You can use a webcam with apps like Skype to make calls over the Internet, or other apps to have face-to-face, live meetings.

A webcam can be a great way to communicate with friends and family, but it can quickly become risky when you use it for conversations with strangers.

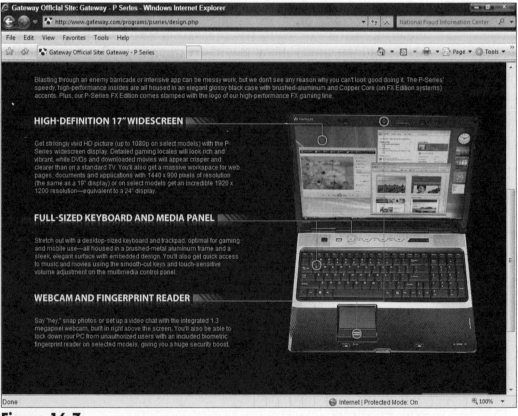

Figure 16-7

➠ Giving your image away, especially one that may show your emotional reactions to a stranger's statements in real time, simply reveals too much information that can put you at risk.

➠ If you use a webcam to meet with someone you don't know online, that person may expose you to behavior you'd rather not see.

➠ Note that webcams can also be hijacked and turned on remotely. This allows predators to view and listen to individuals without their knowledge. When you aren't using your webcam, consider turning it off or disconnecting it if it isn't a built-in model.

 Teens in particular struggle to use good judgment when using webcams. If you have grandchildren or other children in your care, realize that normal inhibitions seem to fall away when they aren't physically present with the person they're speaking to — and many expose themselves, figuratively and literally. In addition to having a conversation about appropriate webcam use with children and teens, it may be wise to limit access to webcams.

Get an Overview of Collaborative and Social Networking Sites

Although you may think kids are the only active group using social networking, that it isn't the case. In fact, people 35–54 years old make up a large segment of social networkers.

There are several types of sites where people collaborate or communicate socially. The following definitions may be useful:

➠ **Wiki:** A website that allows anyone visiting to contribute (add, edit, or remove) content. Wikipedia, for example, is a virtual encyclopedia built by users providing information in their areas of expertise.

Because of the ease of collaboration, wikis are often used when developing group projects or sharing information collaboratively.

➡ **Blog:** An online journal (*blog* is short for *web log*) that may be entirely private, open to select friends or family, or available to the general public. You can usually adjust your blog settings to restrict visitors from commenting on your blog entries, if you'd like.

➡ **Social networking site:** This type of website (see Figure 16-8) allows people to build and maintain a web page and create networks of people that they're somehow connected to — their friends, work associates, and/or other members with similar interests. Most social networking sites also host blogs and have social networking functions that allow people to view information about others and contact each other.

➡ **Social journaling site:** Sites such as Twitter allow people to post short notes online, notes that are typically about what they're doing at the moment. Many companies and celebrities are now *tweeting,* as posting comments on Twitter is referred to. You can follow individuals on Twitter so you're always informed if somebody you're a fan of makes a post.

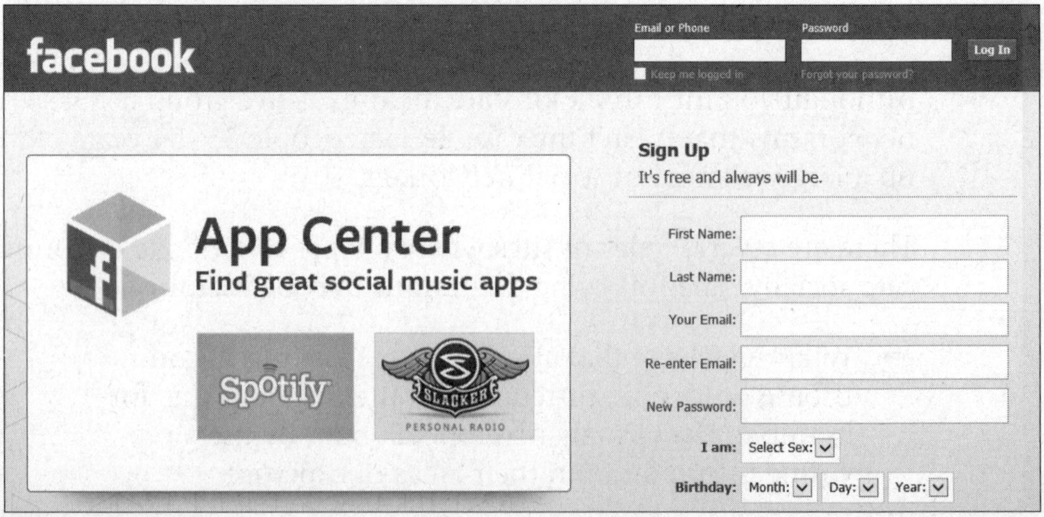

Figure 16-8

Sign Up for a Social Networking Service

Many social networking sites, such as Facebook or MySpace, are general in nature and attract a wide variety of users. Facebook, which was begun by some students at Harvard, has become today's most popular general site, and many seniors use its features to blog, exchange virtual gifts, and post photos. Other social networking sites revolve around particular interests or age groups.

When signing up for a service, understand what is *required* information and what is optional. You should clearly understand why a web service needs any of your personally identifiable information and how it may use that information — before providing it. Consider carefully the questions that sites ask users to complete in creating a profile.

 Accepting a social networking service's default settings may expose more information than you intend.

Walk through the signup process for Facebook to see the kinds of information it asks for. Follow these instructions to do so:

1. Type this URL into your browser's address line: www.facebook.com.

2. In the signup form that appears (see **Figure 16-9**), enter your name, e-mail address, a password, your gender, and birthdate. Note that the site requires your birthdate to verify that you are old enough to use the service, but you can choose to hide this information from others later if you don't want it displayed. (I recommend hiding your birthdate.)

3. Click the Sign Up button. On the screen that appears (see **Figure 16-10**), click the Find Friends link if you want to find people from your contacts who are using the various services listed, or click Skip This Step and click Skip again in the dialog box that appears to move on without adding friends if you don't want to invite everybody on your contacts list to be your friend.

Figure 16-9

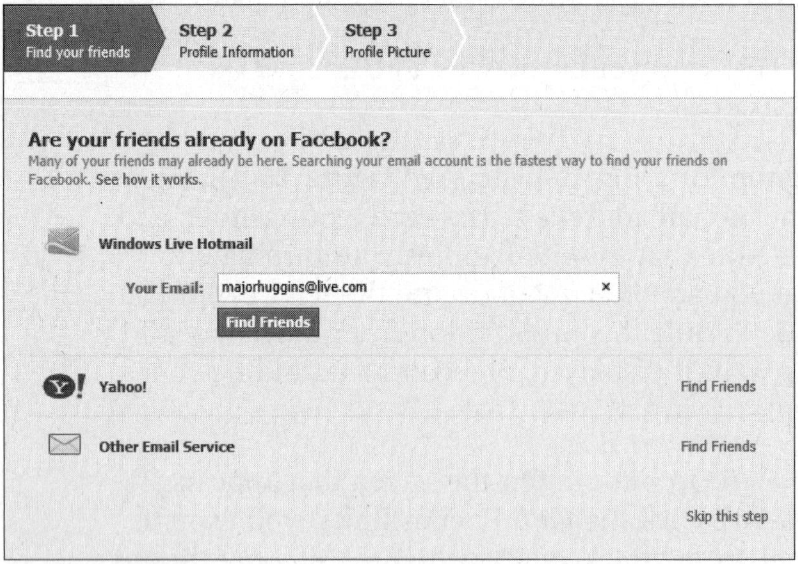

Figure 16-10

4. You now have a Facebook account, and can continue to fill out profile information for Facebook on the following screens, clicking Save and Continue between screens.

Remember that social networking sites sometimes ask for information during signup that they use to provide you with a customized experience that suits your needs. But sometimes the information isn't needed for the service they're providing you at all — they simply want it for marketing purposes, to show to other members, or to sell.

 It's often very difficult to remove information from sites if you later regret the amount of information you've shared. It's best to be conservative in the information you share during the signup process; you can always add more later.

Understand How Online Dating Works

Many seniors are making connections with others via online dating services, and if you've been wondering if this route could be for you, here's how you can jump into the world of online dating:

➡ Choose a reputable dating site. (See the section, "Select a Dating Service," later in this chapter.)

➡ Sign up and provide information about your likes, dislikes, preferences, and so on. This often takes the form of a self-guided interview process.

➡ Create and modify your profile to both avoid exposing too much personal information and ensure that you're sending the right message about yourself to prospective dates.

➡ Use search features on the site (see **Figure 16-11**) to find people who interest you. Send them messages or invitations to view your profile.

➡ You'll get messages from other members of the site, to which you can respond (or not). Use the site's chat and e-mail features to interact with potential dates. You may also be able to read comments about the person from others who've dated him or her, if the site has that feature.

➡ When you're comfortable with the person and feel there might be a spark, decide if you want to meet the person offline.

 Formal dating sites aren't the only places where people meet online, but they typically have the best safeguards in place. If you want to interact with people you meet on other sites, you should provide your own safeguards. Create a separate e-mail account (so you can remain anonymous and abandon the e-mail address if needed). Many dating sites screen participants and provide strong reporting measures that are missing on other types of sites, so be particularly careful. Take your time getting to know someone first before connecting.

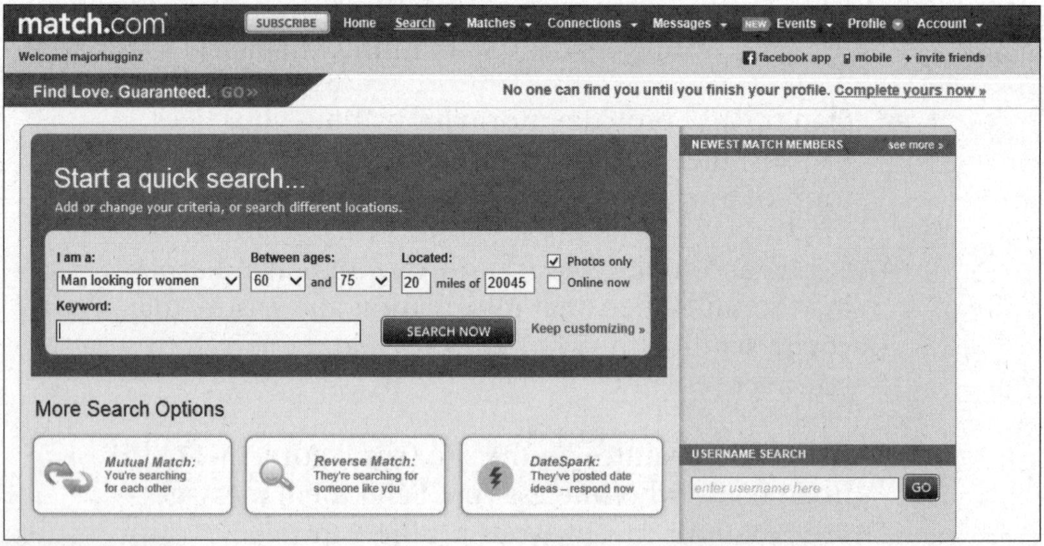

Figure 16-11

Select a Dating Service

Select your online dating service carefully.

➡ Look for an established, popular site with plenty of members and a philosophy that matches your own.

➡ Review the site's policy regarding your privacy and its procedures for screening members. Make sure you're comfortable with them.

➡ Use a service that provides an e-mail system (sometimes called *private messaging*) that you use for contacting other members only. By using the site's e-mail rather than your own e-mail address, you can maintain your privacy.

➡ Some sites, such as www.eharmony.com/senior-dating (shown in **Figure 16-12)** and http://saferdates.com offer stronger levels of authenticating members. Safer Dates, for example, uses fingerprint identification and screening to make you more confident that you know who you're interacting with.

➡ Visit a site such as www.consumer-rankings.comdating for comparisons of sites. Whether you choose a senior-specific dating site such as DatingForSeniors.com or a general-population site such as PerfectMatch.com, reading reviews about them ahead of time will help you make the best choice.

🎯 If you try a site and experience an unpleasant incident involving another member, report it and make sure the service follows through to enforce its policies. If it doesn't, find another service.

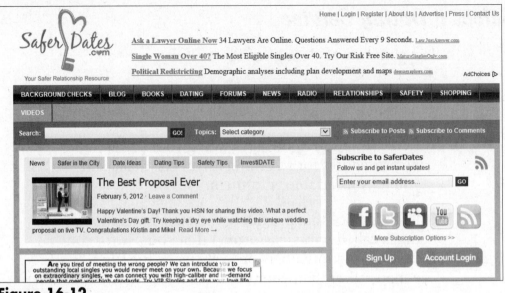

Figure 16-12

Share Content with Others

Windows 8 apps allow you to share various types of content with others via e-mail or several social networking services.

For example, if you display My Music from the Music app — or you're searching the web and find an interesting site — press Win+C to display the Charms bar, click the Share charm, and then click either Mail or People (see **Figure 16-13**).

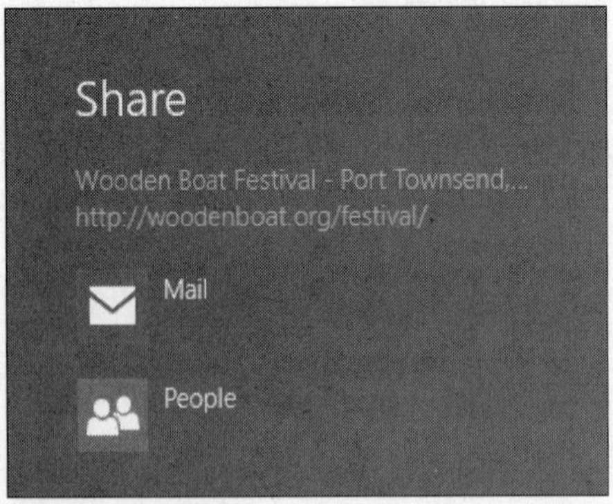

Share

Wooden Boat Festival - Port Townsend,...
http://woodenboat.org/festival/

Mail

People

Figure 16-13

Clicking Mail allows you to forward the item (a music file or a web link, for example) via e-mail. Clicking People lets you view Facebook or Twitter contacts and post the info or link to them on one of those services. Note that the options offered for sharing will vary by app and which services' accounts you've set up.

Part IV
Having Fun

The 5th Wave   By Rich Tennant

"It's really quite an entertaining piece of software. There's roller coaster action, suspense and drama, where skill and strategy are matched against winning and losing. And I thought managing our budget would be dull."

Getting Visual: Using Windows Media Player, Video, and Camera

Chapter 17

The world has discovered that it's fun and easy to share photos online, and that's probably why everybody is in on the digital image craze. Most people today have access to a digital camera (even if only on their cellphones) and have started manipulating and swapping photos like crazy, both online and off.

But today your phone, tablet, and computer not only let you upload and view pictures: You can use a built-in camera and the Windows 8 Camera app to take your own pictures or record videos and play them back. You can also buy videos (movies and TV shows, for example) and play them on your computer or other device, such as a tablet.

In this chapter, you discover how to buy and play video, including movies and TV shows. I also give you some guidelines for uploading photos and videos from your digital camera, and explain how to view and share your photos.

Get ready to . . .

➞ Work with Media Software 284

➞ Buy Video Content at the Windows Store 286

➞ Play Movies with Windows Media Player.................... 289

➞ Upload Photos from Your Digital Camera 291

➞ Take Pictures and Videos with the Windows 8 Camera App 292

➞ View a Digital Image in the Photos App 293

➞ Share a Photo.................... 295

➞ Run a Slide Show in Photos 297

Work with Media Software

Your computer is a doorway into a media-rich world full of music, digital photos, and video. It provides you with all kinds of possibilities for working with media. Windows 8 has a useful media player built right into it: Windows Media Player. The Photos app provides another option for viewing photos. In addition, the Camera and Video apps, both new in Windows 8, help you create and view photos and video.

Here's what you can do with each of these programs:

➥ **Windows Media Player:** Is just what its name suggests: As you see in **Figure 17-1,** it's a program you can use to play music, watch movies, or view photos. It also offers handy tools to create *playlists* (customized lists of music you can build and play) and set up libraries of media to keep things organized. You can even burn media to a DVD so you can play it on your DVD player or another computer.

Figure 17-1

➡ **Photos app:** Enables you to view digital photos; it opens automatically when you double-click a photo (as shown in **Figure 17-2**) in File Explorer and when you click the Photos tile on the Start screen. You can also share photos from within the Photos app by e-mail or by uploading to the SkyDrive file-sharing site.

➡ **Video app:** Takes you to the Windows Store (see **Figure 17-3**), where you can find TV shows and movies to buy and play on your computer or tablet.

➡ **Camera app:** Allows anybody who has a computer with a built-in or external camera or webcam to take photos and record videos.

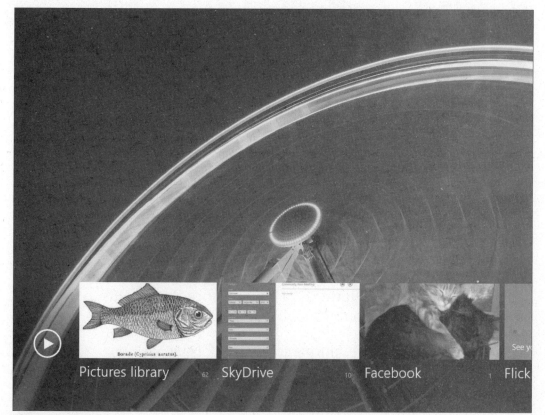

Figure 17-2

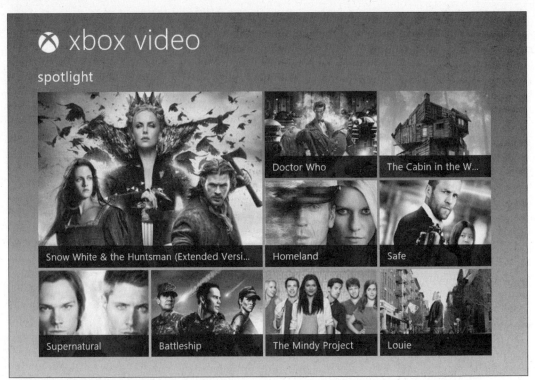

Figure 17-3

Buy Video Content at the Windows Store

1. The Windows Store offers a wonderful world of content that you can buy and play on your computer. To shop for video, you use the Video app, which you access through a tile on the Start screen. Click the Video app tile to get started.

2. Click a featured title in the Windows Store.

3. Click Buy (see **Figure 17-4**). If you click Rent at this point you're taken through a similar sequence of steps.

4. On the Viewing Options screen, click Next.

5. On the Confirm Purchase screen shown in **Figure 17-5**, click Buy Points.

Snow White & the Huntsman (Extended Version)

2012, NR, SD, Action/Adventure, Drama, Romance, Sci-Fi/Fantasy, 2 hr 11 min

From the Producer of Alice in Wonderland comes a new vision that turns a legendary tale into an action-adventure epic. The evil Queen Ravenna (Academy Award- winner Charlize Theron) will rule forever if she can take the life of Snow White (Kristen Stewart), so she dispatches the Huntsman (Chris Hemsworth) to track her down. But the wicked ruler never imagined that the Huntsman would train the girl to become a brave warrior, skilled in the art of war. Filled with intense battles and spectacular visual effects, Snow White & the Huntsman is a thrilling experience that "shouldn't be missed" – Shawn Edwards, Fox-TV.

Buy

Rent

Explore movie

Play trailer

Click this option

Figure 17-4

Confirm Purchase

Buy - 1200

Current balance	320
Price	1200
You don't have enough points.	-880

Goats
2012
Rating: R
Audio: English
SD Download and Stream

You need more Microsoft Points to complete this purchase. To get more, click Buy Points.

Buy Points   Cancel

Click Buy Points

Figure 17-5

6. On the Add Microsoft Points screen shown in **Figure 17-6,** choose the amount of points you'd like to purchase and click Next.

7. On the following screen, choose the credit payment option you prefer, or click Add a New Credit Card to fill in your credit card information. Then click Confirm Purchase.

8. You see a message confirming your purchase of Microsoft Points; click Done.

9. On the final screen, confirm the purchase of your movie.

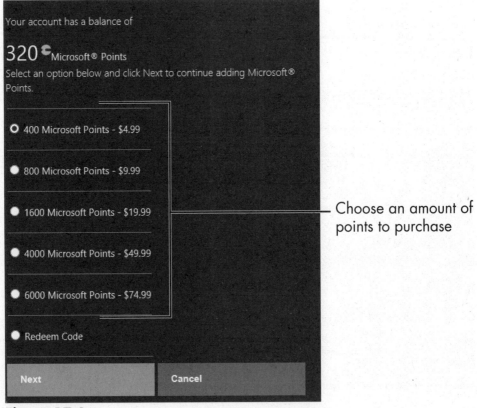

Choose an amount of points to purchase

Figure 17-6

There's a handy way to find videos you want. Just start typing the name of the video on the Start screen. When the Search screen appears, click Video in the list on the right side of the screen. When a result appears from the video marketplace, click to view more details or buy it.

Play Movies with Windows Media Player

1. From the Start screen, begin typing Windows Media Player. Click the app name in the results that appear. If this is your first time using the player, you may be prompted to make some basic settings.

2. Click the Maximize button in the resulting Media Player window. (Maximize is in the upper-right corner of the window, next to the X-shaped Close button, and it has a square icon.)

3. Click Videos in the Navigation pane to the left.

4. In the window listing video files, click the movie you want to play (as shown in **Figure 17-7**).

5. Double-click a file to begin the playback (see **Figure 17-8**). Use tools at the bottom of the screen to do the following (if they disappear during playback, just move your mouse or tap the screen to display them again):

- **Adjust the volume** of any soundtrack by clicking and dragging the slider left (to make it softer) or right (to make it louder). Click the megaphone-shaped volume icon to mute the sound (and click it again to turn the sound back on).

- **Pause the playback** by clicking the round Pause button in the center of the toolbar.

Click the movie to play

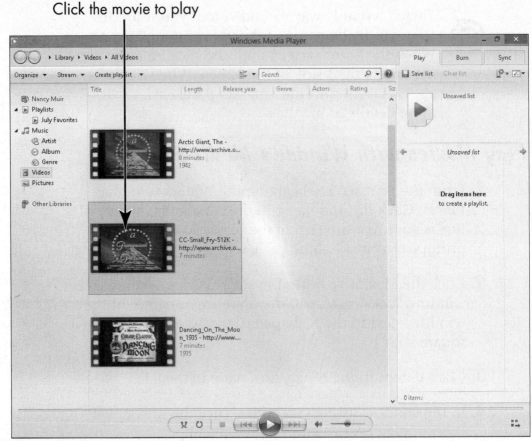

Figure 17-7

- **Stop the playback** by clicking the square-shaped Stop button to the left of the Pause/Play button.

- **Skip to the next or previous movie** by clicking the arrow buttons to the left or right of the Pause button.

6. Click the Close button to close Media Player.

You can also use the Video app to play video content. Just click the Video tile on the Start screen, locate the video in the My Videos section, scroll to the left, and click to play it. The playback controls are almost identical to those discussed for Windows Media Player.

Figure 17-8

Upload Photos from Your Digital Camera

Uploading photos from a camera to your computer is a very simple process, but it helps to understand what's involved. (This is similar to the process you can use to upload movies from a camcorder — in both cases, check your manual for details.) Here are some highlights:

➡ **Making the connection:** Uploading photos from a digital camera to a computer requires that you connect the camera to a USB port on your computer using a USB cable that typically comes with the camera. Power on the camera or change its setting to a playback mode as instructed by your user's manual.

➠ **Installing software:** Digital cameras also typically come with software that makes uploading photos to your computer easy. Install the software and then follow the easy-to-use instructions to upload photos. If you're missing such software, you can simply connect your camera to your computer and use File Explorer to locate the camera device on your computer and copy and paste photo files into a folder on your hard drive. (Chapter 3 tells you how to use File Explorer.)

➠ **Printing straight from the camera:** Digital cameras save photos onto a memory card, and many printers include a slot where you can insert the memory card from the camera and print directly from it without having to first upload pictures. Some cameras also connect directly to printers. However, if you want to keep a copy of the photo and clear up space in your camera's memory, you should upload the photos to your computer or an external storage medium such as a DVD or USB stick, even if you can print without uploading.

Take Pictures and Videos with the Windows 8 Camera App

1. The Camera app was new with Windows 8. If your computer or computing device has a camera (in the case of a computer, what you have may be a webcam), you can use the Camera app features to take both still photos and videos. Click the Camera app tile on the Start screen.

2. If the Video Mode button is gray and not white (see **Figure 17-9**), you're in photo mode. Aim your computer or computing device toward the subject of your picture and click anywhere on the screen (in Windows 8.1, click the Camera button). The photo is captured.

Video Mode button

Figure 17-9

3. Click the Video Mode button to change to video mode.

4. Click the screen (in Windows 8.1, click the Video button) to begin the video recording.

5. Click the screen (or Video button in Windows 8.1) again to stop recording.

 When you take a photo you can click on the picture and buttons appear that you can use to crop the picture or delete it. If you take multiple pictures use the arrows that appear when you move your mouse to the sides of the screen to scroll through the photos.

 To adjust photo resolution or make settings for audio recordings when you're recording a video, click the Camera Options button on the Video app screen and then click the Exposure button and use a slider to adjust exposure brightness.

View a Digital Image in the Photos App

1. To peruse your photos and open them in the Photos app, click the Photos tile on the Start screen.

2. In the Photos app, double-click a photo library to display files within it. Double-click a photo and move the mouse on the picture; arrows appear on the sides and a small - + appears at the bottom-right corner. Click these to zoom in and out.

- You can then right-click the photo and use the tools shown in **Figure 17-10** to do any of the following:

Click the share charm

Figure 17-10

- Click the Set As button to set the image as your lock screen image, the image background for the Photos app tile, or as an app background.

- The **Delete** button deletes the selected image.

- Click the **Slide Show** button to run a slide show (a topic covered later in this chapter).

You can also press Win+I and then click the Settings link (see Figure 17-11) to display settings for how your photos are displayed and shared.

Options link

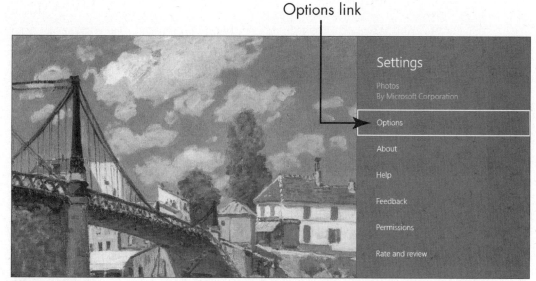

Figure 17-11

Share a Photo

1. Click the Photos app tile on the Start screen. Locate a photo you want to share and then press Win+C.

2. Click the Share charm (see **Figure 17-12**) for more sharing options in Photos. Click Mail.

Click the Share charm

Figure 17-12

3. In the e-mail form that appears (see **Figure 17-13**), enter an e-mail address or addresses, subject, and a message.

4. Click the Send button. An e-mail is sent from your default e-mail with your photo attached.

 If your photo is large, consider clicking the Send using SkyDrive Instead link to upload it to your SkyDrive account and share it with the recipient. See Chapter 15 for more about using the SkyDrive file-sharing service.

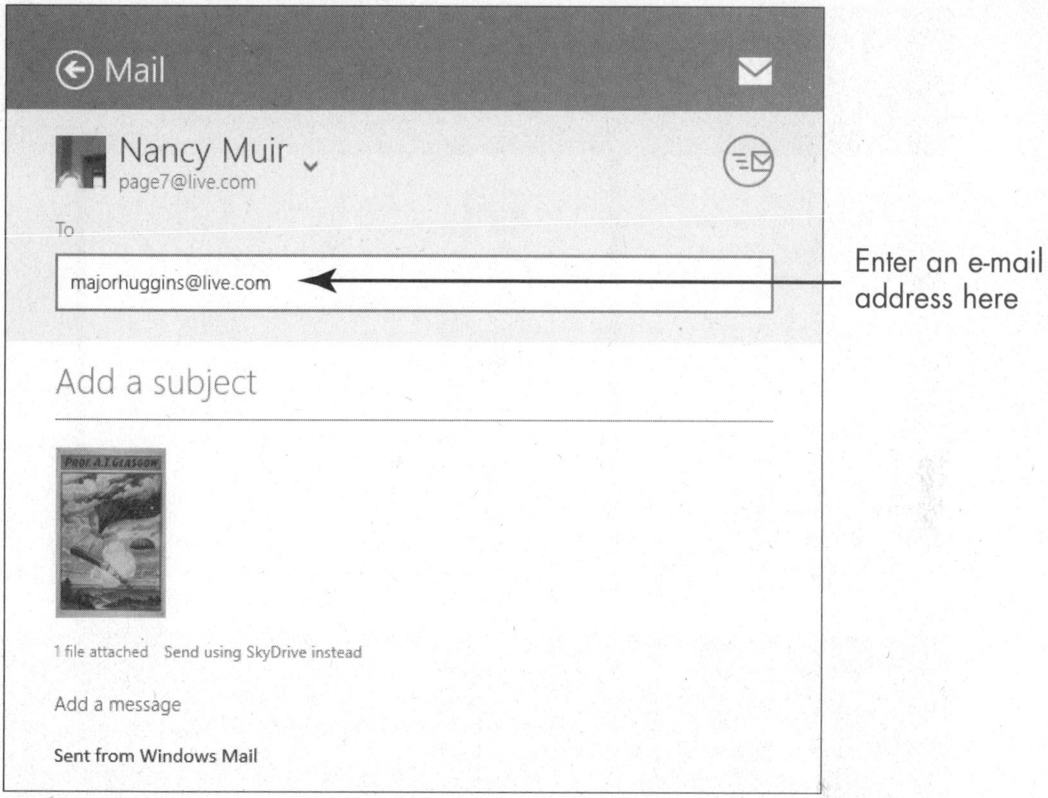

Enter an e-mail address here

Figure 17-13

Run a Slide Show in Photos

1. You can use Photos to play a slide show, which continues until you stop it. Click the Photos tile on the Start screen and click a photo album or library to open it.

2. Right-click and then click the Slide Show button shown in **Figure 17-14**.

3. Click anywhere on the screen to stop the slide show.

Click this button

Figure 17-14

Playing Music in Windows 8

Music is the universal language, and your computer opens up many opportunities for appreciating it. Your computer makes it possible for you to listen to your favorite music, download music from the Internet, play audio CDs and DVDs, and organize your music by creating playlists. You can also save (or *burn*, in computer lingo) music tracks to a CD/DVD or portable music device such as the hugely popular iPod.

With a sound card installed and speakers attached, you can set up your speakers and adjust volume, and then use Windows media programs to play music, manage your music library, burn tracks to a CD/DVD, and use the Music app to buy music.

Chapter 18

Get ready to . . .

➡ Set Up Speakers 300

➡ Adjust System Volume 301

➡ Make Settings for Ripping
 Music 303

➡ Find Music with Windows 8
 Integrated Search 305

➡ Buy Music from the
 Windows Store 306

➡ Create a Playlist 309

➡ Burn Music to a CD/DVD ... 311

➡ Sync with a Music Device... 312

➡ Play Music with Windows
 Media Player 314

Set Up Speakers

1. Attach speakers to your computer by plugging them into the appropriate connection (often labeled with a little megaphone or speaker symbol) on your CPU, laptop, or monitor.

2. On the Start screen, begin typing **Control Panel**, and then click Control Panel in the results.

3. Click Hardware and Sound; then click the Manage Audio Devices link (under the Sound category).

4. In the resulting Sound dialog box (see **Figure 18-1**), double-click the Speakers item and then click the Properties button.

5. In the resulting Speakers Properties dialog box, click the Levels tab, shown in **Figure 18-2,** and then use the Speakers/Headphone slider to adjust the speaker volume. *Note:* If you see a small red x on the Speaker button, click it to activate the speakers.

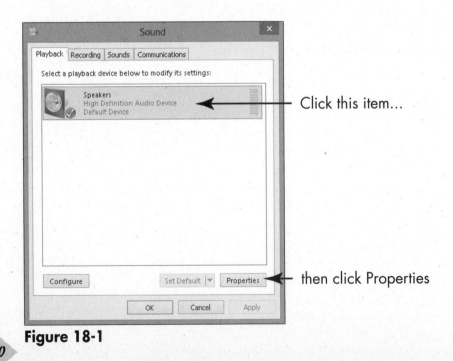

Click this item...

then click Properties

Figure 18-1

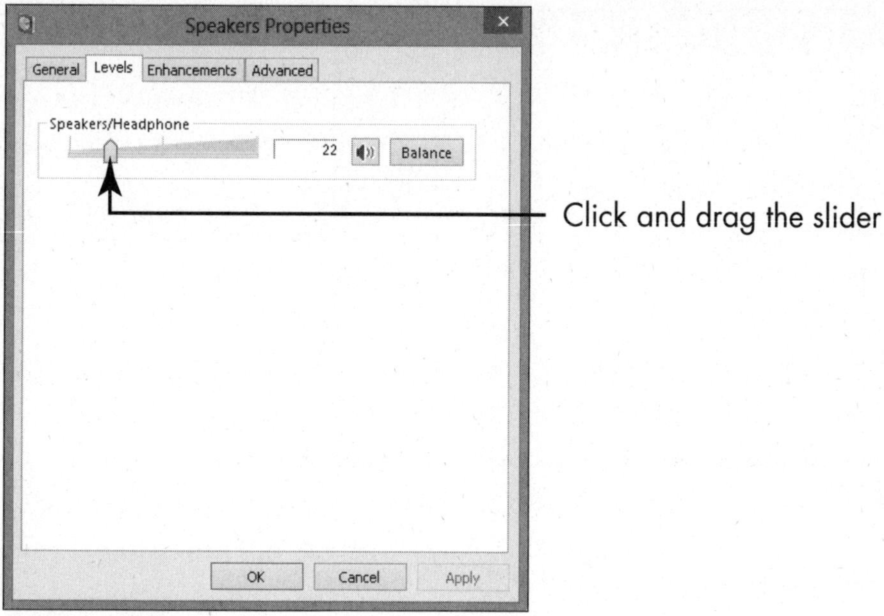

Click and drag the slider

Figure 18-2

6. Click the Balance button. In the resulting Balance dialog box, use the L(eft) and R(ight) sliders to adjust the balance of sounds between the two speakers.

7. Click OK three times to close all the open dialog boxes and save the new settings.

If you use your computer to make or receive phone calls, check out the Communications tab of the Sound dialog box. Here you can make a setting to have Windows automatically adjust sounds to minimize background noise.

Adjust System Volume

1. You can set the master system volume for your computer to be louder or softer. From the Control Panel, click Hardware and Sound.

2. Click the Adjust System Volume link under Sound to display the Volume Mixer dialog box (shown in **Figure 18-3**).

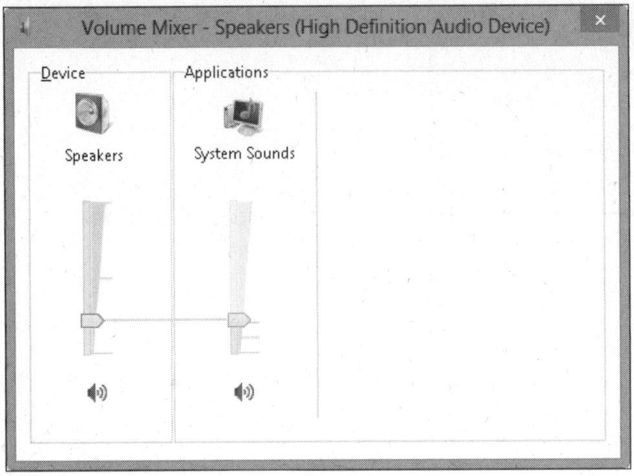

Figure 18-3

3. Make any of the following settings:

- Move the Device slider to adjust the system's speaker volume up and down.

- For sounds played by Windows (called *system sounds*), adjust the volume by moving the Applications slider.

- To mute either the main or application volume, click the speaker icon beneath either slider so that a red no sign appears.

4. Click the Close button twice.

Here's a handy shortcut for quickly adjusting the volume of your default sound device. Click the Volume button (which looks like a little gray speaker) in the notification area on the right side of the taskbar. To adjust the volume, use the slider on the Volume pop-up that appears, or click the Mute Speakers button to turn off sounds temporarily.

Today, many keyboards include volume controls and a mute button to control sounds from your computer. Some even include buttons to play, pause, and stop audio playback. Having these buttons and other controls at your fingertips can be worth a little extra in the price of your keyboard.

Make Settings for Ripping Music

1. If you place a CD/DVD in your disc drive, Windows Media Player will ask if you want to *rip* the music from the disc to your computer. Doing so stores all the tracks on your computer. To control how ripping works, with Windows Media Player open, click the Organize button and choose Options.

2. Click the Rip Music tab to display it.

3. In the Options dialog box (see **Figure** 18-4) you can make the following settings:

Click a library

Figure 18-4

- Click the **Change** button to change the location where ripped music is stored; the default location is your Music folder.

- Click the **File Name** button to choose the information to include in the filenames for music that is ripped to your computer (see **Figure 18-5**).

- Choose the audio format to use by clicking the **Format** drop-down list.

- Many audio files are copyright protected. If you have permission to copy and distribute the music, you may not want to choose the **Copy Protect Music** check box; however, if you're downloading music you paid for and therefore should not give away copies of, you should ethically choose to copy-protect music so that Windows prompts you or others using your computer to download media rights or purchase another copy of the music when you copy it to another location.

- If you don't want to be prompted to rip music from CD/DVDs you insert in your drive, but instead want all music ripped automatically, select the **Rip CD Automatically** check box.

Click the Organize button

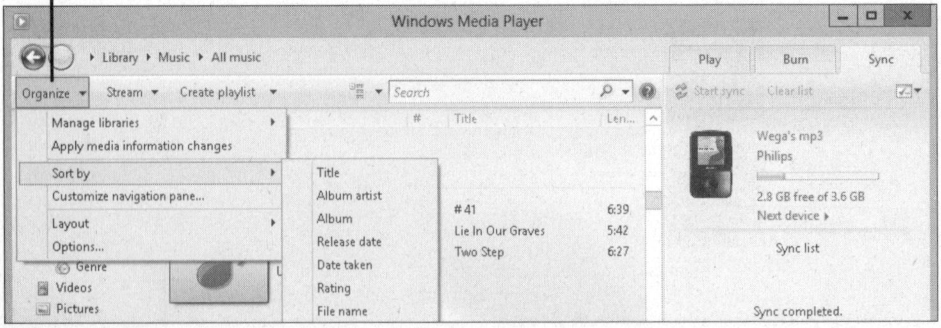

Figure 18-5

- If you want the CD/DVD to eject automatically after ripping is complete, select the **Eject CD after Ripping** check box.

4. When you finish making settings, click the OK button to save them and close the Options dialog box.

 Use the Audio Quality slider to adjust the quality of the ripped music. The smallest size file will save space on your computer by compressing the file, but this causes a loss of audio quality. The Best Quality will provide optimum sound, but these files can be rather large. The choice is yours based on your tastes and your computer's capacity!

Find Music with Windows 8's Integrated Search

1. Windows 8's integrated search feature provides a great way to search for new music. From the Start screen begin to type an artist name or song title.

2. In the search results, click the Music category. Results appear as shown in **Figure 18-6**.

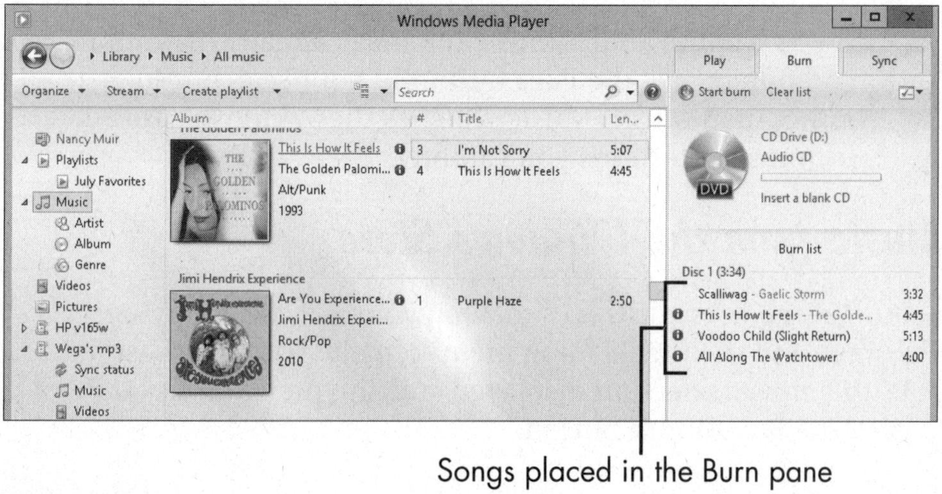

Songs placed in the Burn pane

Figure 18-6

3. Click anywhere in the results, and the scrollbar appears. Click and drag the scrollbar to review music options.

4. Click an item to view more details about tracks and artist, to play it using the Music app player, or to buy it (see **Figure 18-7**).

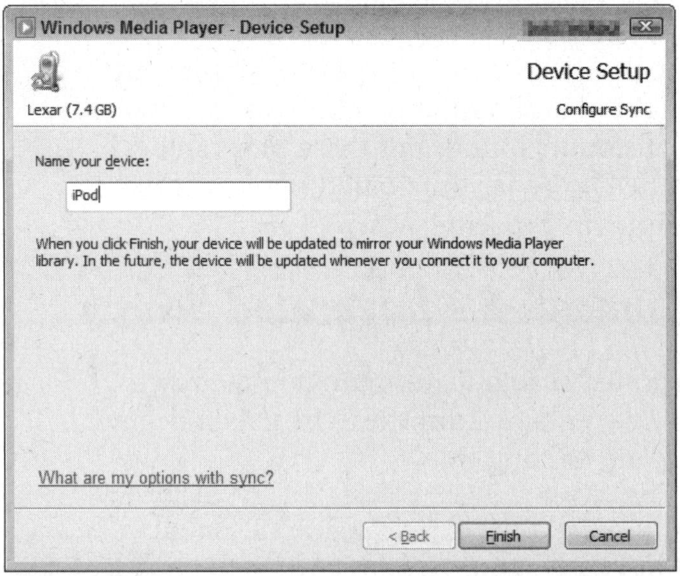

Windows Media Player - Device Setup

Device Setup

Lexar (7.4 GB)   Configure Sync

Name your device:

iPod

When you click Finish, your device will be updated to mirror your Windows Media Player library. In the future, the device will be updated whenever you connect it to your computer.

What are my options with sync?

< Back   Finish   Cancel

Figure 18-7

 If you want to find a music file that's already on your computer, click the Files button in your search results rather than Music. Music searches the Windows Store for music selections you can buy.

Buy Music from the Windows Store

1. Purchasing music involves making your selection, buying points, and then redeeming them to make your purchase. With a music selection displayed (see the previous task) click the Buy Album button.

2. In the screen that appears (see **Figure 18-8**), click the Buy Points button to purchase credit in the Zune store.

3. Click the number of points you want to purchase (see **Figure 18-9**) and then click Next.

4. On the next screen, choose the credit card option you prefer, or click Add a New Credit Card to fill in your credit card information. Click Confirm Purchase.

5. On the following screen shown in **Figure 18-10,** confirm your purchase of Microsoft Points and click Done.

6. On the next screen, click Confirm to finalize the purchase of your music.

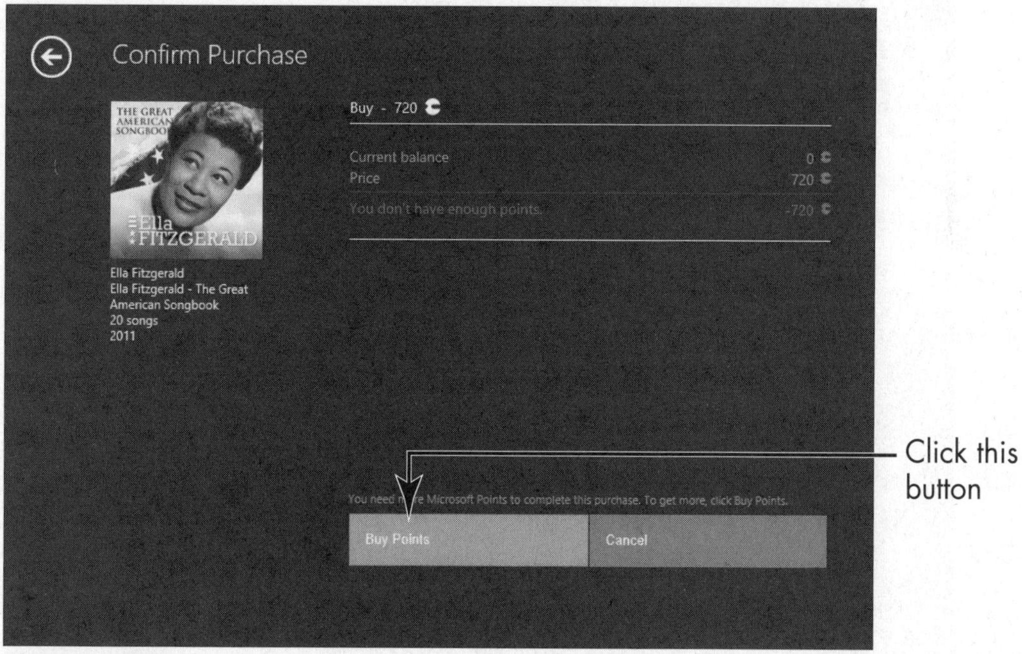

Click this button

Figure 18-8

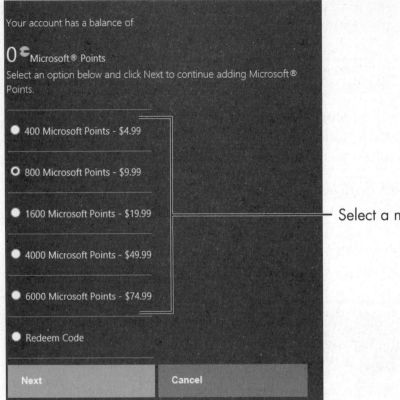

Your account has a balance of
0 Microsoft® Points
Select an option below and click Next to continue adding Microsoft® Points.
400 Microsoft Points - $4.99
800 Microsoft Points - $9.99
1600 Microsoft Points - $19.99
4000 Microsoft Points - $49.99
6000 Microsoft Points - $74.99
Redeem Code
Next
Cancel
Select a number of points

Figure 18-9

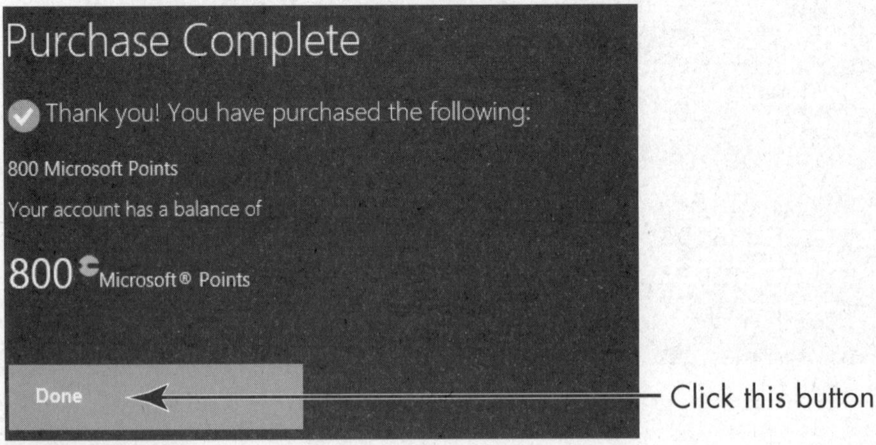

Purchase Complete
Thank you! You have purchased the following:
800 Microsoft Points
Your account has a balance of
800 Microsoft® Points
Done
Click this button

Figure 18-10

Create a Playlist

1. A *playlist* is a saved set of music tracks you can create yourself — like building a personal music album. From the Start screen, begin to type **Windows Media Player** and then click Windows Media Player app in the results.

2. Click a Library in the Navigation pane and then click the Create Playlist button. A new playlist appears in the Navigation pane. Type a name for the playlist, and then click anywhere outside the playlist to save the name.

3. Click a category (for example, Music) to display libraries, and then click a library in the left pane; the library contents appear (see **Figure 18-11**). Click an item and then drag it to the new playlist in the Navigation pane. Repeat this step to locate additional titles to add to the playlist.

4. To play a playlist, click it in the Library pane and then click the Play button at the bottom of the screen.

5. You can organize playlists by clicking the Organize button (see **Figure 18-12**) and then choosing Sort By. In the submenu that appears, sort by features such as title, artist, or release date.

 You can also right-click a playlist in the Library pane and choose Play to play it or choose Delete to delete the list, though the original tracks that were added to the list still exist.

Click a library

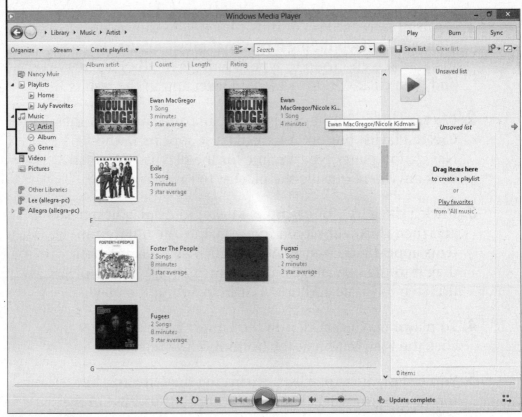

Figure 18-11

Click the Organize button

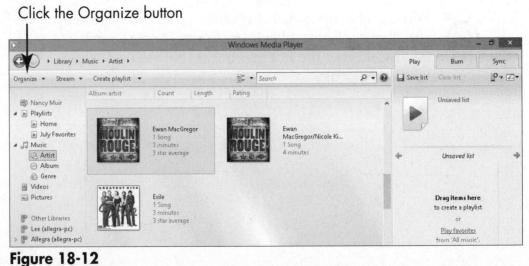

Figure 18-12

Burn Music to a CD/DVD

1. Saving music files to a storage medium such as a CD or DVD is referred to as *burning*. You might burn music to a disc so you can take it to a party or another computer location. Insert a blank CD or DVD suitable for storing audio files in your computer's CD/DVD-RW drive.

2. Open Windows Media Player, click the Burn tab, and then click one or more songs, albums, or playlists in the middle of the screen and drag them to the Burn pane on the right (see **Figure 18-13**).

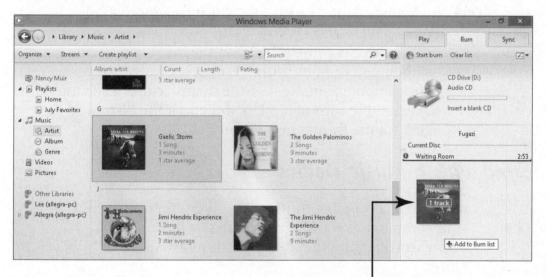

Songs placed in the Burn pane

Figure 18-13

3. Click Start Burn in the right side of the screen. Windows Media Player begins to burn the items to the disc. The Status column for the first song title reads Writing to Disc and changes to Complete when the track is copied.

4. When the burn is complete, your disc is ejected, although you can change this option by clicking the Burn Options button (a small button on the top right of the Burn tab) and choosing Eject Disc After Burning to deselect it.

 If you swap music online through various music-sharing services and then copy them to CD/DVD and pass them around to your friends, always do a virus check on the files before handing them off. Also, be sure you have the legal right to download and swap that music with others.

 Note that optical discs come in different types, including CD-R (readable), CD-RW(read/writable), DVD+, DVD– and DVD+/–. You must be sure your optical drive is compatible with the disc type you're using or you can't burn the disc successfully. Check your computer's manual or the manufacturer's site to see what disc format it takes and check the disc packaging for the format before you buy!

Sync with a Music Device

1. If you have a portable music player, you can sync it to your computer to transfer music files to it. Connect a device to your computer and open Windows Media Player.

2. Click the Sync tab; a Device Setup dialog box appears (see **Figure 18-14**).

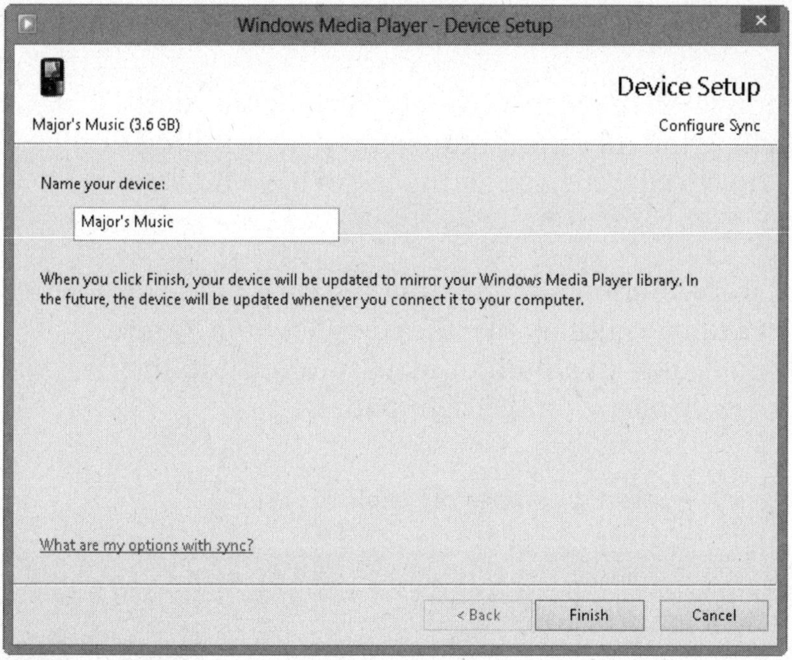

Windows Media Player - Device Setup

Device Setup

Major's Music (3.6 GB)   Configure Sync

Name your device:

Major's Music

When you click Finish, your device will be updated to mirror your Windows Media Player library. In the future, the device will be updated whenever you connect it to your computer.

What are my options with sync?

< Back   Finish   Cancel

Figure 18-14

3. Name the device, and click Finish. The device is now synced with Windows Media Player and will be automatically updated whenever you connect it to your computer.

 To add items to be synced to a device, with the Sync tab displayed, simply drag items to the right pane. If your device is connected, or the next time you connect it, the items are copied onto the device automatically.

 If you want to be sure that the sync is progressing, click the Sync Options button (it's on the far right of the top of the Sync tab and looks like a little box with a check mark in it) and choose View Sync Status.

Play Music with Windows Media Player

1. Open Windows Media Player by right-clicking the Start screen, clicking the All Apps button, and then scrolling to the right and clicking the app in the list of apps that appears.

2. Click the Library button and then double-click Music or Playlists to display a library like the one shown in **Figure 18-15**. Double-click an album or playlist to open it; the song titles are displayed in the right pane.

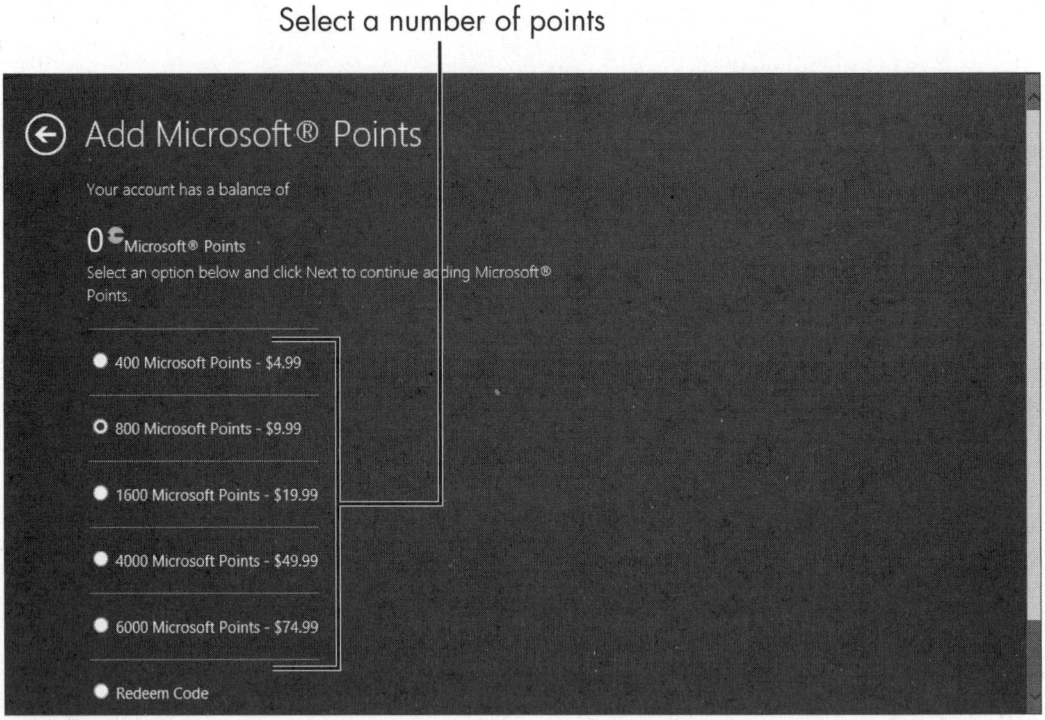

Select a number of points

Figure 18-15

3. Use the buttons on the bottom of the Player window (as shown in **Figure 18-16**) to do the following:

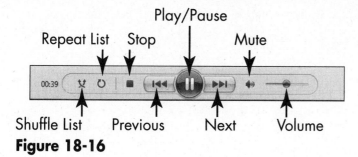

Figure 18-16

- Click a track, and then click the **Play** button to play it. When a song is playing, this button changes to the **Pause** button.

- Click the **Stop** button to stop playback.

- Click the **Next** or **Previous** button to move to the next or previous track in an album or playlist.

- Use the **Mute** and **Volume** controls to pump the sound up or down without having to modify the Windows volume settings.

 Tired of the order in which your tracks play? You can use the List Options button on the Play pane and choose Shuffle List to have Windows Media Player move around the tracks on your album randomly. Click this button again (it sports wavy arrows) to turn the shuffle feature off.

 To jump to another track, rather than using the Next and Previous buttons you can double-click a track in the track list in the Media Player window. This can be much quicker if you want to jump several tracks ahead or behind the currently playing track.

Searching for music with Windows 8.1

Search in Windows 8.1 works a bit differently than in Windows 8. In both versions you type a search term on the Start screen. In Windows 8, you then see a full screen with a list of results on the left and a list of categories, such as music, apps, and maps, in a panel on the right. You can click a result or a category to narrow the results.

In Windows 8.1, you type a search term and then see only a panel on the right with search results listed. When you click a result for a music search (for example, if you type the name of an artist or song) you get web results that will typically include articles, images, shopping choices, news, and more items relevant to that search.

The figure shows the results for the search phrase *The Beatles*.

Going Shopping Online

Chapter
19

*I*f you consider shopping fun, this chapter is for you. Shopping online offers the convenience of looking for what you need 24/7, as well as having items delivered right to your door. You can comparison shop to your heart's delight, finding the best items at the best prices. You can also choose between a retail shopping experience and an online auction, which is kind of like browsing a big, virtual flea market.

Of course, you have to make sure you're doing business with a reputable company that has policies that protect consumers. Online shopping also provides the opportunity to read reviews by other consumers to make sure that what you can't see in person is what you want to get.

When you find what you want, you can also find discount coupons to save you money. Armed with your coupons, you can load products into your online shopping cart, arrange for payment, and choose your shipping method. If your purchase doesn't pan out, you should also understand your return options.

In this chapter, you discover the ins and outs of becoming a very savvy online shopper.

Get ready to . . .

➠ Search for Items 318

➠ Find Price Comparisons 319

➠ Verify If a Store is Trustworthy 320

➠ Read Customer Reviews 321

➠ Buy through Auction Sites ... 322

➠ Find Coupons 323

➠ Manage a Shopping Cart ... 324

➠ Use Various Payment Methods 326

➠ Understand Shipping Options 327

Search for Items

There are so many products online and so many places where you can buy them that the process can be a bit overwhelming. Luckily you have several options for finding what you need when shopping online:

➡ Use search engines. If you type a word or phrase on the Start screen and then click Internet Explorer, you're taken online with results from the Bing search engine (see **Figure 19-1**). You can also open a browser such as Internet Explorer and enter a search term.

 When you view search results, be aware that clicking any kind of sponsored results or ads could be a bit risky, as your activities or identity might be tracked. If you're interested in a sponsored site, simply type the address in the browser address bar.

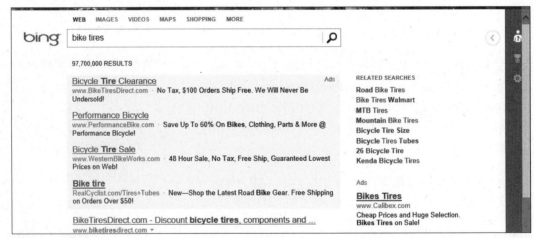

Figure 19-1

➡ Browse retail sites. You can go to a site such as Amazon.com or Zappos.com and use the search feature at that retail site to search for products.

➡ Tap into social sites. Some social sites such as Facebook allow you to include your friends in your search. By letting your friends know what you're looking for, you can get recommendations of great online stores and wonderful items you might want to buy.

Compare Prices

One of the great features of shopping online is the ability to comparison shop. Not only can you compare the price of an item by visiting two or three online stores without having to drive around town; you can also use comparison tools on sites such as `www.pricegrabber.com`, `www.nextag.com`, `www.bizrate.com`, `www.pricewatch.com`, and `http://price.com` that search the Internet for the best prices among hundreds of stores.

Sites such as Nextag.com, shown in **Figure 19-2**, can provide lots of information, such as whether items are in stock at various vendors, customer ratings, any special offers such as free shipping or discounts, and related items. You can go to a particular store using handy links, such as the See Store button at Nextag.com.

Figure 19-2

Verify If a Store is Trustworthy

Before you buy anything on a site, it's a good idea to assess if that store is trustworthy. There are several ways to do this:

➡️ Check out the free Better Business Bureau (`www.bbb.org`) or Online Business Bureau (`www.onlinebusinessbureau.com`), or visit paid sites such as Angie's List (`www.angieslist.com`), shown in **Figure 19-3**, for complaints against or rankings of online stores.

➡️ Read customer reviews on the store's own site; some product reviews include comments about the service and ethical behavior of the business itself.

➡️ When you purchase an item, be sure that the prefix *https* shows in your browser's address field. The *s* in *https* ensures that the store is using technology that protects your payment information such as credit card numbers from prying eyes.

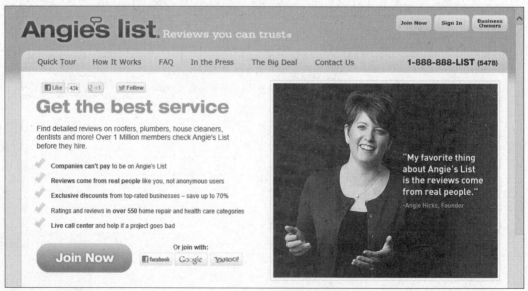

Figure 19-3

➡ Do business with a store you know from the bricks-and-mortar world. If you've been a customer of a store such as Sears or Macy's in the offline world, expect to find similar efficiency, ethics, and customer service in its online store.

➡ Locate and read privacy policies. A site may give you a good deal, but may be data mining your private information and selling it to other companies. *Data mining* is a practice whereby a website takes many pieces of information about you, from your address, to your shopping habits, health conditions, or clothing size and sells that information to others who may or may not be trustworthy. Check privacy policies to make sure your information isn't sold or shared with others.

If you check a free online organization such as BBB. com for complaints or reviews, remember that businesses pay to be members of such organizations. Paid services such as Angie's List may cost you, but businesses have no control over how these sites rank them.

Read Customer Reviews

Customer reviews and expert rankings are good sources of information about the quality of products or services that you buy online. For example, on a retail site such as Amazon.com, shown in **Figure 19-4,** customers can post their ratings of products and a description of their experience with them. By reading these reviews, you can try to find customers who have similar taste to yours and weigh their reviews more heavily.

You can also find reviews from professional reviewers on sites such as CNET (www.cnet.com) for electronics and Consumer Reports (www. consumerreports.org) for reviews on a variety of products. These review sites may or may not get payments in the form of advertising from businesses, so check their credentials and credibility.

Figure 19-4

Buy through Auction Sites

Auction sites such as www.ebay.com or http://ebid.net allow you to name your price on products. The bidding process usually involves you becoming a member and providing information for a payment method such as a credit card or PayPal account. Remember that on an auction site you're dealing with thousands of sellers, from individuals to small- or medium-size companies, and you have to be careful about checking the trustworthiness of a seller before completing a transaction.

Auction sites, such as eBay (see **Figure 19-5**), have placed different consumer protection regulations on their sites, so it's worth reviewing their policies. In addition, many use a system whereby your payment is held until you verify that you received the merchandise and it's in the condition described in the seller listing.

Figure 19-5

 For more advice about buying or selling items using an auction site, check out *eBay For Dummies*, by Marsha Collier.

Find Coupons

Many of us have come to depend on paper coupons to get discounts at retail stores. Online, you can look for coupons that give you everything from free shipping to a percentage off your purchase price or a free gift.

You can visit coupon sites to search for discounts from online retailers and then enter the coupon codes into a field typically labeled *Coupon* or *Discount Code* when you check out (see the next task for more about checking out). Note that the effectiveness of these coupon codes varies, and most sites rank how often each coupon works.

Start by visiting some of these popular sites to get a sampling of discounts:

➡ RetailMeNot

➡ Google's Offers

➡ Groupon.com (see **Figure 19-6**)

➡ FatWallet.com

Figure 19-6

Manage a Shopping Cart

When you shop at an online site, you typically use a mechanism called a *shopping cart*. Though it comes with different names on different sites, the idea is that you place items in this holding area. When you're ready to check out, you open your shopping cart and enter payment and shipping information. You can see an example of a shopping cart on Amazon.com in **Figure 19-7**.

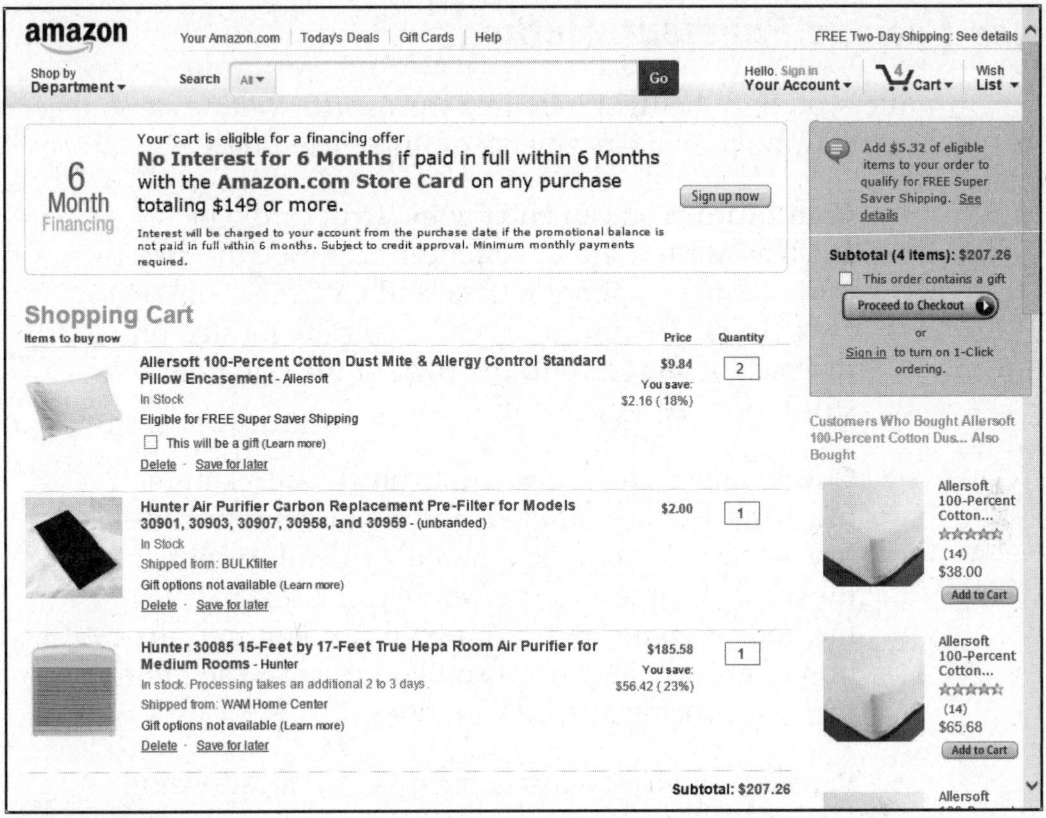

Figure 19-7

During the checkout process, you can also typically change your order, adding or deleting items, changing sizes or colors, and supplying both a billing and a shipping address, in case these differ. This is also the point at which you can enter coupon and discount codes (see the previous section).

You often have the option of saving payment information for future use on a retail site. This can be very convenient, and if you trust the site, probably poses no safety concerns. However, keep in mind that others who use your computer could use this saved payment information to make a purchase, so consider carefully whether you want to save such information.

Use Various Payment Methods

After you find the right item in a trustworthy online store, there are several ways to make payments online, including

➡ **Credit card:** You can enter your credit card type (such as MasterCard or American Express), the credit card number, expiration date, and CVC, CSC or CVV (a credit card verification) code typically located on the back of your card to the right of the signature strip) to make a payment.

➡ **Check:** Many sites allow you to enter a check number, bank account number, and routing number to pay by virtual check. Be especially careful to verify the trustworthiness of site before using this payment method, as giving away your bank account information offers no safety net if somebody steals the information, as using a credit card does.

➡ **Payment services:** Services such as PayPal, shown in **Figure 19-8,** allow you to pay by various accounts such as credit cards, debit cards, or a check through a bank account. The huge benefit to these services is that the seller never sees your payment information.

 Some sites ask you to create an account or use a guest login. If you think you'll use the account often, consider creating an account. If you'll use it only occasionally, it might be better to use a guest account to avoid providing some payment and personal information that will be stored or even shared with other sites.

Figure 19-8

Understand Shipping Options

When you purchase items online, consider how they'll be shipped to you. The two key considerations here, as with many things in life, are time and money.

You can often find free or low-cost shipping offered by online retail sites. This free shipping may be based on a minimum purchase amount, but whatever the criteria, it's worth looking for a site that ships items for free. Also, sites may or may not hit you with sales tax, depending on their locations and yours.

Most online retailers ship items to arrive in three to five business days. If time is a factor and you want expedited shipping, you'll pay for it. Remember that the expedited shipping clock may not start ticking immediately; it may take a few days to process your order before it ships. Also, some items that are out of stock, or back ordered, may take weeks to ship, so your expedited shipping costs might be wasted. Read your order confirmation carefully to see if estimated shipping dates make expedited shipping worthwhile.

After you place an order most online sites offer a way to track its progress and estimated arrival date, sometimes via the carrier's system such as FedEx or UPS.

 Amazon Prime is an interesting fee-based shipping alternative offered by Amazon. You pay $79 per year for Amazon Prime, but for that fee you get free two-day shipping on all Prime-eligible items. Not every item on this giant retailer's site is eligible, but enough are that you'll probably pay for the yearly fee with just a few free, fast shipments. In addition, Amazon Prime offers access to thousands of free e-books and instant- streaming videos with the membership.

 Remember that if you're not satisfied with a product you order online, most sites don't cover return shipping costs. If a piece of clothing doesn't fit or a product doesn't match its description, you may be out $10 or more in return shipping. If an item is defective, however, most reputable sites will pay for return shipping. You can check to see if the store you ordered from has brick-and-mortar stores; sometimes the local version of the store accepts returns of goods ordered online.

Windows 8.1: Search for free stuff

In Windows 8.1, when you type a word or phrase from the Start screen and press Enter, you're taken to integrated search results that could include images, articles, news stories, and media. For example, if you type *Doris Day*, Internet Explorer displays items such as photos, her official website, a Wikipedia article, and links to movies, TV shows, and albums. Follow these and you end up in Xbox Music or Xbox Video where you can sometimes play the music or videos for free and in other cases purchase them.

Part V
Windows Toolkit

The 5th Wave   By Rich Tennant

"A centralized security management system
sounds fine, but then what would we do
with all the dogs?"

Working with Networks

A computer network allows you to share information and devices among computers.

You can connect your computer to other computers by setting up a wired or wireless network, for example. Devices connected to a single Homegroup on a network can share hardware such as a printer, an Internet connection, and more.

In addition to a computer network, you can use Bluetooth technology to connect to devices at a short range. For example, you might use your computer's built-in Bluetooth capability to connect to a Bluetooth mouse that sits next to it on your work surface.

You can also use your cellphone's 3G or 4G network to go online through a process called *tethering*.

In this chapter, you'll explore several options for getting connected to other devices and sharing information.

Chapter 20

Get ready to . . .

➡ Join a Homegroup 332

➡ Make a Connection to a Network 333

➡ Specify What to Share over a Network 334

➡ Set Up a Wireless Network 336

➡ Make Your Computer Discoverable to Bluetooth ... 338

➡ Connect to Bluetooth Devices 339

➡ Go Online Using Your Cellular Network.............. 340

Join a Homegroup

1. When you set up a network, you have to arrange to include each computer on the network in a Homegroup so that they can connect. If somebody has set up a Homegroup on another computer, you can join that network with a few steps. Start by pressing Win+I.

2. Click Change PC Settings.

3. Click HomeGroup, and then enter a Homegroup password on the screen that appears (see **Figure 20-1**).

4. Click Join to make your computer part of that Homegroup.

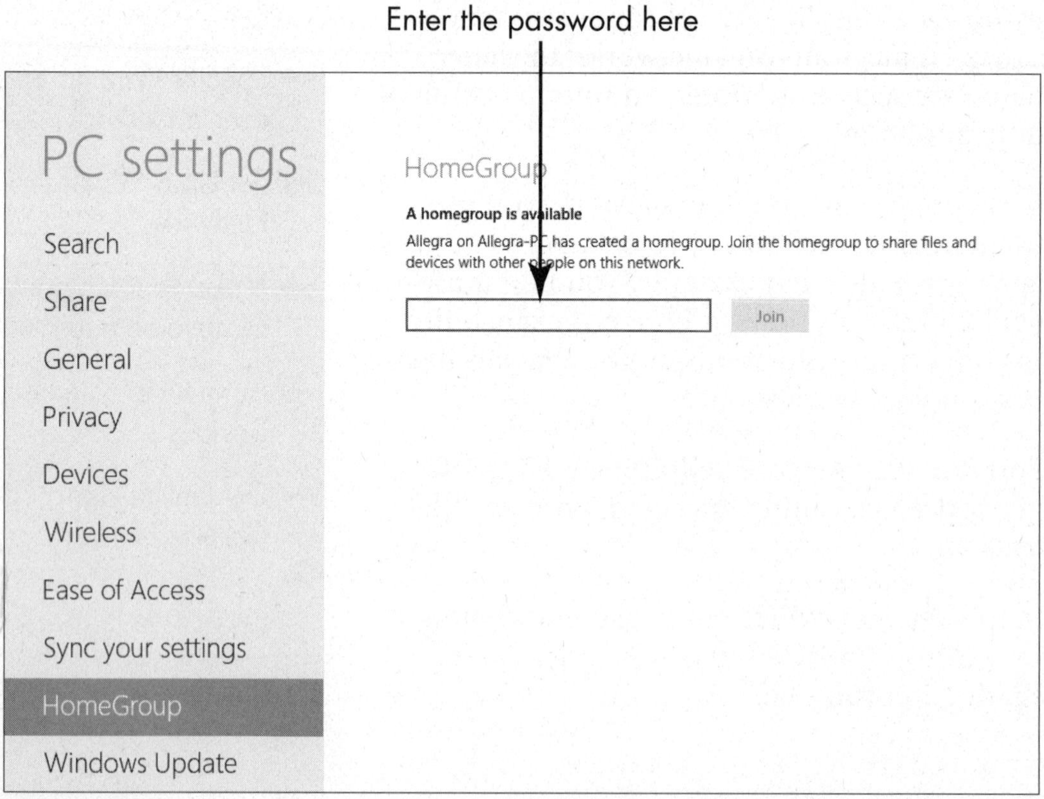

Enter the password here

PC settings

Search

Share

General

Privacy

Devices

Wireless

Ease of Access

Sync your settings

HomeGroup

Windows Update

HomeGroup

A homegroup is available

Allegra on Allegra-PC has created a homegroup. Join the homegroup to share files and devices with other people on this network.

Join

Figure 20-1

To locate the password for the Homegroup, you need to sign in as a user with administrator status. Then, open the Control Panel, click Network and

Internet⇨Homegroup, and then click View or Print the Homegroup Password. Once you've joined the Homegroup, the password is displayed in the Homegroup settings of the PC Settings screen.

Make a Connection to a Network

1. If you take a computing device with you around town or on the road, you'll find that you often need to connect to networks in locations such as airports, coffee shops, or hotels. These public network connections are called *hotspots*. When you're in range of a hotspot, connect to it by first pressing Win+I.

2. Click the Network shortcut shown in **Figure 20-2**.

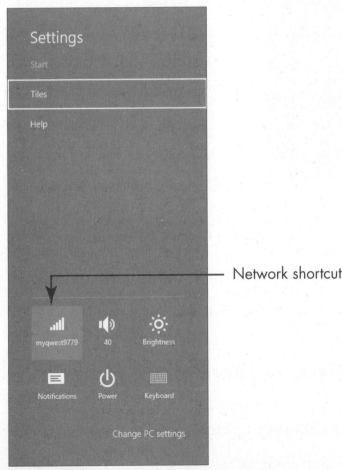

Network shortcut

Figure 20-2

3. Click a network name, as shown in Figure **20-3**.

4. If you want your computer to connect to this network when you come in range of it, you can click the Connect Automatically check box.

5. Click Connect.

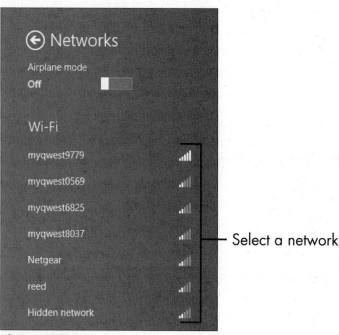

— Select a network

Figure 20-3

 In many cases, you're asked to enter a password for a network after you click Connect in Step 5. You have to ask somebody for this password; it may be pub- licly posted — for example, in a coffee shop — or you may have to ask for the password when you check into a hotel.

Specify What You Want to Share over a Network

1. Many people use networks to share content such as word- processing documents or pictures, or even a printer connection. When you're using a public network, you might not want to share your valuable data with others, so you may want to modify your sharing settings. Be sure you are part of the Homegroup (see the previous "Join a Homegroup" task) and then press Win+I.

2. Click Change PC Settings.

3. Click HomeGroup, and then click the On/Off button for any of the content or devices in the list (see **Figure 20-4**).

4. In the Media Devices section, click the On/Off button to share content with devices other than your computer, such as a game console.

 If you decide you don't want to participate in the network anymore, you can leave it by scrolling down in the window shown in Figure 20-4 and clicking the Leave button.

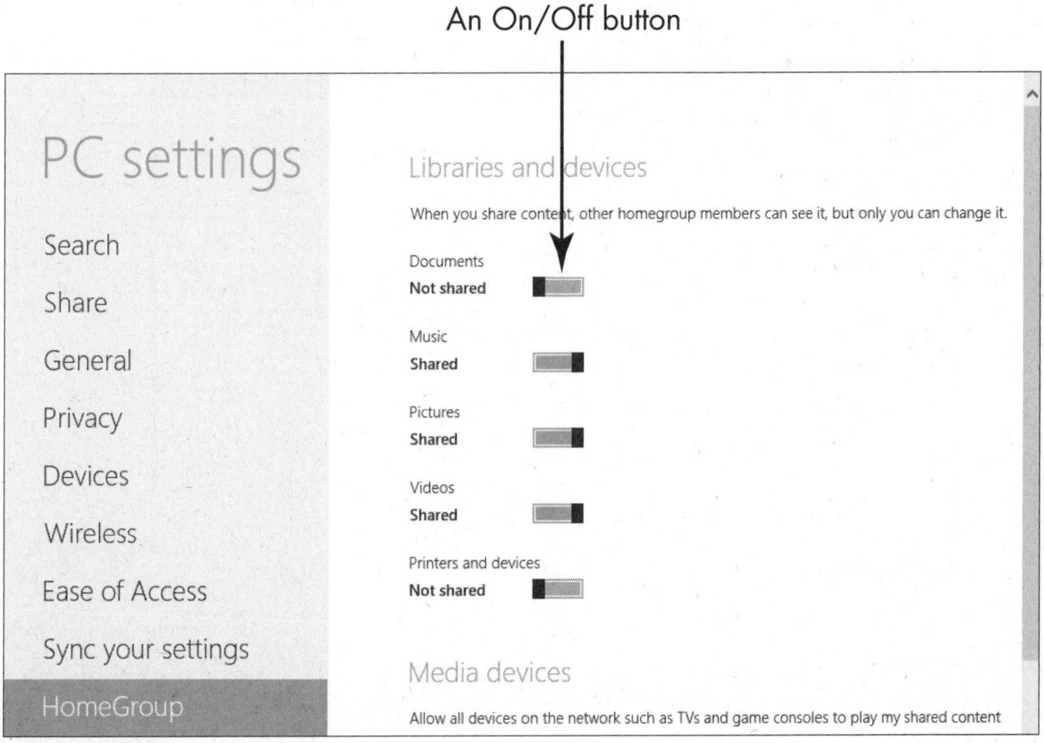

An On/Off button

PC settings

Search

Share

General

Privacy

Devices

Wireless

Ease of Access

Sync your settings

HomeGroup

Libraries and devices

When you share content, other homegroup members can see it, but only you can change it.

Documents
Not shared

Music
Shared

Pictures
Shared

Videos
Shared

Printers and devices
Not shared

Media devices

Allow all devices on the network such as TVs and game consoles to play my shared content

Figure 20-4

Set Up a Wireless Network

1. If you have several computers in your home, you'll find you can save yourself steps by connecting them to each other through a wireless network. No more will you have to walk upstairs to print from a single computer; all your computers on every floor and in every room can share that printer, as well as an Internet connection and documents. Start by connecting a router or other access point hardware to your computer.

2. Start to type **Control Panel** on the Start screen.

3. In the Search results that appear, click the Control Panel app.

4. Click Network and Internet in the Control Panel (see **Figure 20-5**).

Click this option

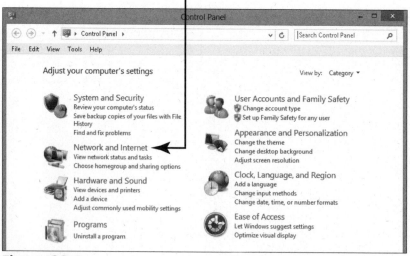

Figure 20-5

5. Click Network and Sharing Center, and then click Set Up a New Connection or Network (see **Figure 20-6**).

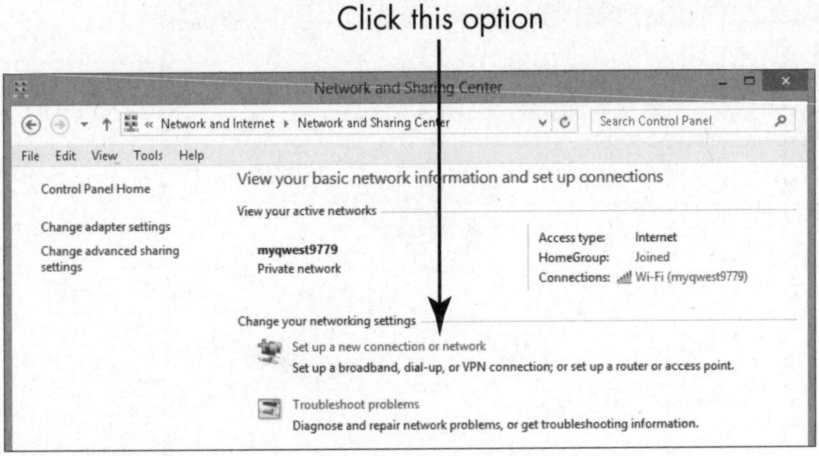

Click this option

Figure 20-6

6. Click Set Up a New Network and then click Next.

7. Click the router or access point to set up and click Next.

8. In the window shown in **Figure 20-7,** enter the PIN number located on the router label and then click Next.

9. Enter a network name and click Next. Windows completes your network setup. Click the Close button to close the window.

You can also share documents using a service such as Microsoft's SkyDrive. You can upload and share files using this service, and a small amount of online storage is free. You can also then access this content from any computer, connected to your network or not. See Chapter 15 for more about SkyDrive.

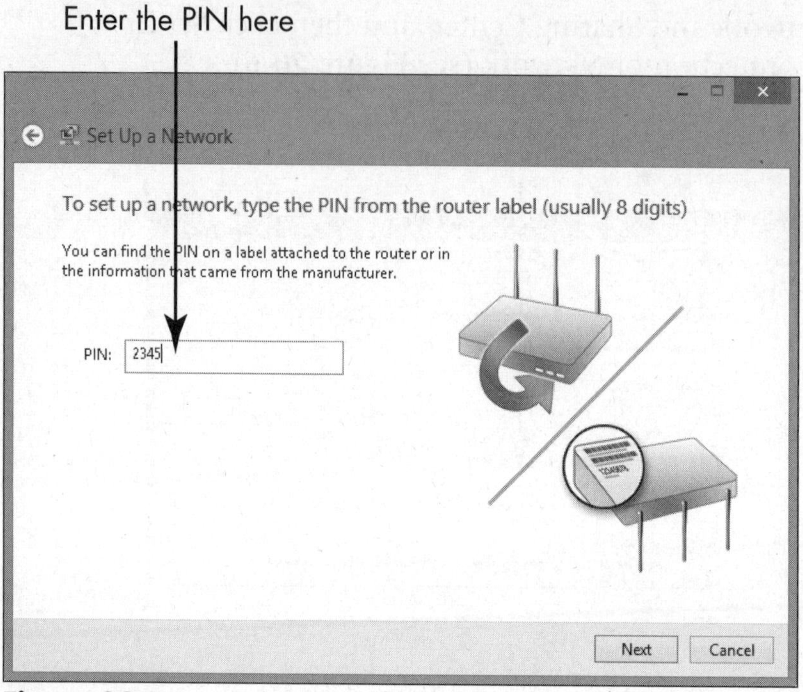

Enter the PIN here

Figure 20-7

Make Your Computer Discoverable to Bluetooth

1. Making a Bluetooth connection involves ensuring that both devices are Bluetooth compatible (check your device specs for this) and making both devices discoverable. Begin typing **Control Panel**.

2. Click the Control Panel app in the Search results.

3. Type the word **Bluetooth** in the Search box.

4. Click Change Bluetooth Settings.

5. Select the Allow Bluetooth Devices to Find This Computer check box (see **Figure 20-8**) and then click OK.

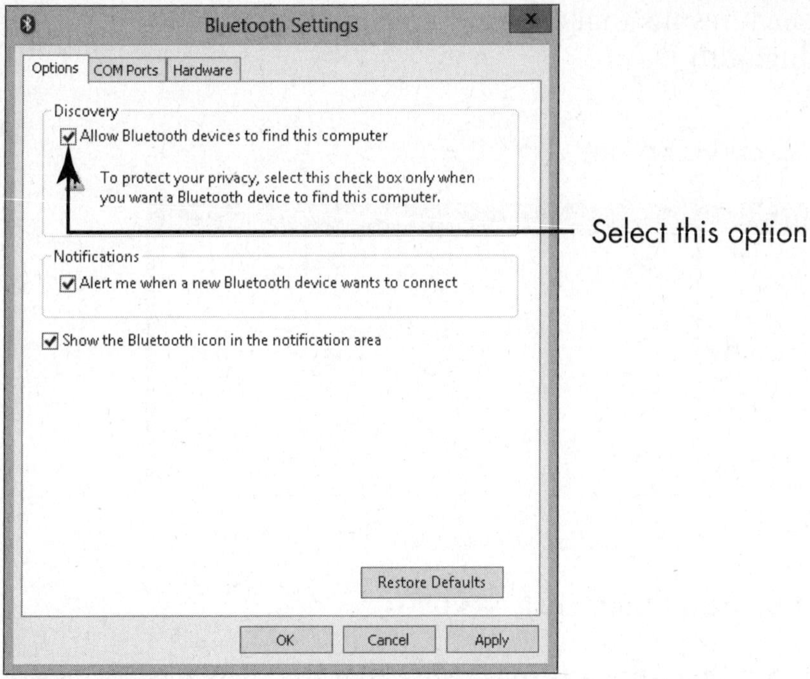

Figure 20-8

 If you're travelling out of your home with your tablet or laptop, set your device to be undiscoverable. That step will protect your computer's contents or settings from people who might try to connect to your computer and steal your data via a Bluetooth connection. Another option is to leave your computer discoverable but select the Alert Me When a New Bluetooth Device Wants to Connect check box in the Bluetooth Settings dialog box.

Connect to Bluetooth Devices

1. After you make your computer discoverable, you can connect to another Bluetooth device that is turned on. Begin by displaying the Control Panel.

2. Type **Bluetooth** in the Search box.

3. In the search results that appear (see **Figure 20-9**), click Add a Bluetooth Device.

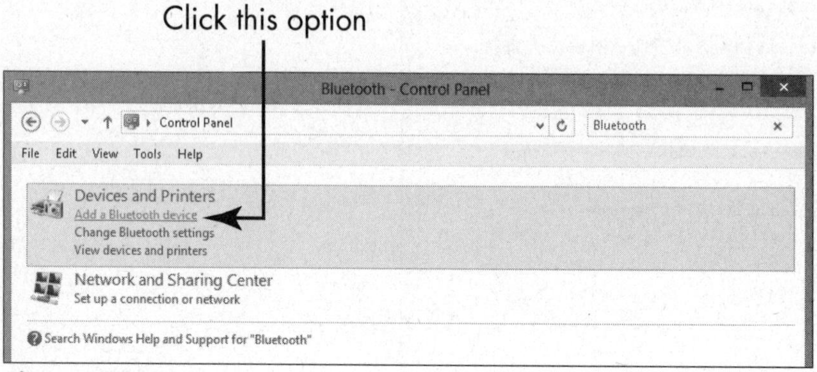

Click this option

Figure 20-9

4. Click a device and then click Next.

5. In the screen that appears, make sure that the displayed passcode on your computer and Bluetooth device match, and click Yes.

6. Click Close.

 Bluetooth devices are improving, but you may find that connections are spotty. If a Bluetooth device such as a headset isn't dependable, consider having a USB or wireless version of the device available as a backup.

Go Online Using Your Cellular Network

1. It's possible to use a smartphone's 3G or 4G connection to connect to the Internet. Usually you have to pay your phone service provider a monthly fee for this service, called *tethering* or *personal hotspot*. In addition, your computer has to be Wi-Fi capable. Start by turning on the hotspot feature on your phone (typically this is found in Network settings).

2. On your computer, press Win+I, and then click the Network setting.

3. Click your phone's Wi-Fi connection, like the one shown in **Figure 20-10**.

Click your phone's connection

Figure 20-10

4. Click Connect and Enter the Security Key.

5. Click Next, and click an option to turn on sharing or leave sharing off.

 Be aware of the drain on your phone's battery when tethering. Connect your phone to a power source when tethering, if possible, and turn off hotspot when you're not using it.

 Some users who switch from Windows 8 to Windows 8.1 have reported problems with network connectivity. In most cases, updating your network card will solve the problem. You can open Windows Update (begin typing Control Panel from the Start screen, click System and Security, and then click Windows Update) and then click Check for Updates and look for any network card updates. Another method is to go to Device Manager under Hardware and Sound in the Control Panel, right-click a network adapter, and then click Update Driver Software (see **Figure 20-11**).

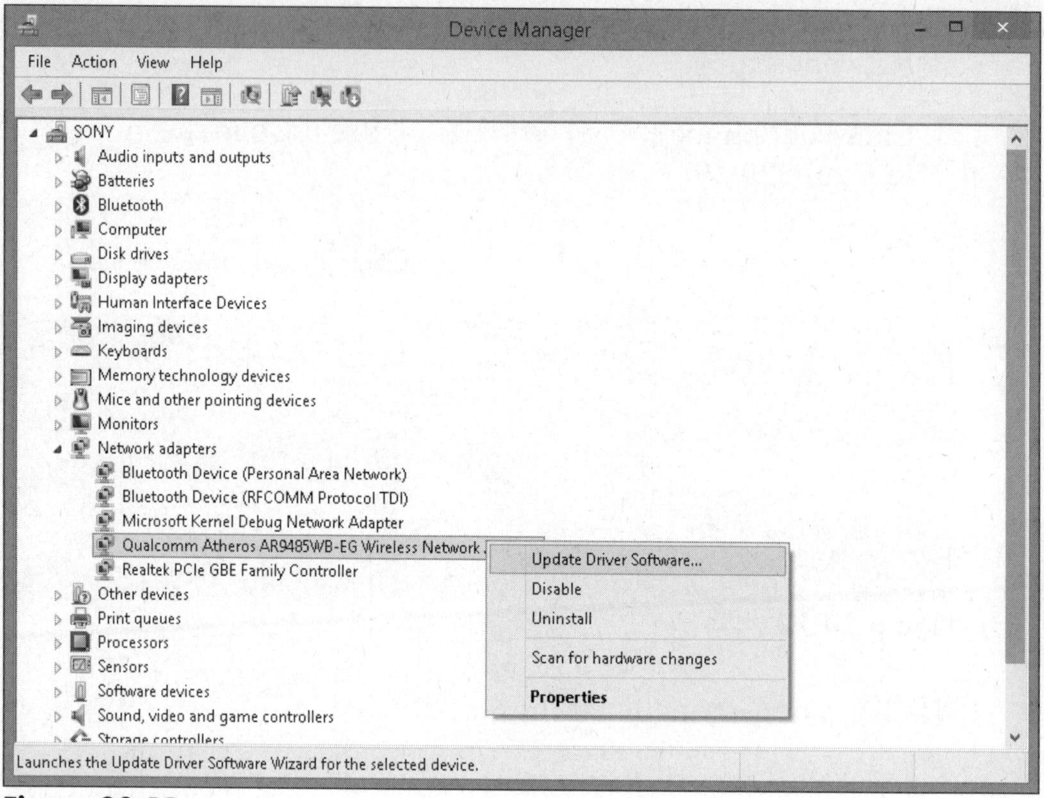
Device Manager
File
Action
View
Help
SONY
Audio inputs and outputs
Batteries
Bluetooth
Computer
Disk drives
Display adapters
Human Interface Devices
Imaging devices
Keyboards
Memory technology devices
Mice and other pointing devices
Monitors
Network adapters
Bluetooth Device (Personal Area Network)
Bluetooth Device (RFCOMM Protocol TDI)
Microsoft Kernel Debug Network Adapter
Qualcomm Atheros AR9485WB-EG Wireless Network
Realtek PCIe GBE Family Controller
Other devices
Print queues
Processors
Sensors
Software devices
Sound, video and game controllers
Update Driver Software...
Disable
Uninstall
Scan for hardware changes
Properties
Launches the Update Driver Software Wizard for the selected device.

Figure 20-11

Protecting Windows

Chapter

21

*Y*our computer contains software and files that can be damaged in several different ways. One major source of damage is from malicious attacks that are delivered via the Internet. Some people create damaging programs called *viruses* specifically designed to get into your computer's hard drive and destroy or scramble data. Companies might download *adware* on your computer, which causes pop-up ads to appear, slowing down your computer's performance. Spyware is another form of malicious software that you might download by clicking a link or opening a file attachment; *spyware* sits on your computer and tracks your activities, whether for use by a legitimate company in selling products to you or by a criminal element to steal your identity.

Microsoft provides security features within Windows 8 that help to keep your computer and information safe, whether you're at home or travelling with a laptop computer.

In this chapter, I introduce you to the major concepts of computer security and cover Windows 8 security features that allow you to do the following:

Get ready to . . .

➡ Understand Computer Security 344

➡ Understand Windows Update Options 345

➡ Run Windows Update 347

➡ Set Up Trusted and Restricted Websites 348

➡ Enable Windows Firewall ... 351

➡ Change Your Password 353

➡ Allow Firewall Exceptions ... 355

➟ Run periodic updates to Windows, which install security solutions and patches (essentially, *patches* fix problems) to the software.

➟ Enable a *firewall*, which is a security feature that keeps your computer safe from outsiders and helps you avoid several kinds of attacks on your data.

➟ Change the password used to protect your computer from others.

➟ Protect yourself against spyware.

Understand Computer Security

Every day you carry around a wallet full of cash and credit cards, and you take certain measures to protect its contents. Your computer also contains valuable items in the form of data, and it's just as important that you protect it from thieves and damage. Your computer comes with an operating system (such as Microsoft Windows) preinstalled, and that operating system has security features to protect your valuable data. Sometimes the operating system has flaws or new threats emerge, and you need to get an update to keep your computer secure.

In addition, as you use your computer you're exposing it to dangerous conditions and situations that you have to guard against. Threats to your computer security can come from a file you copy from a disc you insert into your computer, but most of the time the danger is from a program that you downloaded from the Internet. These downloads can happen when you click a link, open an attachment in an e-mail, or download a piece of software without realizing that the malware is attached to it.

You can use Windows security tools such as Windows Defender, or third-party antivirus or antispyware programs (see **Figure 21-1**) to protect your computer from dangerous computer programs collectively known as *malware*. See Chapter 13 for more detail about threats and protections from malware.

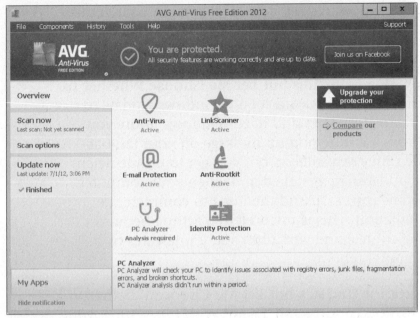

Figure 21-1

Understand Windows Update Options

When a new operating system such as Windows 8 is released, it has been thoroughly tested; however, when the product is in general use, the manufacturer begins to find a few problems or security gaps that it couldn't anticipate. For that reason, companies such as Microsoft release updates to their software, both to fix those problems and deal with new threats to computers that appear after the software release.

Windows Update is a tool you can use to make sure your computer has the most up-to-date security measures in place. You can set Windows Update to work in a few different ways from the Control Panel by choosing System and Security⇨Windows Update⇨Change Settings. In the resulting dialog box (see **Figure 21-2**), click the Important Updates drop-down list and you find these settings:

⇒ **Install Updates Automatically:** With this setting, Windows Update starts at a time of day you specify, but your computer must be on for it to work. If you've turned off your computer, the automatic

update will start when you next turn on your computer, and it might shut down your computer in the
middle of your work to complete the installation.

➡ **Download Updates but Let Me Choose Whether to
Install Them:** You can set up Windows Update to
download updates and have Windows notify you
(through a little pop-up message on your taskbar)
when they're available, but you get to decide when
the updates are installed and when your computer
reboots (turns off and then on) to complete the
installation. This is my preferred setting because I
have control and won't be caught unawares by a
computer reboot.

➡ **Check for Updates but Let Me Choose Whether to
Download and Install Them:** With this setting, you
neither download nor install updates until you say
so, but Windows notifies you that new updates are
available.

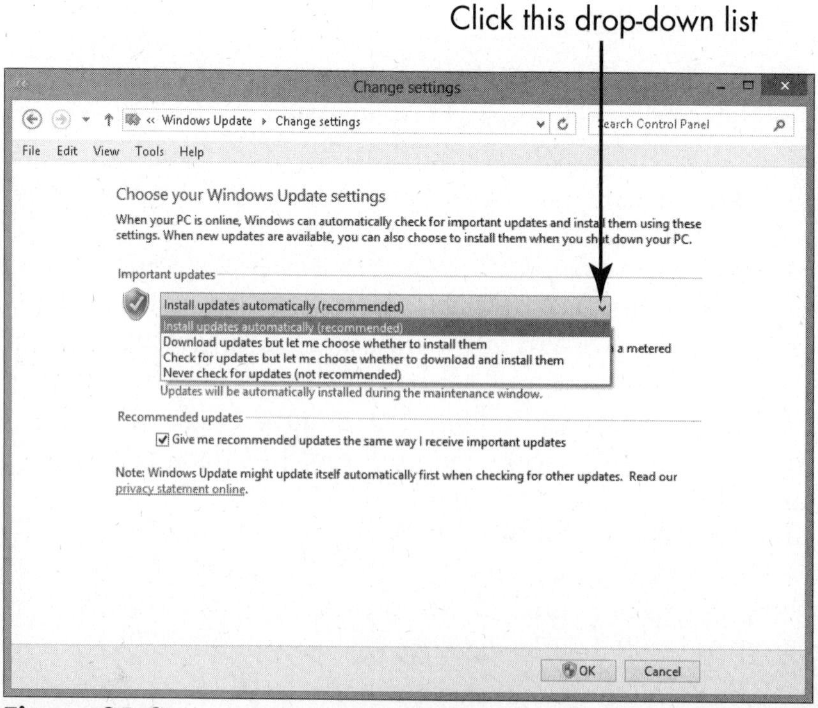

Click this drop-down list

Figure 21-2

➟ **Never Check for Updates:** You can stop Windows from checking for updates and check for them yourself, manually (see the following task). This puts your computer at a bit more risk, but it's useful for you to know how to perform a manual update. For instance, you might discover that you can't proceed with a certain task (such printing a document or using French in your correspondence) until you run a specific update.

Run Windows Update

1. Press Win+I and click Change PC Settings. In the PC Settings window, click Windows Update.

2. In the resulting window, as shown in **Figure 21-3,** click the Check for Updates Now link to see all updates.

Click this link

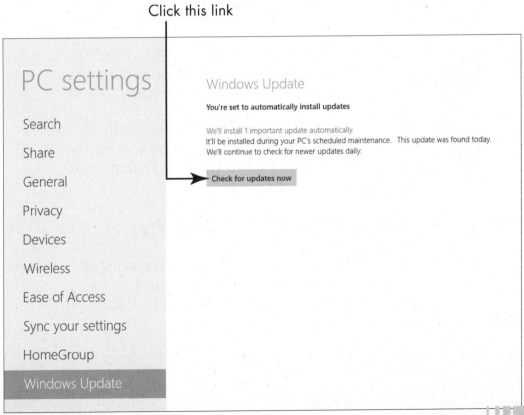

PC settings

Search

Share

General

Privacy

Devices

Wireless

Ease of Access

Sync your settings

HomeGroup

Windows Update

Windows Update

You're set to automatically install updates

We'll install 1 important update automatically.
It'll be installed during your PC's scheduled maintenance. This update was found today.
We'll continue to check for newer updates daily.

Check for updates now

Figure 21-3

3. In the following window, which shows the available updates (see **Figure 21-4**), click to select available critical or optional updates that you want to install. Then click the Install button.

> **1 important update**
>
> **Visual Studio 2008**
>
>   Security Update for Microsoft Visual C++ 2008 Service Pack 1 Redis...
>
> Choose important updates to install, or install optional updates.
>
>   Install

Figure 21-4

4. A window appears, showing the progress of your installation. When the installation is complete, you might get a message telling you that it's a good idea to restart your computer to complete the installation. Click Restart Now.

 If you keep the Windows Update to Never Check for Updates setting selected, it's very important that you perform a manual update on a regular basis.

 Running Windows Update either automatically or manually on a regular basis ensures that you get the latest security updates to the operating system, and it's a good idea to stay current.

Set Up Trusted and Restricted Websites

1. You can set up Internet Explorer to recognize websites you trust and those you don't want IE to take you to. Click the Internet Explorer icon in the desktop taskbar to start your browser.

2. Choose Tools⇨Internet Options.

3. In the Internet Options dialog box (see **Figure 21-5**), click the Security tab.

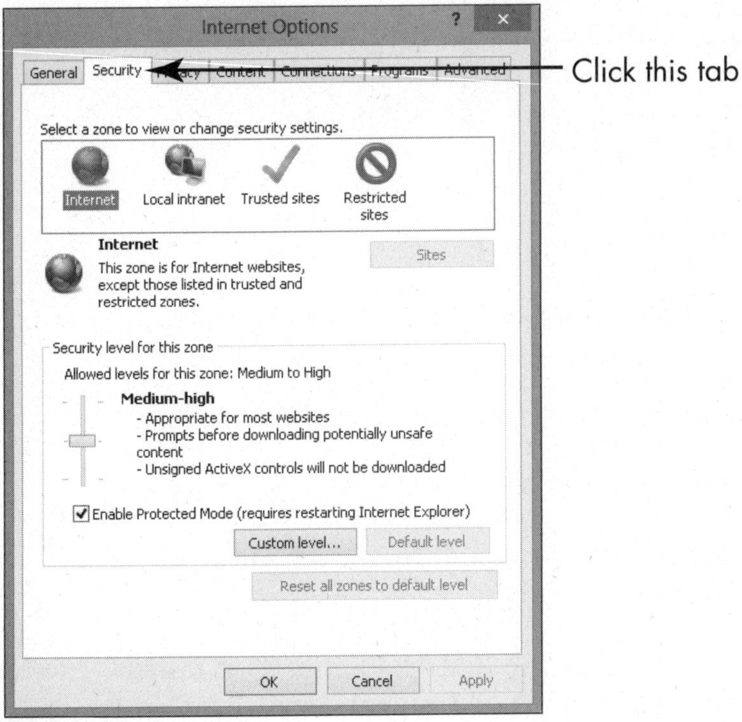

Figure 21-5

4. Click the Trusted Sites icon and then click the Sites button.

5. In the resulting Trusted Sites dialog box, enter a URL in the Add This Web Site to the Zone text box for a website you want to allow your computer to access. If you want any locations for a particular company, such as Microsoft, to be allowed, you can use a wild card in the form of an asterisk, as shown in **Figure 21-6**.

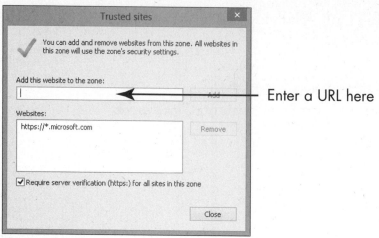

Enter a URL here

Figure 21-6

6. Click Add to add the site to the list of websites.

7. Repeat Steps 3–6 to add more sites.

8. When you're done, click Close and then click OK to close the Internet Options dialog box.

9. Repeat Steps 1–8, clicking the Restricted Sites icon rather than Trusted Sites (in Step 4) to designate sites that you don't want your computer to access.

 If the Require Server Verification (https:) for All Sites in This Zone check box is selected in the Trusted Sites dialog box, any trusted site you add must use the *https* prefix, which indicates that the site has a secure connection that can protect you during online payment transactions.

 You can establish a Privacy setting on the Privacy tab of the Internet Options dialog box to control which sites are allowed to download *cookies* to your computer. *Cookies* are tiny files that a site uses to track your online activity and recognize you when you return to the source site. *Trusted sites* are sites that you allow to download cookies to your computer even though the privacy setting you've made might not allow any other sites to do so. *Restricted sites*, on the other hand, can never download cookies to your computer, no matter what your privacy setting is. See Chapter 13 for more information about the options on the Privacy tab.

Enable Windows Firewall

1. A firewall keeps outsiders from accessing your computer via an Internet connection. Begin typing **Control Panel** from the Start screen and click Control Panel in the search results.

2. Click System and Security⇨Windows Firewall.

3. In the Windows Firewall window that appears (see **Figure 21-7**), make sure that Windows Firewall is On. If it isn't, click the Turn Windows Firewall On or Off link in the left pane of the window.

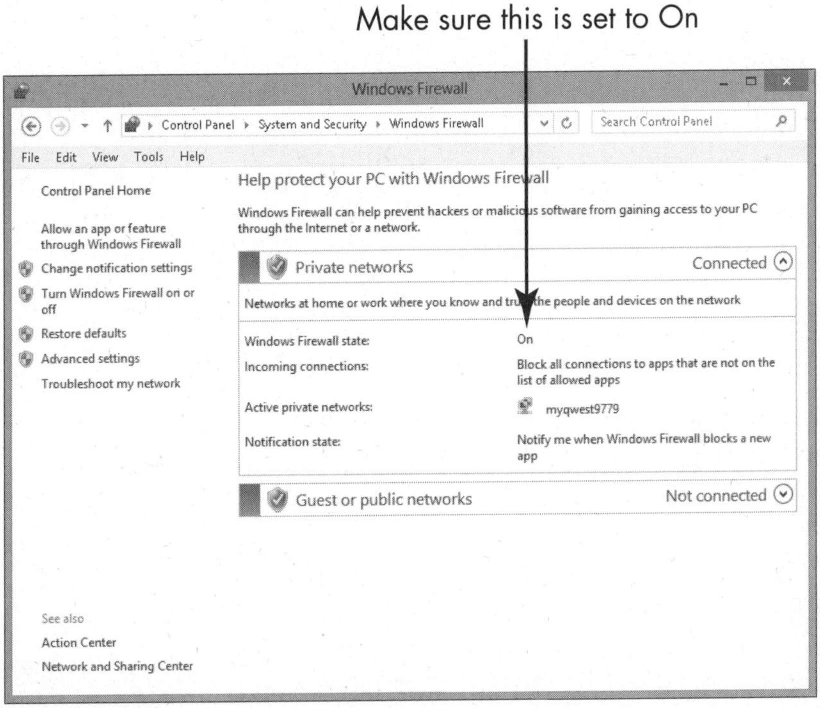

Make sure this is set to On

Figure 21-7

4. In the resulting Customize Settings window (see **Figure 21-8**), select the Turn on Windows Firewall radio button for Private Networks (such as your home network) and/or Public Networks (such as a coffee shop) and then click OK.

Turn either/both of these options on

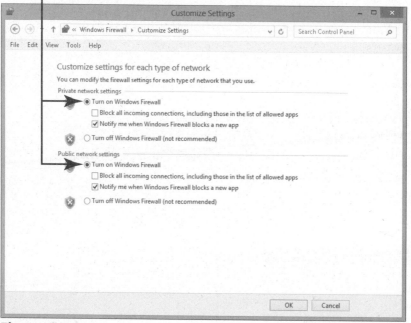

Figure 21-8

5. Click the Close button to close Windows Security Center and the Control Panel.

 A *firewall* is a program that protects your computer from the outside world. This is generally a good thing, unless you use a Virtual Private Network (VPN), often used by corporations. Using a firewall with a VPN can restrict you from sharing files and using some other VPN features.

 Antivirus and security software programs may offer their own firewall protection and may display a message asking if you want to switch. Check their features against Windows and then decide, but usually most firewall features are comparable. The important thing is to have one activated.

Change Your Password

1. If you log into Windows using an online account, your password is the password associated with your Windows Live account. If you set up a local account not associated with an online account, you create a password when you set up the account. To change a password, press Win+I, click Change PC Settings, and then click Users.

2. In the Users panel, shown in **Figure 21-9,** click the Change Your Password link.

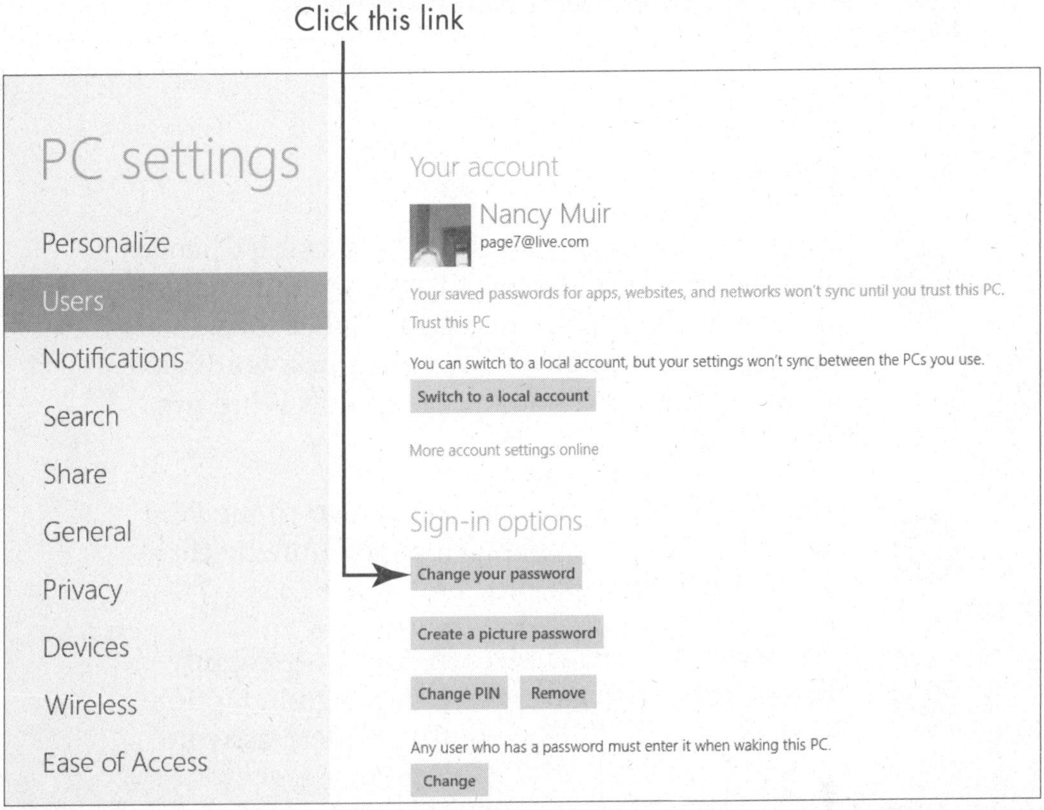

Click this link

Figure 21-9

3. In the Change Your Password screen, shown in **Figure 21-10,** enter your current password, and then enter the new password and confirm it.

Change your Microsoft account password

Nancy Muir
page7@live.com

Old password ••••••••••••

Forgot your password?

New password ••••••••••••

Reenter password ••••••••••••

Figure 21-10

4. Click Next.

5. Click Finish.

You can use a similar procedure by clicking Change PIN in the PC User Settings to assign a four-character PIN for logging into your account, rather than a password. PINs are typically shorter than passwords, so they save you time if you log on and off Windows during the day.

After you create a password, you can go to the PC Settings window and change it at any time by clicking Change Your Password.

In Windows 8.1, the choices in Step 2 are slightly different: In the Accounts panel, click Sign-In Options, and then click the Change button under Password.

Allow Firewall Exceptions

1. When you have a firewall active you can allow certain programs to communicate through that firewall. For example, you might want to allow live apps such as Weather or Video to send information or content to your computer. Begin typing **Control Panel** and then click the Control Panel app in the results. Click System and Security.

2. In the resulting System and Security window (see **Figure 21-11**), click Windows Firewall and then click Allow an App through Windows Firewall.

Click this option

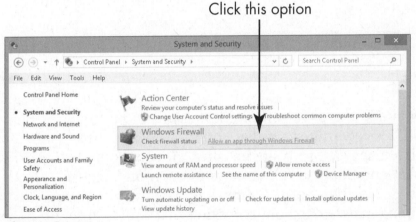

Figure 21-11

3. In the Allowed Apps window that appears (see **Figure 21-12**), click the Change Settings button, and then select the check box for apps on your computer that you want to allow to communicate over the Internet without being stopped by Firewall.

4. Click the Private and Public check box to narrow down whether you want just networks that are secure to allow this communication, or also public and nonsecure networks to do so.

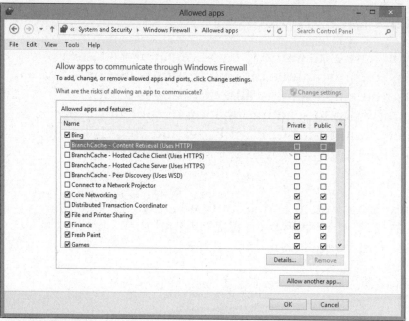

Figure 21-12

5. Click OK.

 If you allow apps to communicate across your fire-wall, it's very important that you do have antivirus and antispyware software installed on your computer, and that you run updates to them on a regular basis. These types of programs help you avoid down-loading malware to your computer that could cause advertising pop-ups, slow your computer's perfor-mance, damage computer files, or even track your keystrokes as you type to steal your identity and more. If you don't want to pay for such a program, consider a free solution such as Spyware Terminator (www.spywareterminator.com).

Maintaining Windows

All the wonderful hardware that you've spent your hard-earned money on doesn't mean a thing if the software driving it goes flooey. If any program causes your system to *crash* (meaning it freezes up and you have to take drastic measures to revive it), you can try a variety of tasks to fix it. You can also keep your system in good shape to help avoid those crashes. In this chapter, you find out how to take good care of your programs and operating system in these ways:

➡ When a program crashes, you can simply shut that program down by using Windows Task Manager. This utility keeps track of all the programs and processes that are running on your computer.

➡ If you've got problems and Windows isn't responding, sometimes it helps to restart in Safe Mode, which requires only basic files and drivers. Restarting in Safe Mode often allows you to troubleshoot what's going on, and you can restart Windows in its regular mode after the problem is solved.

➡ Use the System Restore feature to first create a *system restore point* (a point in time when your settings and programs all

Get ready to . . .

➡ Shut Down a Nonresponsive Application 358

➡ Create a System Restore Point..................... 359

➡ Restore Your PC................ 361

➡ Refresh Your PC................ 364

➡ Reset Your PC................... 365

➡ Defragment a Hard Drive... 367

➡ Free Disk Space................ 368

➡ Delete Temporary Internet Files by Using Internet Explorer.......................... 370

➡ Schedule Maintenance Tasks 372

➡ Troubleshoot Software Problems......................... 374

seem to be humming along just fine), and then restore Windows to that point when trouble hits.

➠ You can clean up your system to delete unused files, free up disk space, and schedule maintenance tasks.

➠ If you need a little help, you might run a trouble-shooting program to help you figure out a problem you're experiencing with a program.

Shut Down a Nonresponsive Application

1. If your computer freezes and won't let you proceed with what you were doing, press Ctrl+Alt+Delete.

2. In the Windows screen that appears, click Task Manager.

3. In the resulting Task Manager dialog box, click More Details, click the Processes tab (see **Figure 22-1**), and select the application that you were in when your system stopped responding.

4. Click the End Task button.

5. The app shuts down. Click the Close button to close Task Manager.

 If pressing Ctrl+Alt+Delete doesn't bring up the Task Manager, you're in bigger trouble than you thought. You might need to press and hold your computer's power button to shut down. Note that some applications use an AutoSave feature that keeps an interim version of the document that you were working in. You might be able to save some of your work by opening that last-saved version. Other programs don't have such a safety net, and you simply lose whatever changes you made to your document since the last time you saved it. The moral? Save, and save often.

Click this tab

| | | | 8% | 73% | 4% | 0% |
Name	Status		CPU	Memory	Disk	Network

Task Manager

File Options View

Processes | Performance | App history | Startup | Users | Details | Services

Apps (8)

Camera	0%	7.4 MB	0 MB/s	0 Mbps
Internet Explorer	0%	105.7 MB	0 MB/s	0 Mbps
▷ Internet Explorer (4)	4.4%	447.8 MB	0.1 MB/s	0 Mbps
Music	0%	206.6 MB	0 MB/s	0 Mbps
PC settings	0%	40.6 MB	0 MB/s	0 Mbps
Photos	0%	65.4 MB	0 MB/s	0 Mbps
▷ Task Manager	0.5%	8.4 MB	0 MB/s	0 Mbps
Video	0%	77.4 MB	0 MB/s	0 Mbps

Background processes (26)

Adobe® Flash® Player Utility	0%	1.9 MB	0 MB/s	0 Mbps
▷ Bluetooth Radio Management S...	0%	0.6 MB	0 MB/s	0 Mbps
COM Surrogate	0%	1.2 MB	0 MB/s	0 Mbps
COM Surrogate	0%	1.7 MB	0 MB/s	0 Mbps

⌃ Fewer details   End task

Figure 22-1

You may see a dialog box appear when an application shuts down that asks if you want to report the problem to Microsoft. If you say yes, information is sent to Microsoft to help it provide advice or fix the problem down the road.

Create a System Restore Point

1. You can back up your system files, which creates a restore point you can later use to return your computer to earlier settings if you experience problems. Begin to type **control panel** from the Start Screen and then click the Control Panel app in the search results.

2. Click System and Security and, in the resulting window, click the System link.

3. In the System window, click the System Protection link in the left panel. In the System Properties dialog box that appears (see **Figure 22-2**) on the System Protection tab, click the Create button.

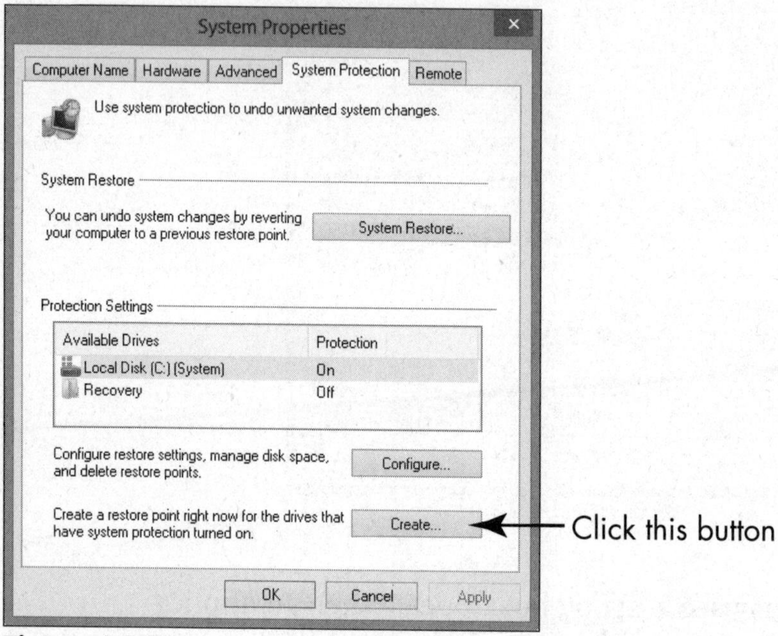

Figure 22-2

4. In the Create a Restore Point dialog box that appears, enter a name to identify the restore point, such as the current date or the name of a program you are about to install, and click Create.

5. Windows displays a progress window. When the restore point is created, the message shown in **Figure 22-3** appears. Click Close to close the message box, click Close to close the System Protection dialog box, and Close again to close the Control Panel.

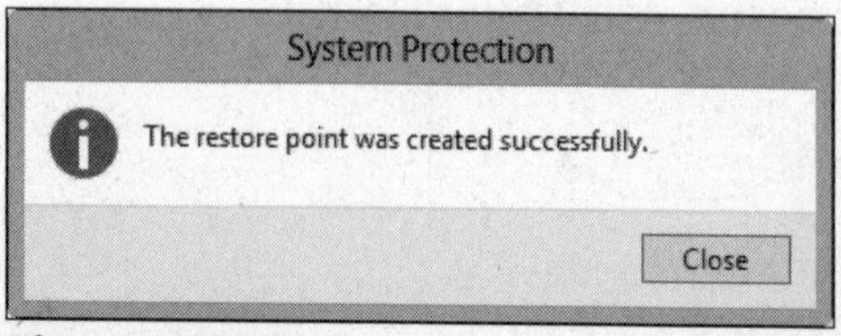

Figure 22-3

Every once in a while, when you install some software and make some new settings in Windows, and when things seem to be running just fine, create a system restore point. It's good computer practice, just like backing up your files, only you're backing up your settings. Once a month or once every couple of months works for most people, but if you frequently make changes, create a system restore point more often.

Restore Your PC

1. From the Control Panel, click System and Security, and then click System on the following screen.

2. Click the System Protection link on the left side of the window.

3. In the System Properties dialog box that appears, click the System Protection tab and then click the System Restore button, as shown in Figure 22-4.

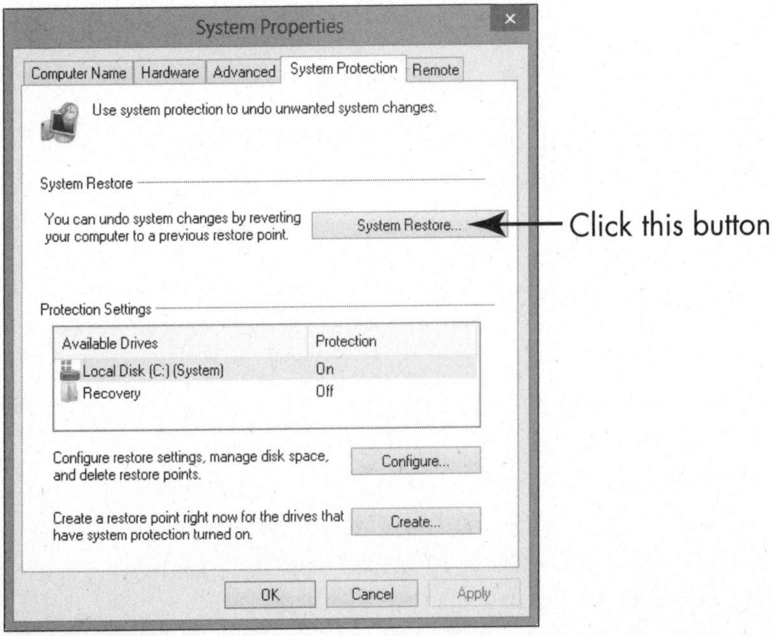

— Click this button

Figure 22-4

4. In the System Restore window, click Next. In the window that appears, click the Choose a Different Restore Point button, choose the date and time of the restore point (see **Figure 22-5**), and then click Next.

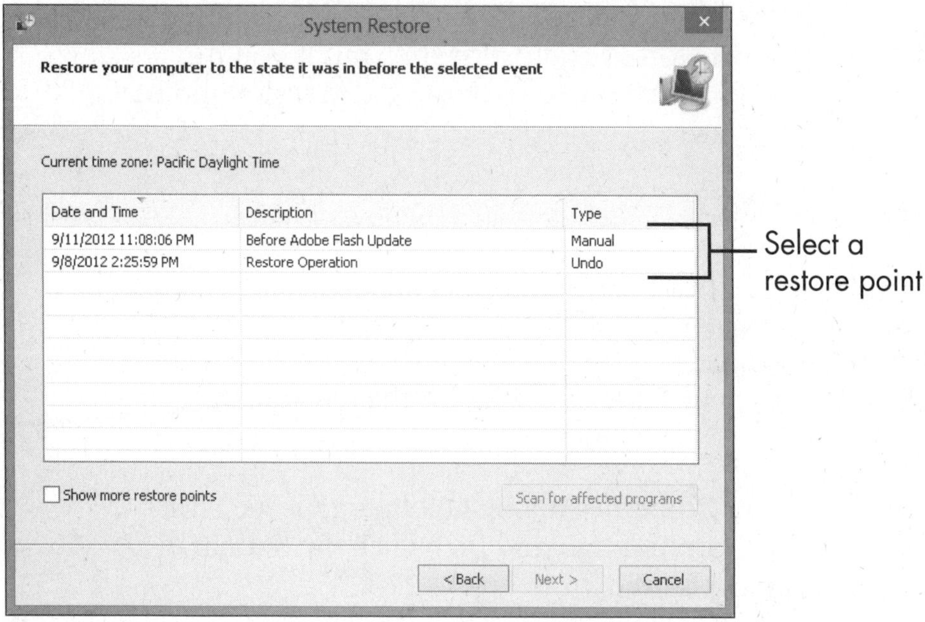

Date and Time	Description	Type
9/11/2012 11:08:06 PM	Before Adobe Flash Update	Manual
9/8/2012 2:25:59 PM	Restore Operation	Undo

System Restore

Restore your computer to the state it was in before the selected event

Current time zone: Pacific Daylight Time

☐ Show more restore points   Scan for affected programs

< Back   Next >   Cancel

Select a restore point

Figure 22-5

5. Click the Finish button to start the restore.

6. A dialog box confirms that you want to run System Restore and informs you that System Restore can't be interrupted — and in most cases can't be undone. Close any open files or programs, and then click Yes to proceed. The system goes through a shutdown and restart sequence.

System Restore doesn't get rid of files that you've saved, so you don't lose your Ph.D. dissertation. System Restore simply reverts to Windows settings as of the restore point. This can help if you or some piece of installed software made a setting that's causing some conflict in your system, making your computer sluggish or prone to crashes. If you're concerned about what changes will happen, click the Scan for Affected Programs button shown in the window displayed in **Figure 22-6.**

System Restore doesn't always solve the problem. Your very best bet is to be sure you create a set of backup discs for your computer when you buy it. If you didn't do that, and you can't get things running right again, contact your computer manufacturer. It may be able to send you a set of recovery discs, though it may charge a small fee. These discs restore your computer to its state when it left the factory, and in this case you lose applications you installed and documents you created, but you can get your computer running again.

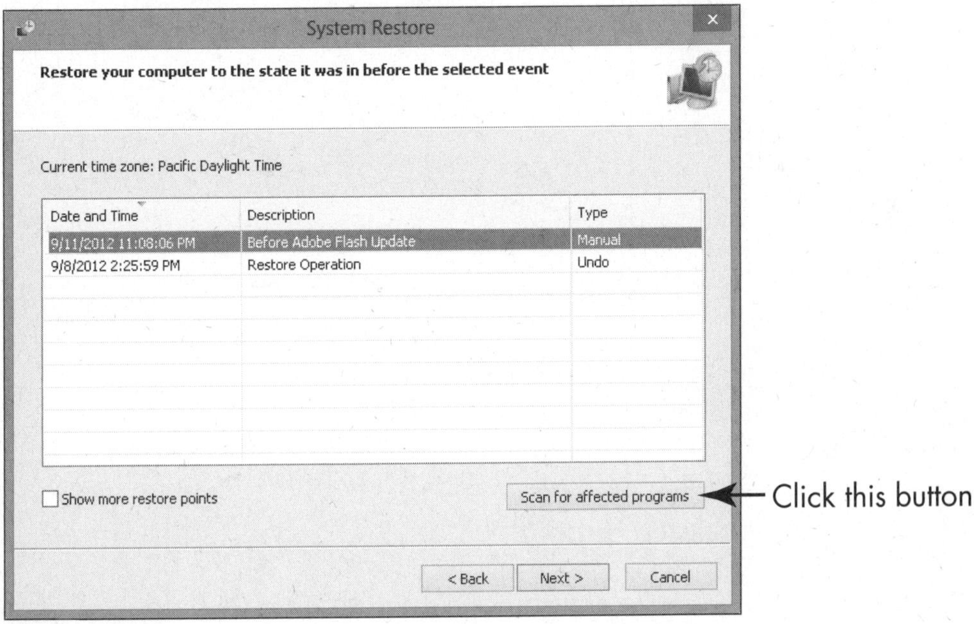

Figure 22-6

Refresh Your PC

1. Refreshing your computer is a way to get a sluggish device to perform better by resetting your system files to default settings, while leaving your personal files alone. Press Win+I to display the Settings panel.

2. Click Change PC Settings, and then click General.

3. Scroll down the right panel until you see the Refresh your PC without Affecting Your Files setting (see **Figure 22-7**).

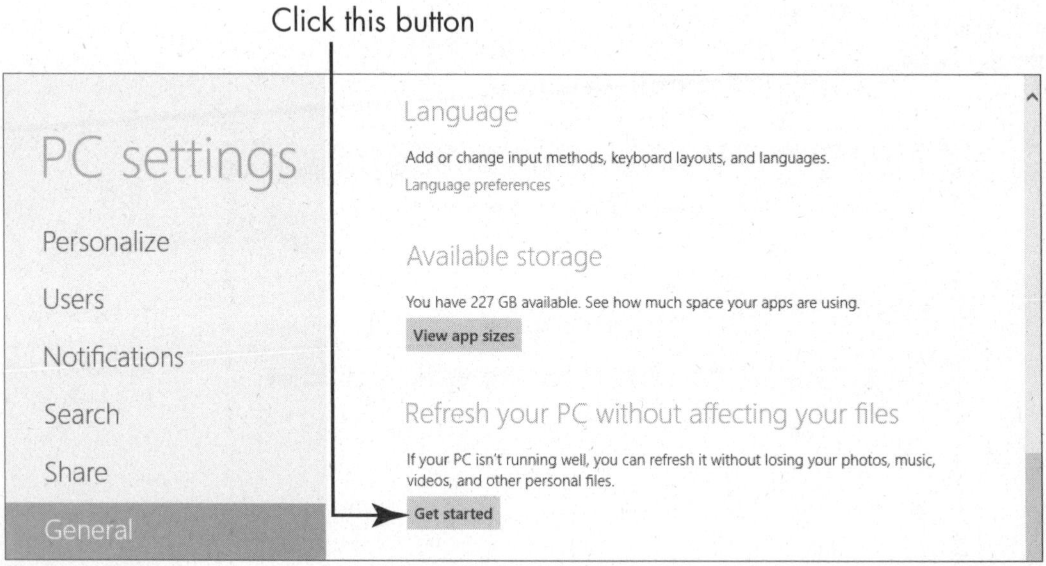

Click this button

PC settings

Personalize

Users

Notifications

Search

Share

General

Language

Add or change input methods, keyboard layouts, and languages.
Language preferences

Available storage

You have 227 GB available. See how much space your apps are using.
View app sizes

Refresh your PC without affecting your files

If your PC isn't running well, you can refresh it without losing your photos, music, videos, and other personal files.
Get started

Figure 22-7

4. Click the Get Started button.

5. A message appears, explaining what will happen when you run Refresh. Click Next to proceed.

6. On the next screen (see **Figure 22-8**) click Refresh to proceed, or Cancel to cancel the Refresh. When the Refresh is finished, a list of the apps that were removed appears on your desktop.

Figure 22-8

 Remember that using the Refresh procedure retains apps you bought from the Windows Store, but you'll lose apps you installed from other sources, such as a DVD or an online source.

Reset Your PC

1. Whereas refreshing a PC resets system files to factory defaults and retains all your files and some apps, resetting your PC not only resets system files, it gets rid of all your personal files and apps you installed. Resetting is for those times when nothing else has gotten your computer working again. To begin, press Win +I and click the Change PC Settings link.

2. Click General and scroll down in the right panel until you see the Remove Everything and Reinstall Windows setting.

 In Windows 8.1, you click Update & Recovery and then click Recovery.

3. Click the Get Started button.

4. In the next screen, shown in **Figure 22-9,** read the description of what Reset will do, and then click Next.

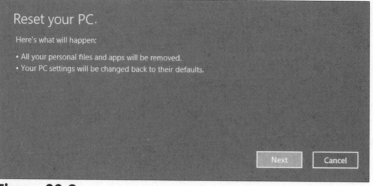

Figure 22-9

5. In the following screen, shown in **Figure 22-10,** choose which drive to remove files from: Only the Drive where Windows is Installed or All Drives.

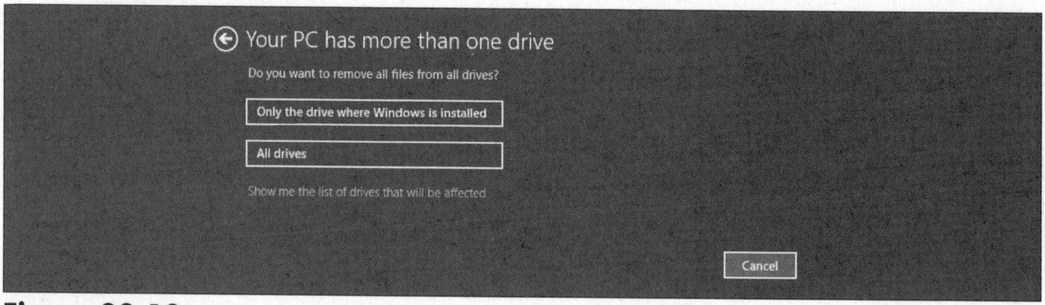

![Your PC has more than one drive screen]

Figure 22-10

6. In the following screen, choose either a thorough or quick reset.

7. In the Ready to Reset your PC screen, if you're positive you want to proceed, click the Reset button.

 The Reset procedure is a somewhat drastic step that will remove any apps you installed and files you saved. Remember, you can back out of the Reset procedure at any time up until you hit the Reset button. Just click Cancel.

Defragment a Hard Drive

1. To clean up files on your hard drive, from the Control Panel choose System and Security and then click Defragment and Optimize Your Drives in the Administrative Tools window.

2. In the resulting Optimize Drives window (see **Figure 22-11**), to the left of the Optimize button is the Analyze button. Use this to check whether your disk requires defragmenting. When the analysis is complete, click the Optimize button. A notation appears (see **Figure 22-12**) showing the progress of defragmenting your drive.

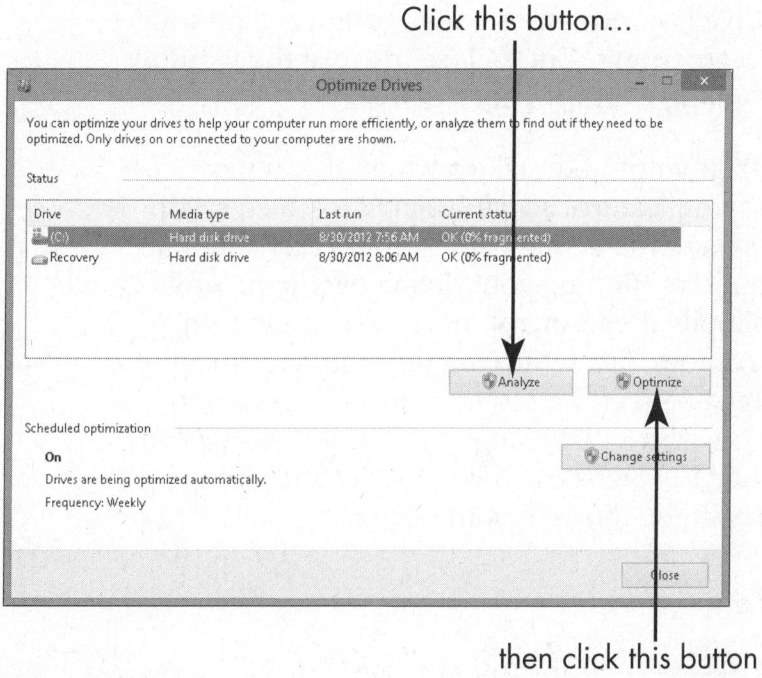

Click this button...

then click this button

Figure 22-11

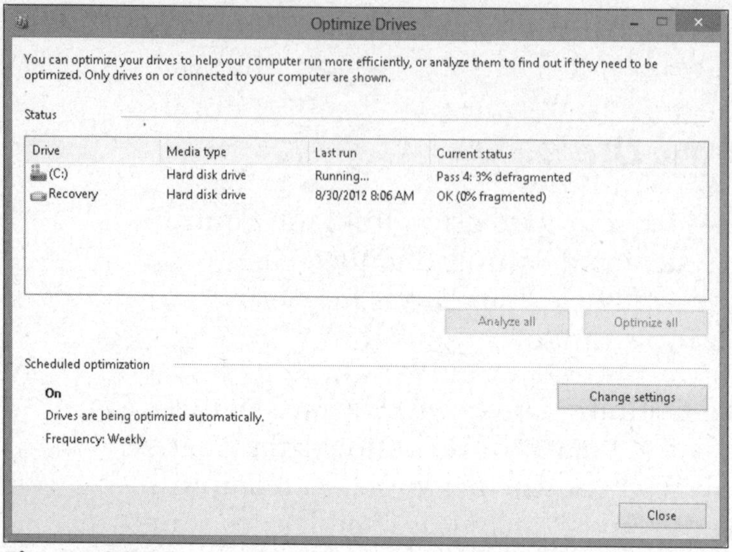

Figure 22-12

3. When the defragmenting process is complete, the Optimize Drives window shows that your drive no longer requires defragmenting. Click Close to close the window, and then close the Control Panel.

> Disk defragmenting can take a while. If you have energy-saving features active (such as a screen saver), they can cause the defragmenter to stop and start all over again. Try running your defrag overnight while you're happily dreaming of much more interesting things. You can also set up the procedure to run automatically at a preset period of time — such as once every two weeks — by using the Change Settings button in the Disk Defragmenter window and choosing a frequency in the dialog box that appears.

Free Disk Space

1. To run a process that cleans unused files and fragments of data from your hard drive to free up space, begin typing **control panel** from the Start screen and then click the Control Panel app in the results.

2. Click System and Security and then click Free Up Disk Space in the Administrative Tools.

3. In the Disk Cleanup: Drive Selection dialog box that appears (see **Figure 22-13**), choose the drive you want to clean up from the drop-down list and click OK. Disk Cleanup calculates how much space you will be able to free up.

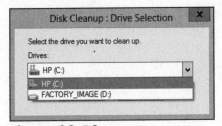

Figure 22-13

4. The resulting dialog box, shown in **Figure 22-14**, tells you that Disk Cleanup calculated how much space can be cleared on your hard drive and displays the suggested files to delete in a list (those to be deleted have a check mark). If you want to select additional files in the list to delete, click to place a check mark next to them.

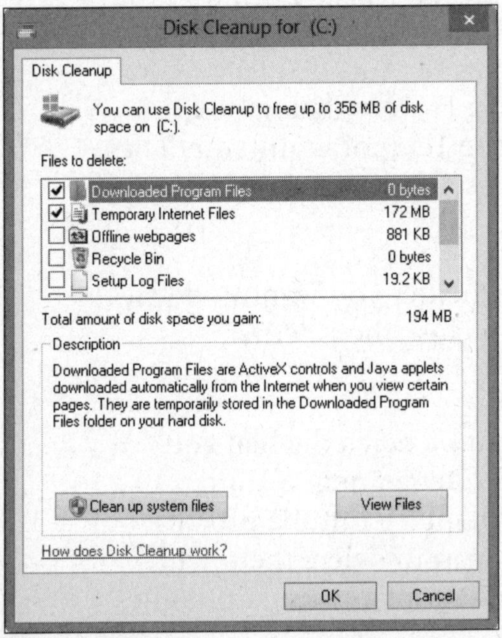

Figure 22-14

5. After you select all the files to delete, click OK. The selected files are deleted. Click the Close button to close the Control Panel.

 Click the View Files button in the Disk Cleanup dialog box to see more details about the files that Windows proposes to delete, including the size of the files and when they were created or last accessed.

Delete Temporary Internet Files by Using Internet Explorer

1. When you roam the Internet, various files may be downloaded to your computer to temporarily allow you to access sites or services. To clear these away, first open Internet Explorer from the desktop.

2. In the upper-right corner, choose Tools⇨Internet Options.

3. On the General tab of the resulting Internet Options dialog box (see **Figure 22-15**), click the Delete button in the Browsing History section.

4. In the resulting Delete Browsing History dialog box, shown in **Figure 22-16,** click the Temporary Internet Files and Website Files check box to select it, if it's not already selected, and click Delete.

5. A confirmation message asks whether you want to delete the files. Click Yes. Click OK to close the Internet Options dialog box.

 Temporary Internet files can be deleted when you run Disk Cleanup (see the "Defragment a Hard Drive" task earlier in this chapter), but the process that I describe here allows you to delete them without having to make choices about deleting other files on your system.

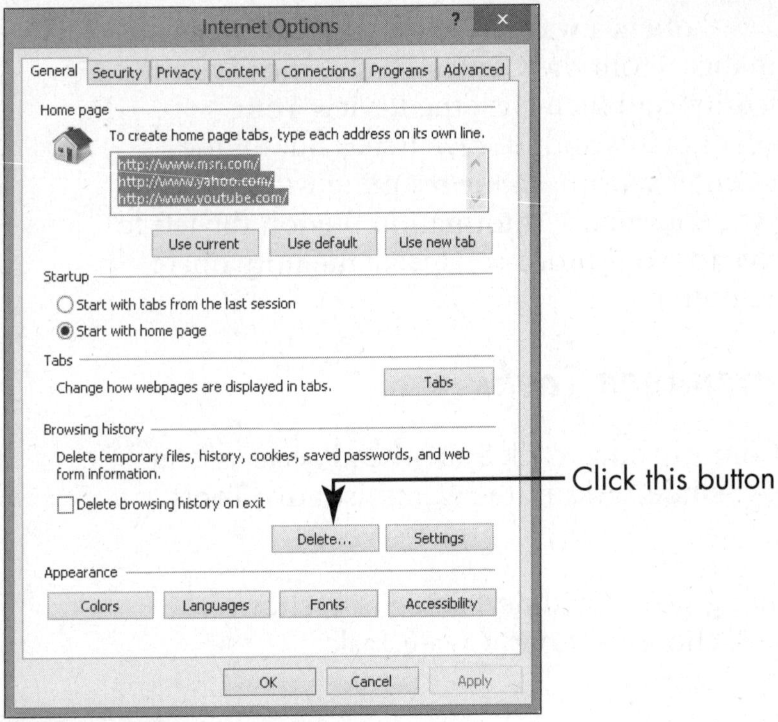

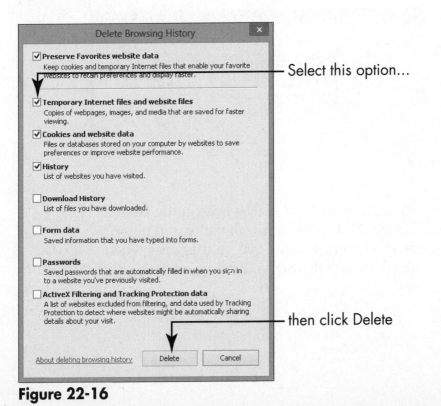

Figure 22-15

Figure 22-16

Windows 8 offers a way to review your computer's performance. From the Control Panel, click System and Security, and then click the Review Your Computer's Status and Resolve Issues link in the Action Center section. In the resulting window, click the View Performance Information link on the left to get scores for your processor speed, memory operations, and more.

Schedule Maintenance Tasks

1. From the Control Panel, click System and Security and then click Schedule Tasks in the Administrative Tools window.

2. In the resulting Task Scheduler dialog box, shown in **Figure 22-17**, choose Action⇨Create Task.

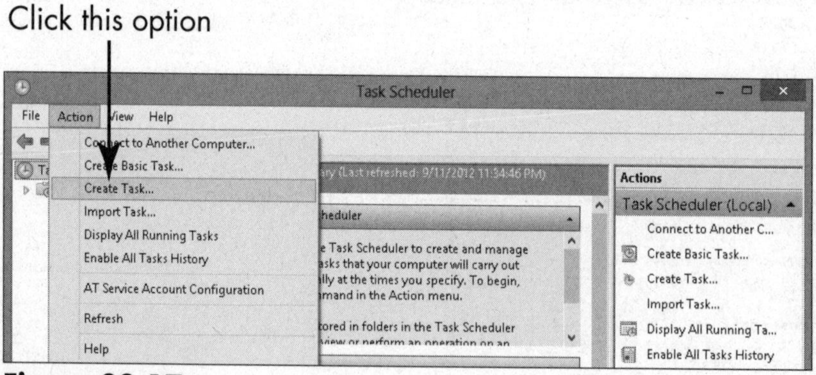

Click this option

Figure 22-17

3. In the resulting Create Task dialog box on the General tab (see **Figure 22-18**), enter a task name and description. Choose when to run the task (either only when you're logged on, or whether you're logged on or not).

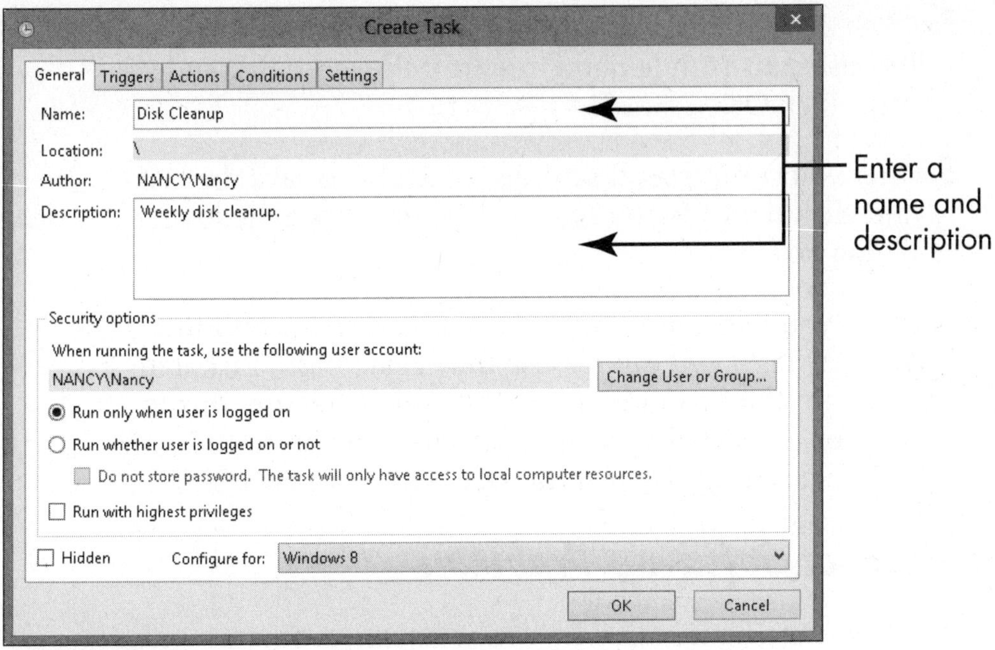

Enter a name and description

Figure 22-18

4. Click the Triggers tab and then click New. In the New Trigger dialog box, choose a criteria in the Begin the Task drop-down list and use the settings to specify how often to perform the task as well as when and at what time of day to begin. Click OK.

5. Click the Actions tab and then click New. In the New Action dialog box, choose the action that will occur from the Action drop-down list. These include starting a program, sending an e-mail, or displaying a message. Depending on what you choose here, different action dialog boxes appear. For example, if you want to send an e-mail, you get an e-mail form to fill in. Click OK.

6. If you want to set conditions in addition to those that trigger the action and those that control whether it should occur, click the Conditions tab and choose from the options there, such as starting the task when the computer has been idle for a time or only if the computer isn't running on a battery.

7. Click the Settings tab and make settings that control how the task runs (on demand, restart if the task fails, and so on). Click OK.

8. After you complete all settings, click OK to save the task and click the Close button to close the Task Scheduler dialog box.

 If you like a more wizardlike interface for building a new task, you can choose the Create Basic Task item from the Action menu in the Task Scheduler dialog box. This walks you through the most basic and minimal settings you can make to create a new task.

Troubleshoot Software Problems

1. If you can't figure out why you're having problems with a piece of software, from the Control Panel click Find and Fix Problems (under System and Security).

2. In the resulting Troubleshooting window (see **Figure 22-19**), click Programs.

Click this option

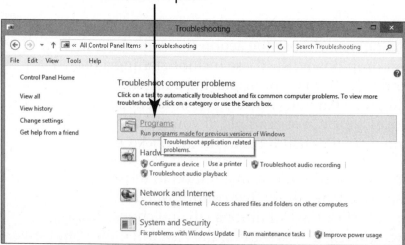

Figure 22-19

3. In the resulting Troubleshooting Problems – Programs
window, choose what you want to troubleshoot:

- **Network:** Allows you to troubleshoot a connection
  to the Internet.

- **Web Browser:** Helps you figure out problems you
  may have with the Internet Explorer browser.

- **Programs:** Is a good choice if you have an older
  program that doesn't seem to be functioning well
  with this version of Windows. Program compatibility is a common cause of problems with running software.

- **Printing:** Allows you to find out why you're having difficulty with your printer, including checking
  for the correct printer driver software.

- **Media Player:** Troubleshooting can be used to pin-
  point problems with general settings, media files,
  or playing DVDs.

4. Follow the sequence of instructions for the item you
selected to let Windows help you resolve your problem
(see **Figure 22-20**).

 In some cases, you'll be asked for administrator permission for the troubleshooter to perform an action,
so it's a good idea to run the troubleshooting wizard
through an administrator-level user account. See
Chapter 2 for more about user accounts and
administrators.

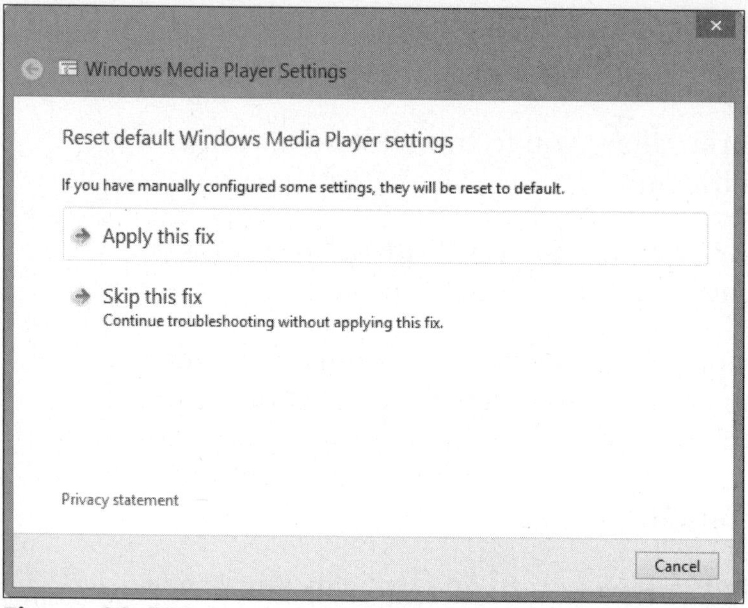

Figure 22-20

Free disk space differences in Windows 8.1

In the Free Disk Space task in this chapter, things work differently if you have Windows 8.1 installed:

1. Open Control Panel.

2. Click System and Security and then click Administrative Tools.

3. Double-click Disk Cleanup, and in the Disk Cleanup for Windows dialog box that appears, click the files you want to delete and click OK. A message asks you to confirm that you want to delete this material. Click the Delete Files button.

4. The resulting dialog box shows the Disk Cleanup progress.

Index

• A •

access speed, 23
accessing
 frequently viewed sites, 183
 pinned sites, 183
 Recently Used Items, 138–139
 Windows Live Mail, 236
accounts
 changing pictures, 67–69
 Internet-based, 230–232
 setting up in Mail app, 232–234
 settings in Mail app, 244–247
adding
 contacts in People app, 159–161
 events to calendars, 167–169
 files to Favorites list, 150–151
 files to SkyDrive, 252–253
 functions to taskbar, 53
 items to be synced, 313
 printers manually, 95–98
 websites to Favorites, 197–198
address, privacy of, 222
Adobe (website), 213
Advanced Settings link, 64
adware, 209
AIM (website), 267
allowing firewall exceptions, 355–356
Alt+Tab, 51
Amazon Prime, 328
Amazon.com (website), 321, 322
Angie's List (website), 320

antiadware programs, 209
antispyware programs, 209
antivirus programs, 13, 209,
 352–353
AOL, 231
AOL Instant Messenger (website), 267
appearance, customizing for
 windows, 62–63
applications. *See also* software
 Calendar, 153, 167–169
 Camera, 69, 285, 292–293
 financial, 251–252
 Mail, 229–247
 Messaging, 267–270
 Music, 17
 opening with File Explorer, 56–57
 People, 153, 159–167, 239
 Photos, 285, 293–298
 searching for, 47–49
 shutting down nonresponsive,
 358–359
 using online, 250–252
 Video, 285, 286, 290
 Weather, 153–159
 Word Web, 257
applying desktop themes, 70–71
arranging icons on desktop, 54–55
attachments, e-mail, 225–226
auction sites, 18, 322–323
Audio port, 28
Audio Quality slider, 305
AVG Free, 209, 210

• *B* •

background
  desktop, 62, 70–71
  Start screen, 62, 65–66
backing up files, 152
Better Business Bureau (website), 320
Bing Weather, 154–155
bizrate (website), 319
blogs, 262–264, 272
Blu-ray discs, 21
Bluetooth
  connecting to devices, 339–340
  making computer discoverable to,
    338–339
broadband Internet connection,
    24, 178
browsers
  defined, 174
  tabs in, 184–185
browsing the web. *See* web browsing
built-in modems, 178
burning
  defined, 299
  music to CD/DVD, 311–312
buying
  music from Windows Store, 306–308
  video content at Windows Store,
    286–289

• *C* •

cable connection, 176
Calendar app
  about, 153
  adding events to calendars, 167–169
  inviting people to events, 169
camera, 69, 291–292

Camera app, 69, 285, 292–293
Camera button, 69
capital letters, in e-mail, 239
car information, privacy of, 223
CardBus adapter PC card, 178
CDs
  burning music to, 311–312
  compared with DVDs, 21
cellular networks, 340–341
central processing unit (CPU), 11
changing
  account picture, 67–69
  cursor, 91–92
  desktop background, 70–71
  Lock Screen picture, 66–67
  passwords, 353–354
  photo resolution, 293
  privacy settings, 216–218
  Start screen background/color,
    65–66
  system volume, 301–303
  user account type, 38–40
  volume in Windows Media
    Player, 289
Character Repeat settings, 88–89
Charms bar
  about, 33–35
  displaying, 46–47
chat rooms, 261, 264–266
checking for updates, 346
checks, for payments in shopping
    carts, 326
choosing
  an online dating service, 277–278
  monitors, 19–20
  optical drives, 21–22
  price range, 17–19
  settings for Sync, 258–259

cleaning out Favorites list, 198
clicking and dragging files, 142
clicking and dragging the mouse, 30
clicking the mouse, 29
clients, e-mail, 250
cloud
  about, 249
  adding files to SkyDrive, 252–253
  choosing Sync settings, 258–259
  creating new SkyDrive folders,
    255–256
  defined, 22
  enabling Sync feature, 257–258
  sharing files using SkyDrive,
    253–255
  sharing SkyDrive folder, 256–257
  using applications online, 250–252
clubs, information exposure by, 219
CNET (website), 321
collaborative sites, 271–272
Collier, Marsha (author)
  eBay For Dummies, 323
color schemes, 91
color, Start screen, 65–66
Color/Grayscale option (Printing
  Preferences dialog box), 100
comparing prices, 319
compressed files/folders, creating,
  148–150
computers. *See also specific topics*
  about, 7
  benefits of having, 8–10
  customized, 25–26
  hardware, 11–13
  Internet connections, 24–25,
    176–180
  memory, 22–23
  monitors, selecting, 19–20

optical drives, choosing, 21–22
price range, choosing, 17–19
processor speed, 22–23
software, 11–13
types, 13–16
Windows versions, 16–17
connections
  Internet, 24–25, 176–180
  keyboard, 28
  making to networks, 333–334
  monitor, 28
  mouse, 28
  to Bluetooth devices, 339–340
Consumer Reports (website), 321
consumer-rankings (website), 277
contacts
  adding in People app, 159–161
  editing information in People app,
    161–162
  pinning, 166–167
  unpinning, 167
content
  finding on web pages, 195–196
  illegal, 270
  sharing, 278–279
conventions, explained, 1
cookies, 350
cost, monitor, 20
coupons, finding, 323–324
CPU (central processing unit), 11
creating
  compressed files/folders, 148–150
  desktop shortcuts, 51–53
  e-mail messages, 238–240
  folders, 137, 148–150
  passwords, 208, 226–228
  playlists, 309–310
  projects, 9

creating *(continued)*
  shortcuts to files/folders, 57–58,
    146–147
  SkyDrive folders, 255–256
  system restore points, 359–361
  user accounts, 35–37
credit card, for payments in shopping
    carts, 326
credit status, privacy of, 223
Ctrl+Alt+Delete, 358
cursor, changing, 91–92
customer reviews, reading, 321–322
customizing
  computers, 25–26
  Internet Explorer toolbar, 201–202
  mouse behavior, 89–91
  window appearance, 62–63

• *D* •

data mining, 261
data organization, 136–138
date, setting, 33–35
DDR2, 22
defragmenting hard drives, 367–368
deleting
  files from SkyDrive, 253
  files/folders, 147–148, 253
  temporary Internet files, 370–372
Dell, 25
desktop
  about, 14–15, 50–52
  applying themes, 70–71
  arranging icons on, 54–55
  background, 62, 70–71
  changing background, 70–71
  IE app, 183–184, 185, 186–188,
    191–192, 199–201

restoring, 58
  shortcuts, 51, 53
devices
  Bluetooth, 339–340
  syncing music with, 312–313
dexterity, vision and hearing
    challenges
  about, 75–76
  changing cursor, 91–92
  customizing mouse behavior, 89–91
  modifying keyboard, 84–86
  onscreen keyboard feature, 86–88
  replacing sounds with visual cues,
    78–79
  resizing text, 79–81
  setting up keyboard repeat rates,
    88–89
  setting up speech recognition,
    81–84
  tools for visually challenged, 76–78
dialup Internet connection, 24, 177,
    178
digital cameras, uploading photos
    from, 291–292
Digital Scrapbook, 137
Digital Subscriber Line (DSL), 24,
    176, 178
discoverable devices, 338–339
discs, recovery, 22
discussion boards, 262–264
Disk Cleanup, 368–370
Disk Defragmenter, 367–368
disk space, freeing, 368–370
display
  about, 61–62
  changing account picture, 67–69

changing desktop background, 70–71

changing Lock Screen picture, 66–67

changing Start screen background and color, 65–66

choosing desktop theme, 72–73

customizing windows appearance, 62–63

setting screen resolution, 63–64

setting up screen saver, 63, 73–74

displaying
Charms bar, 46–47
events, 168
weather views, 154–156

Documents folder, 136

downloading
files, 212–214
updates, 346

DRAM, 22

drives
DVD, 21
flash, 136
hard, 367–368
saving files to, 152

DSL (Digital Subscriber Line), 24, 176, 178

dual-core, 23

DVD drives, 21

DVDs
burning music to, 311–312
compared with CDs, 21

• **E** •

e-commerce, 174. *See also* online shopping

e-mail. *See also* Mail app
about, 229–230
attachments, 225–226, 240–241
capital letters in, 239
clients, 250
creating messages, 238–240
etiquette, 239
forwarding messages, 243–244
links in messages, 224–225
opening, 236–238
reading messages, 241–242
receiving messages, 236–238
replying to messages, 242–243
sending attachments, 240–241
sending messages, 238–240
sending to contacts, 163–164
setting up Internet-based accounts, 230–232

e-mail alias, 231

e-mail fraud, 224–226

eBay (website), 322

eBay For Dummies (Collier), 323

ebid (website), 322

editing
contacts information in People app, 161–162
events, 169

eharmony (website), 277

employers, information exposure by, 219

emptying Recycle Bin, 55–56

enabling
Filter Keys, 85
InPrivate Browsing, 214–215
mouse keys, 84
Sticky Keys, 85
Sync feature, 257–258

enabling *(continued)*
  Toggle Keys, 85
  Windows Firewall, 351–353
Epinions (website), 19
Ethernet cable, 178
etiquette, e-mail, 239
events
  adding to calendars, 167–169
  editing, 169
  inviting people to, 169
  showing, 168
exceptions, firewall, 355–356
exclamation point, in e-mail, 238
exposure of information, 218–222

• F •

Facebook, 269, 273–275
family members, information
    exposure by, 219
family names, privacy of, 222
Favorites list
  adding files to, 150–151
  adding websites to, 197–198
  organizing, 198–199
File Explorer, 56–57
files and folders
  about, 135–136
  accessing Recently Used Items,
    138–139
  adding files to Favorites list,
    150–151
  adding files to SkyDrive, 252–253
  backing up files, 152
  clicking and dragging files, 142
  creating compressed, 148–150
  creating folders, 137, 148–150
  creating shortcuts to, 57–58,
    146–147

creating SkyDrive folders, 255–256
data organization, 136–138
deleting, 147–148, 253
deleting files from SkyDrive, 253
Documents folder, 136
downloading files, 212–214
finding with File Explorer, 56–57
locating, 56–57, 139–141
moving, 142–144
predefined folders, 136–137
renaming, 145–146
right clicking and dragging files, 142
right clicking files, 142
saving files to drives, 152
searching for, 47–49
searching for online content,
    141–142
sharing using SkyDrive, 253–257
SkyDrive, creating, 255–256
SkyDrive, sharing, 256–257
Filter Keys, enabling, 85
filtering, junk-mail, 231–232
financial applications, 251–252
financial management, 10
finding
  content on web pages, 195–196
  coupons, 323–324
  files with File Explorer, 56–57
  files/folders, 56–57, 139–141
  music with Integrated Search,
    305–306
firewalls
  about, 211, 344
  allowing exceptions, 355–356
  defined, 352
flash drive, 136
flat panels, 19, 20
Flickr (website), 250

folders. *See* files and folders
footprint, 19
forwarding e-mail messages,
    243–244
freeing disk space, 368–370
friends, information exposure by, 219
functions, adding to taskbar, 53

• *G* •

Gadgets, 51
games, interactive, 9
gaming, 16
Gateway, 25
GB (gigabytes), 23
gestures, 30–31, 50
getting started, with Windows 8,
    112–114
GHz (gigahertz), 22
gigabytes (GB), 23
gigahertz (GHz), 22
global weather, 157–159
Gmail (website), 230, 231
Google (website), 192, 250
Google Docs, 250
Government agencies, information
    exposure by, 219
graphic links, 175, 181

• *H* •

hard drives, defragmenting, 367–368
hardware
  about, 11–13
  defined, 7
  for Internet connections, 178–179
hearing challenges. *See* dexterity,
    vision and hearing challenges

help
  about, 109–110
  getting started with Windows 8,
    112–114
  Help and Support database, 109,
    110–112
  online compared with offline,
    117–118
  Remote Assistance, 110, 118–122
  Start screen, 114–115
  Windows community, 115–117
hexa-core, 23
High Contrast color scheme, 76
highlighting keyboard shortcuts, 85
history, browsing, 199–201
hobbies online, 9
home pages
  about, 185–186
  removing, 188
  setting up in desktop IE app,
    186–188
Homegroups, joining, 332–333
hotspots, 24, 177
Hover typing mode, 88
https, 320, 350
hyperlinks
  defined, 175
  graphic, 175, 181
  in e-mail messages, 224–225

• *I* •

icons
  arranging on desktop, 54–55
  explained, 1
IE (Internet Explorer)
  about, 189–190
  adding websites to Favorites,
    197–198

IE (Internet Explorer) *(continued)*
  customizing Internet Explorer
    toolbar, 201–202
  customizing toolbar, 201–202
  finding content on Start screen,
    195–196
  Internet Explorer versions, 190–192
  organizing Favorites, 198–199
  pinning web pages to Start screen,
    196–197
  printing web pages, 204–205
  searching, 192–195
  versions, 190–192
  viewing browsing history, 199–201
  viewing RSS feeds, 202–204
IE app
  desktop, 183–184, 185, 186–188,
    191–192, 199–201
  Start screen, 181–183, 185, 190–191,
    195–196
illegal content, 270
IM (instant messaging), 8, 261,
    266–267
image quality, monitor, 19, 20
images. *See* photos
information
  exposure of, 218–222
  privacy of, 222–224
InPrivate Browsing, enabling,
    214–215
installing
  plug-and-play scanners, 105
  printers, 94–95
  scanners manually, 105–106
  software, 292
  updates automatically, 345–346
instant messaging (IM), 8, 261,
    266–267

Integrated Search, finding music
    with, 305–306
interactive games, 9
interface, 41
Internet
  about, 173–175
  benefits of, 8
  connections, 24–25, 176–180
  desktop IE app, 183–184, 185, 186–
    188, 191–192, 199–201
  determining connections, 24–25
  files, deleting, 370–372
  home pages, 185–188
  setting up connections, 179–180
  setting up home pages in desktop
    IE, 186–188
  Start screen IE app, 181–183, 185,
    190–191, 195–196
  tabs in browsers, 184–185
Internet Explorer. *See* IE
Internet service provider (ISP), 176,
    230, 231
inviting people to events, 169
iPad, 15
ISP (Internet Service Provider), 176,
    230, 231

• J •

joining Homegroups, 332–333
junk-mail filtering, 231–232

• K •

keyboard
  about, 11
  connecting, 28
  modifying, 84–86

onscreen keyboard feature, 86–88
repeat rates, 88–89
keyboard shortcuts, 31, 85
keystroke combinations, 87
Kindle Fire, 15

• L •

laptop, 14
launching programs, 126–128
LCD (liquid crystal display), 19
LinkedIn, 269
links
  defined, 175
  graphic, 175, 181
  in e-mail messages, 224–225
liquid crystal display (LCD), 19
local access numbers, 177
locating
  content on web pages, 195–196
  coupons, 323–324
  files with File Explorer, 56–57
  files/folders, 56–57, 139–141
  music with Integrated Search,
    305–306
Lock Screen, changing picture, 66–67
logging on to Windows 8, 31–32

• M •

Magnifier feature, 77–78
maiden names, privacy of, 222
Mail app
  about, 229–230, 234–236
  account settings, 244–247
  creating e-mail, 238–240
  forwarding e-mail, 243–244
  opening mail, 236–238
  reading messages, 241–242

receiving messages, 236–238
replying to messages, 242–243
sending attachments, 240–241
sending e-mail, 238–240
setting up an account, 232–234
maintaining Windows
  about, 357–358
  creating system restore points,
    359–361
  defragmenting hard drives, 367–368
  deleting temporary Internet files,
    370–372
  freeing disk space, 368–370
  refreshing PCs, 364–365
  resetting PCs, 365–366
  restoring PCs, 361–363
  scheduling maintenance tasks,
    372–374
  shutting down nonresponsive
    applications, 358–359
  troubleshooting software problems,
    374–376
malware, 344
managing
  shopping carts, 324–325
  windows, 85
Maximize button, 51
media
  about, 283
  software, 284–286
megahertz (MHz), 23
memory, 22–23
messages, e-mail. *See also* Mail app
  about, 229–230
  attachments, 225–226, 240–241
  capital letters in, 239
  creating, 238–240
  e-mail clients, 250

messages, e-mail *(continued)*
  etiquette, 239
  forwarding, 243–244
  links in, 224–225
  opening, 236–238
  reading, 241–242
  receiving, 236–238
  replying to, 242–243
  sending, 238–240
  sending attachments, 240–241
  sending to contacts, 163–164
  setting up Internet-based accounts,
    230–232
Messaging app, 267–270
MHz (megahertz), 23
Microsoft, 110
Microsoft SkyDrive. *See* SkyDrive
Minimize button, 51, 60
Mint (website), 252
modems, 178
monitors
  about, 11
  connecting, 28
  selecting, 19–20
mouse
  about, 11–12
  click and drag, 30
  clicking, 29
  connecting, 28
  customizing behavior, 89–91
  enabling keys, 84
  right clicking, 29
  using, 29

moving
  files/folders, 142–144
  information between programs,
    128–130
  messages from Inbox in Mail
    app, 236
multimedia models, 16
multiple core, 23
multitasking, 23
music
  about, 299
  adjusting system volume, 301–303
  burning to CD/DVD, 311–312
  buying from Windows Store,
    306–308
  creating playlists, 309–310
  finding with Integrated Search,
    305–306
  playing with Windows Media
    Player, 314–315
  setting up speakers, 300–301
  settings for ripping, 303–305
  syncing with devices, 312–313
Music app, 278
mute button, 302
MySpace, 273

• *N* •

Narrator feature, 76
navigating
  about, 41
  arranging icons on desktop, 54–55
  changes in Windows 8, 42–43

creating shortcuts to files/folders, 57–58

desktop, 50–52

displaying Charms bar, 46–47

emptying Recycle Bin, 55–56

File Explorer, 56–57

frequently used programs, 52–53

resizing windows, 59–60

searching for files, settings, and apps, 47–49

Start screen, 43–45

switching between programs, 58–59

touchscreen, 50

viewing Recent Apps, 49–50

networks

about, 331

Bluetooth, making computer discoverable to, 338–339

cellular, 340–341

connecting to Bluetooth devices, 339–340

joining Homegroups, 332–333

making connections to, 333–334

sharing specifications, 334–335

wireless, setting up, 336–338

NewEgg (website), 17

newspapers, information exposure by, 220

Nextag (website), 10, 19, 319

notification area, 51

• O •

offline help, compared with online help, 117–118

online auctions, 18, 322–323

Online Business Bureau (website), 320

online content, searching for, 141–142

online dating

about, 275–276

choosing a service, 277–278

online directories, information exposure by, 220–221

online help, compared with offline help, 117–118

Online Investment Portfolio (website), 251

online shopping

about, 10, 317

auction sites, 18, 322–323

comparing prices, 319

finding coupons, 323–324

managing shopping carts, 324–325

payment methods, 326–327

reading customer reviews, 321–322

searching for items, 318–319

shipping options, 327–328

trustworthiness of stores, 320–321

onscreen keyboard feature, 86–88

opening

applications with File Explorer, 56–57

e-mail, 236–238

tabs in Start screen IE app, 185

operating system. *See* OS
optical discs, 312
optical drives, choosing, 21–22
organizations, information exposure
    by, 219
organizing
  data, 136–138
  Favorites list, 198–199
OS (operating system)
  about, 13–15
  versions, 16–17

• P •

Paper Size option (Printing
    Preferences dialog box), 101
Paper Source option (Printing
    Preferences dialog box), 101
Parallel port, 28
passwords
  changing, 353–354
  creating, 208, 226–228
  Homegroups, 332–333
  networks, 334
pausing playback in Windows Media
    Player, 289
payment methods, for online
    shopping, 326–327
PayPal, for payments in shopping
    carts, 326, 327
PC Tools' Spyware Doctor, 210
PCs
  refreshing, 364–365
  resetting, 365–366
  restoring, 361–363
People app
  about, 153
  adding contacts, 159–161
  addressing e-mail from, 239
  editing contact information,
    161–162
  pinning contacts, 166–167
  sending e-mail to contacts,
    163–164
  viewing postings by contacts,
    164–166
peripherals, 12
personal hotspot, 340–341
phishing scams, 224–226
phone number, privacy of, 222
photo-sharing sites, 250
photos
  about, 283
  account, 67–69
  adjusting resolution, 293
  Camera app, 285
  Lock Screen, 66–67
  sending using SkyDrive, 296
  sharing, 9–10, 295–297
  software, 284–286
  taking with Camera app, 292–293
  uploading from digital cameras,
    291–292
  viewing in Photos app, 293–295
Photos app
  about, 285
  running slide shows in, 297–298
  sharing photos, 295–297
  viewing photos, 293–295
pictures. *See* photos
PIN numbers, 37, 354
pinch gesture, 30, 50
pinning
  contacts, 166–167
  web pages to Start screen, 196–197
pixels, 19

playing
  movies with Windows Media Player,
    289–291
  music with Windows Media Player,
    314–315
  video content with Video app, 290
playlists, creating, 309–310
plug-and-play scanners, installing, 105
pointer speed, 91
pop-up blocker settings, 218
ports, 28
postings, viewing by contacts,
    164–166
predefined folders, 136–137
preferences, printer, 100–102
Price Grabber (website), 319
price range, choosing, 17–19
price.com (website), 319
prices, comparing, 319
pricewatch (website), 319
printer driver, 93
printers and printing
  about, 93
  adding manually, 95–98
  from cameras, 292
  installing, 94–95
  modifying printer properties,
    99–100
  removing, 104–105
  setting default, 98–100
  setting preferences, 100–102
  viewing installed, 103–104
  web pages, 204–205
privacy
  changing settings, 216–218
  of information, 222–224
privacy policies, 321
private messaging, 277

processor speed, 22–23
programs. See also software
  frequently used, 52–53
  launching, 126–128
  moving information between,
    128–130
  removing, 131–133
  setting defaults, 130–131
  switching between, 58–59
projects, creating, 9
properties
  printer, 99–100
  Recycle Bin, modifying, 56
provider, 176

• Q •

quad-core, 23
Quality option (Printing Preferences
    dialog box), 100–101
quality, image, monitor, 19, 20

• R •

RAM, 22–23
readable DVD drive, 21
reading
  customer reviews, 321–322
  e-mail messages, 241–242
rebooting, 40
receiving e-mail messages, 236–238
Recent Apps, viewing, 49–50
Recently Used Items, accessing,
    138–139
recovery discs, 22
Recycle Bin, 51, 55–56
Refresh button, 183
refreshing PCs, 364–365
refurbished computers, 18
Remote Assistance, 110, 118–122

removing
  home pages, 188
  printers, 104–105
  programs, 131–133
renaming files/folders, 145–146
replacing sounds with visual cues,
    78–79
replying to e-mail messages, 242–243
researching, 8
resetting PCs, 365–366
resizing
  text, 79–81
  windows, 59–60
resolution
  monitor, 19
  photo, adjusting, 293
  screen, 62, 63–64
restoring
  desktop, 58
  PCs, 361–363
restricted sites, 350
retail sites, for online shopping, 318
right clicking and dragging files, 142
right clicking files, 142
right-click gesture, 50
right-clicking, 181
right-clicking the mouse, 29
ripping music, 303–305
risks, technology, 207, 208–211
router, 178
RSS feeds, viewing, 202–204
running
  slide shows in Photos app, 297–298
  Windows Update, 347–348

• S •

Safe Mode, 357
saferdates (website), 277

satellite connection, 177
saving
  attachments to storage disc, 242
  custom themes, 73
  files to drives, 152
scanners
  about, 93
  installing manually, 105–106
  modifying settings, 106–108
  plug-and-play, installing, 105
scheduling maintenance tasks,
    372–374
screen resolution, 62, 63–64
screen savers, 63, 73–74
scrolling gesture, 155
scrolling the mouse, 30
SDRAM, 22
search engines, for online shopping,
    318
Search This Site feature, on websites,
    196
searching
  apps, 47–49
  for e-mail providers, 231
  for files, 47–49
  for folders, 47–49
  for items for online shopping,
    318–319
  for online content, 141–142
  settings, 47–49
  web, 192–195
  Windows Help and Support, 109,
    110–112
security
  about, 207–208, 343–345
  allowing firewall exceptions,
    355–356
  changing passwords, 353–354

changing privacy settings, 216–218
creating strong passwords, 208, 226–228
downloading files, 212–214
e-mail fraud, 224–226
enabling InPrivate Browsing, 214–215
enabling Windows Firewall, 351–353
information exposure, 207, 218–222
keeping information private, 222–224
phishing scams, 224–226
risks, 207, 208–211
running Windows Update, 347–348
setting up Trusted and Restricted websites, 348–351
SmartScreen Filter, 215–216
software programs, 352–353
Suggested Sites, 211–212
webcams, 271
Windows update options, 345–347
sending
  e-mail attachments, 240–241
  e-mail messages, 238–240
  e-mail to contacts, 163–164
  photos using SkyDrive, 296
servers, 176
setting(s)
  Character Repeat, 88–89
  date, 33–35
  default printers, 98–100
  for ripping music, 303–305
  Mail app account, 244–247
  pop-up blocker, 218
  printer preferences, 100–102
  privacy, changing, 216–218
  program defaults, 130–131
  scanner, 106–108

screen resolution, 63–64
searching for, 47–49
Sync, choosing, 258–259
time, 33–35
usage rights, 194
View, 64
Viewbook, 250
setup
  about, 27
  accounts in Mail app, 232–234
  changing user account type, 38–40
  creating user accounts, 35–37
  e-mail accounts in Mail app, 230
  home pages in desktop IE app, 186–188
  Internet connection, 179–180
  Internet-based e-mail accounts, 230–232
  keyboard, 28, 88–89
  keyboard repeat rates, 88–89
  logging on to Windows 8, 31–32
  monitor, 28
  mouse, 28, 29–30
  screen savers, 73–74
  setting date and time, 33–35
  shortcuts, 31
  shutting down, 40
  speakers, 300–301
  speech recognition, 81–84
  switching user accounts, 38
  touchscreen, 30–31
  Trusted and Restricted websites, 348–351
  wireless networks, 336–338
sharing
  about, 262
  content, 278–279
  files using SkyDrive, 253–255

sharing *(continued)*
  photos, 9–10, 295–297
  SkyDrive folders, 256–257
  specifications for networks,
    334–335
  videos, 9–10
shipping options for online
    shopping, 327–328
shopping carts, managing, 324–325
shortcut text, 269
shortcuts
  creating to files/folders, 57–58,
    146–147
  desktop, 51, 53
  keyboard, 31, 85
showing
  Charms bar, 46–47
  events, 168
  weather views, 154–156
shutting down
  computers, 40
  nonresponsive applications,
    358–359
signing up, for social networking
    sites, 273–275
size, monitor, 19
skipping to next movie in Windows
    Media Player, 290
SkyDrive (Microsoft)
  about, 249, 337
  adding files to, 252–253
  creating folders, 255–256
  deleting files from, 253
  sending photos using, 296
  sharing files/folders using, 253–257
  viewing contents of, 255
Skype, 12

slide shows, running in Photos app,
    297–298
SmartScreen Filter, 215–216
Snopes (website), 224
social engineering, 261
social journaling site, 272
social networking sites
  about, 271–272
  for online shopping, 318–319
  signing up for, 273–275
socializing
  about, 261–262
  blogs, 262–264
  chat rooms, 264–266
  collaborative sites, 271–272
  discussion boards, 262–264
  instant messaging (IM), 266–267
  Messaging app, 267–270
  online dating, 275–278
  sharing content, 278–279
  social networking sites, 271–275
  webcams, 270–271
software
  about, 11–13, 125
  defined, 7
  installing, 292
  launching programs, 126–128
  media, 284–286
  moving information between
    programs, 128–130
  removing programs, 131–133
  setting program defaults, 130–131
  troubleshooting problems,
    374–376
sound card, 15–16
sounds, replacing with visual cues,
    78–79

speakers, setting up, 300–301

specifying places for weather, 156–157

Speech Recognition feature, 76, 81–84

speed
Internet connection, 177–178
processor, 22–23

Spybot, 210

spyware, 13, 209

Spyware Doctor (PC Tools), 210

Spyware Terminator, 210, 356

standards, DVD, 21

Start screen
about, 42–45
background, 62, 65–66
changing background/color, 65–66
help, 114–115
IE app, 181–183, 185, 190–191, 195–196
pinning web pages to, 196–197

Sticky Keys, enabling, 85

stopping
playback in Windows Media Player, 290
Speech Recognition feature, 84

subfolders, 137

Suggested Sites feature, 211–212

swalk (website), 269

swipe gesture, 30, 31, 50

switching
between programs, 58–59
user accounts, 38

Sync feature
about, 249
adding items to be synced, 313
choosing settings, 258–259

enabling, 257–258
syncing music with devices, 312–313

Sync Options button, 313

system restore points
creating, 359–361
defined, 357–358

system volume, adjusting, 301–303

• T •

tablets, 15

tabs, in browsers, 184–185

tap gesture, 30, 50

taskbar, 50, 53

temporary Internet files, deleting, 370–372

Terms of Use, 266

tethering, 25, 331, 340–341

text
resizing, 79–81
shortcut, 269

text links, 175, 181

themes
about, 62–63, 73
desktop, 70–71

tiles, 42

time, setting, 33–35

Tip icon, 1

Toggle Keys, enabling, 85

toolbar, Internet Explorer, customizing, 201–202

tools, for visually challenged, 76–78

touchscreen
gestures, 50
technology, 20
working with, 30–31

troubleshooting software problems, 374–376

Trusted and Restricted websites, setting up, 348–351
trusted sites, 350
trustworthiness of stores, 320–321
Truth or Fiction (website), 224
tweeting, 272
Twitter, 272

• U •

undiscoverable devices, 339
uninstalling software, 13
Universal Resource Locator (URL), 175
unpinning
  contacts, 167
  web pages, 197
updates
  checking for, 346
  downloading, 346
  installing automatically, 345–346
uploading
  about, 9
  photos from digital cameras, 291–292
urgent designation, in e-mail, 238
URL (Universal Resource Locator), 175
usage rights settings, 194
USB connection, 291
USB port, 28
used computers, 18
user accounts
  changing type, 38–40
  creating, 35–37
  switching, 38
usernames, e-mail, 232
utilities, 13

• V •

versions
  Internet Explorer, 190–192
  Windows, 16–17
VGA port, 28
Video app, 285, 286, 290
videos
  about, 283
  buying content at Windows Store, 286–289
  Camera app, 285
  playing with Windows Media Player, 289–291
  sharing, 9–10
  software, 284–286
  taking with Camera app, 292–293
  Videos app, 285
View settings, 64
Viewbook (website), 250
viewing
  browsing history, 199–201
  contents of SkyDrive, 255
  installed printers, 103–104
  photos in Photos app, 293–295
  postings by contacts, 164–166
  Recent Apps, 49–50
  RSS feeds, 202–204
views, weather, displaying, 154–156
virus, 209, 343
vision challenges. *See* dexterity, vision and hearing challenges
visual elements, 15–16
VoIP (Voice over Internet Protocol), 8

volume
  system, adjusting, 301–303
  Windows Media Player, adjusting in, 289
Volume button, 302

• W •

WDT, 155
Weather app
  about, 153
  displaying weather views, 154–156
  global weather, 157–159
  specifying places, 156–157
Weather Underground, 155
web, 174. *See also* Internet
web browsing
  about, 189–190
  adding websites to Favorites, 197–198
  customizing Internet Explorer toolbar, 201–202
  finding content on Start screen, 195–196
  Internet Explorer versions, 190–192
  organizing Favorites, 198–199
  pinning web pages to Start screen, 196–197
  printing web pages, 204–205
  searching, 192–195
  viewing browsing history, 199–201
  viewing RSS feeds, 202–204
web pages
  defined, 174
  finding content on, 195–196
  pinning to Start screen, 196–197

printing, 204–205
  unpinning, 197
web searching, 192–195
webcams, 270–271
websites. *See also specific websites*
  adding to Favorites, 197–198
  collaborative, 271–272
  defined, 174
  gestures, 31
  restricted, 350
  Search This feature, 196
  social networking, 271–275, 318–319
White Pages (website), 220
wiki, 271–272
windows
  customizing appearance, 62–63
  managing, 85
  resizing, 59–60
Windows 8
  about, 16
  changes in, 42–43
  getting started, 112–114
  keyboard shortcuts, 31
  logging on, 31–32
  touchscreen gestures, 50
Windows 8 Pro, 16–17
Windows community, 115–117
Windows Defender, 13, 210, 344
Windows Firewall, enabling, 351–353
Windows Live, 160
Windows Live Mail, 236
Windows Media Player
  about, 284
  burning music to CD/DVDs, 311–312

Windows Media Player *(continued)*
  playing movies with, 289–291
  playing music with, 314–315
Windows Store
  buying music from, 306–308
  buying video content, 286–289
Windows Update
  options, 345–347
  running, 347–348
Windows versions, 16–17
Windows-based tablets, 15
wireless CardBus adapter PC card, 178
wireless hotspots, 177
wireless Internet connection, 24–25
wireless networks, setting up,
    336–338

wireless router, 178
Wireless Wide Area Network
    (WWAN), 24–25
Word Web app, 257
work history, privacy of, 223
World Wide Web, 174. *See also*
    Internet
writeable DVD drive, 21
WWAN (Wireless Wide Area
    Network), 24–25

• Y •

Yahoo, 231
Yahoo! Messenger (website), 267